Praise for *Loving Him without Losing You*

"This book is both powerful and practical in its approach to the problem. Women should read it to regain the strength and vitality that made them attractive to their partners. Men should read it both to understand the female perspective and to regain a whole, loving mate."

—Robert Epstein, Ph.D., Editor-in-Chief, *Psychology Today,* University Research Professor, United States International University

"The glib tricksters of the self-help movement have met their match in Beverly Engel. Instead of false promises, Engel tells it like it is and delivers a comprehensive, informative, and inspiring book that is much more than a self-help guide. She offers insightful strategies for change—both real and human—and intersperses her up-to-date research with surprising tales about famous women as well as her own life. She brings women a book that truly can help them in the transformation from Disappearing Women to Women of Substance. It's a terrific read, too."

—Annie Culver, Editor-at-Large and writer for UnderWire (underwire.msn.com)

"*Loving Him without Losing You* is a powerful and practical guide to relationships that every woman should read!"

—Barbara De Angelis, Ph.D., author of *Secrets about Life Every Woman Should Know* and *Are You the One for Me?*

"Again, Beverly Engel has identified a widespread problem and provided women with wise guidelines for bursting through it. She writes with compassion and insight. If you think you are a Disappearing Woman, you will drink in this book as if it were a health-giving elixir. It is!"

—Susan Page, author of *How One of You Can Bring the Two of You Together* and *If I'm So Wonderful, Why Am I Still Single?*

"This remarkably helpful book offers new insights into why so many women surrender their individuality in relationships. Its strategies for relating fulfillingly to a man can rescue even the most vulnerable woman from sacrificing herself on the altar of love. Don't wait until your hair is on fire to read it."

—Maxine Schnall, founder and executive director of Wives Self Help, the first marital hotline in America, and author of *Limits* and *Every Woman Can Be Adored*

"This book clearly explains why so many women find themselves in fantasy marriages and romances with real men. Beverly Engel urges women to think, evaluate, and risk rejection before they repeatedly jump into the same trap. In a gentle voice, she offers commonsense guidelines for telling the truth, learning to trust perceptions, and using solitude."

—Evelyn Streit Cohen, M.S., M.A., marriage and family therapist and coauthor of *Couple Fits: How to Live with the Person You Love*

"When I was in college, we were all Disappearing Women. We didn't even think about it; that's just the way things were. If we all had had this book, our lives might have turned out much differently. This book will help Disappearing Women find their authentic selves. Buy it for yourself or someone you love."

—Randi Kreger, coauthor of *Stop Walking on Eggshells*

"Loving Him without Losing You is a wonderful resource and guide to finding oneself and to tapping into creativity as a part of one's foundation for a life well lived."

—Lucia Capacchione, Ph.D., author of *Visioning: Ten Steps to Designing the Life of Your Dreams* and *The Creative Journal*

"This is a book of depth and power. I highly recommend it not only to women who lose themselves in their relationships with men but to the parents of adolescent girls who need to be taught how to view themselves as valuable beings separate from their relationships with men and boys."

—Michael Gurian, author of *The Good Son: Shaping the Moral Development of Our Boys and Young Men* and *A Fine Young Man*

"A terrific book, written with authority and sensitivity to men as well as women . . . full of useful, fresh information."

—Bradley Gerstman, Esq., Christopher Pizzo, CPA, and Rich Seldes, M.D., authors of *What Men Want* and *Marry Me!*

"An abundant supply of useful strategies. . . . unique for its readers."

—Sheila A. Rogovin, Ph.D., psychotherapist and coauthor of *Couple Fits: How to Live with the Person You Love*

"Powerful wisdom and insight. . . . Unlike so many others, Beverly Engel doesn't take the easy way out by blaming men but instead she explores the phenomenon from a biological, cultural, and psychological perspective and offers women empowering suggestions as to how to take responsibility for changing their situation."

—Patti McDermott, author of *How to Talk to Your Husband, How to Talk to Your Wife*

"Groundbreaking, provocative, and substantial, this book will light the fire of every woman who seeks true intimacy and strength."

—Salli Rasberry, coauthor of *Living Your Life Out Loud*

Loving Him
without
Losing You

Also by Beverly Engel:

The Right to Innocence

Divorcing a Parent

The Emotionally Abused Woman

Encouragements for the Emotionally Abused Woman

Partners in Recovery

Families in Recovery

Raising Your Sexual Self-Esteem

Beyond the Birds and the Bees

Blessings from the Fall

The Parenthood Decision

Sensual Sex

Loving Him
without
Losing You

How to Stop Disappearing
and Start Being Yourself

Beverly Engel

JOHN WILEY & SONS, INC.

New York   Chichester   Weinheim   Brisbane   Singapore   Toronto

This book is dedicated to all the courageous women
I've worked with through the years who have transformed
themselves from Disappearing Women to Women of Substance,
as well as those who are in the process.

Excerpt from Frida Kahlo's diary reproduced with the permission of the Banco de Mexico, Subgerencia Juridica Fiduciaria, Mexico City, and the Instituto National de Bellas Artes, Mexico City.

Design and production by Navta Associates, Inc.

This publication is designed to provide accurate and authoritative information in regard to the subject matter covered. It is sold with the understanding that the publisher is not engaged in rendering professional services. If professional advice or other expert assistance is required, the services of a competent professional person should be sought.

Library of Congress Cataloging-in-Publication Data

Engel, Beverly.
  Loving him without losing you: how to stop disappearing and start being yourself / Beverly Engel.
      p.   cm.
  Includes index.
  ISBN 0-471-35558-5 (cloth : alk. paper)
  ISBN 0-471-40979-0 (paper)
  1. Relationship addiction.   2. Codependency.   3. Women—Mental health.   I. Title.
RC552.R44 E53   2000
616.86—dc21   99-052075

Printed in the United States of America

15 14 13

Acknowledgments

First and foremost I wish to thank my wonderful agent, Stedman Mays, who was enthusiastic about the book from the beginning and who provided important feedback throughout. I appreciate your hard work, your constant support, and your wonderful sense of humor.

Next I would like to thank Tom Miller, my editor at Wiley. I have never had an editor who took as much interest in one of my books or who worked harder to create the best version of the book possible. Thank you for your diligence and your brilliance.

A special thank you to the women I interviewed for the book, as well as those clients whose stories added invaluable insight into the Disappearing Woman syndrome.

Thanks also to everyone who read my manuscript and gave me feedback.

The book wouldn't have been as substantial without the research of Carol Gilligan, Michael Gurian, Ernest Hartmann, J. Kreisman, Paul T. Mason, and Randi Kreger, and it would have lacked depth without the work of Carl Jung.

I also owe a debt of gratitude to the Women of Substance who have influenced my life and the book: poet May Sarton; Deena Metzger, author of *Writing for Your Life;* Alice Koller, author of *An Unknown Woman: A Journey of Self-Discovery;* Judith Viorst, author of *Necessary Losses;* Linda Schierse Leonard, author of *The Wounded Woman;* and last but not least, Gloria Steinem.

I would also like to thank Gloria Steinem, Mia Farrow, Claire Bloom, and Drew Barrymore, whose personal stories were used as examples to help other women.

Finally, a heartfelt thank-you to Barbara Stephens, Ph.D., whose brilliant work with me helped me in my quest to become a Woman of Substance.

Contents

Part III. Become a Woman of Substance: Developing a Self and a Life That Satisfies You

Introduction

The problem of women losing themselves in relationships is not a new one. For years women have been grappling with the issue. It's been a major focus of feminism, and therapists often stress the importance of women maintaining their sense of self while in a relationship. Many books have addressed the issue, as have articles in women's magazines. An entire movement was created by the book *Women Who Love Too Much*.

So why address this issue again? Because women are still losing themselves in their relationships with men and still giving their power to the men they date and become romantically involved with.

There are many reasons for this phenomenon. There is an entire generation of women, those in their late teens and early to late twenties, who seem to have missed the information on codependency in the books written more than ten years ago. And many women in their thirties, forties, and fifties seem to have forgotten what they learned.

But this is only part of the answer. The fact is that understanding codependency does not necessarily take away a woman's tendency to give her power to men. And there are many ways by which women lose themselves in relationships besides being codependent. The problem is far more complex than codependency or low self-esteem and can only be fully understood by exploring the cultural, biological, and psychological influences on men and women, as well as the differences between women and men that these influences create.

In the past ten years we have become educated about many of the differences between women and men—especially in books such as Deborah Tannen's *You Just Don't Understand* and John Gray's *Men Are from Mars, Women Are from Venus*. Although these books are helpful, they fail to explain fully why women tend to lose themselves in relationships and do not offer enough strategies for change.

By reading *Loving Him without Losing You,* women will come to understand more fully how their tendency to lose themselves in relationships with men is partly a natural by-product of their cultural conditioning and biological hardwiring.

Loving Him without Losing You does not blame men for all the problems women encounter, as so many other books have done. Instead it encourages women to take responsibility for making the kinds of changes that will encourage men to respect them as equals.

And unlike *Women Who Love Too Much, Loving Him without Losing You* does not define the problem by the types of men a woman chooses to be with. A "Disappearing Woman"—a woman who tends to sacrifice her individuality, her beliefs, her career, her friends, and sometimes her sanity whenever she is in a romantic relationship—will act primarily the same with a man who is loving and kind as she does with a man who is distant, cruel, or abusive. In fact, she is likely to turn off a healthier man with her insecurities and demands or cause a man who maintains a life outside the relationship to lose respect for her because of her neediness.

In addition, unlike *Women Who Love Too Much* and other recovery books from the eighties, *Loving Him without Losing You* does not focus primarily on dysfunctional families and abuse. While there will obviously be some references to these causes, most of us know this information by now (for those who don't, I include a Recommended Reading list at the back of this book). I will focus instead on how women can take responsibility for changing their behavior and attitudes in the present.

Much has also been written about the psychological effects of inadequate parenting and bonding experiences and the loss or absence of parents, so I will not repeat this work. What I will do is explain why women react to these psychological factors in very different ways from men, primarily by losing themselves in their relationships with men. I will present a continuum describing the full scope of the Disappearing Woman syndrome, along with an explanation of why some women suffer from only a mild or moderate version of the problem while others suffer from a more extreme version. I will also include recommendations for how women at each point on the continuum can get further help.

More extreme versions of the problem have also been written about, usually only in professional journals and complex textbooks. *Loving Him without Losing You* will explain both the causes and the cures for this personality disorder in language women can understand and relate to.

Understanding a syndrome is one thing, but actually changing it is an entirely different matter. In addition to finally offering definitive answers to questions that have plagued millions of women, this will be the first book to offer effective strategies for change. Women who read *Loving Him without Losing You* will not only learn *why* they are the way they are but also how to go about *changing,* beginning immediately.

This book will teach specific strategies to help you and other women become as strong and as independent in your romantic relationships as you have come to be in other areas of your lives. It also includes suggestions for how you can maintain your sense of self and your individuality so you will attract the kind of man you admire.

How This Book Is Organized

Loving Him without Losing You is divided into four parts, including a section of appendixes in the back of the book. In part I, "Disappearing Women," you will learn how and why women lose themselves in relationships; and in so doing, you will gain understanding of and compassion for yourself. You will also discover to what extent your problem has influenced your life and how extreme your problem actually is.

In part II, "How to Maintain Your Sense of Self while Flourishing in a Relationship," those of you who are single will learn specific strategies to prevent you from losing yourself in new relationships, while those who are already in a relationship will learn how to go about making the necessary changes that will enable you to regain your sense of self.

In part III, "Become a Woman of Substance: Developing a Self and a Life That Satisfies You," we will focus on the more long-term work you will need to do to make deeper changes.

Throughout the book I offer case examples from my many years of working with Disappearing Women. I also include excerpts from interviews I conducted for the book with forty-seven women from all economic and educational backgrounds and from a variety of religions and cultures who identify themselves as Disappearing Women. Although my survey is more anecdotal than scientific, in the process of conducting it I gained invaluable information and was privy to thoughts and feelings that women rarely share with others.

In addition to case examples and dramatic personal stories, I pepper the book with examples of famous women who, in spite of their talent and success, became Disappearing Women in their relationships, including Gloria

Steinem, Frida Kahlo, Claire Bloom, Mia Farrow, and Drew Barrymore. In some cases I follow their relationships from beginning to end, including the steps these women took to discover or regain their sense of self.

About Me

I have dedicated my life to women's issues. I am a psychotherapist with twenty-four years' experience, much of it working with women, and am the author of several self-help books for women.

Through the years I have gained tremendous insight and empathy into the plight of Disappearing Women, both from the experience of working with them and from extensive research. Many years ago I began noticing that almost every woman who came into my office suffered from this problem to some degree. I was appalled when I began to notice the number of very young women who were quick to give themselves away to young men and then suffer the consequences.

I bring to this book a great deal of knowledge about many issues, including object relations, self-esteem and identity issues, human sexuality, child development, and borderline and narcissistic personality disorders. As someone who specialized for years in working with women who had been sexually, emotionally, or physically abused as children or adults, I have worked with many of those who suffer from more extreme versions of the problem, since personality disorders often go hand in hand with a history of abuse and neglect.

I have always felt a special affinity for women with this problem because I also suffered from it for many years, especially when I was in my twenties. I still remember the confusion, anger, and pain I felt whenever I was in a relationship, and the devastation I felt when a relationship inevitably ended. The fact that I have had many of the same experiences will hopefully help you to feel both connected to me and supported by me.

Many women are on the threshold of deciding whether to "give up on love" or to continue seeking equal relationships with men. Of the forty-seven women I interviewed during the course of writing this book, a majority expressed frustration concerning the level of emotional support and involvement they receive from the men they have relationships with. They often asked questions such as, "Why can't men love more, be more emotionally supportive? Why must it always be women who have to make the changes?"

At the same time they expressed a desire to change and not to allow their emotions to rule their lives as much as they have.

In addition, for years women have been in the midst of an important, historic debate—should women stop loving "too much," or should we now expect men to change and become more loving?

What has been referred to as the "feminization of America" in the past three decades has caused harm to both women and men by defining emotional development from a mainly female standard and by holding men to that standard. Men are constantly criticized for not showing their feelings, for not talking about how they feel, for not relating on a more emotional level. Because of this, men have been made to feel inadequate and guilty.

At the same time, the qualities deemed necessary for adulthood, such as the capacity for autonomous thinking, clear decision-making, and responsible action, continue to be those associated with masculinity—whether we like it or not—and are considered undesirable as attributes in women.

In the meantime, in spite of the fact that it is politically incorrect, women give themselves over completely to their emotions when they fall in love, throwing away their careers, their friends, and even their health. And men continue to miss out on the benefits of intimacy and often continue to attempt to dominate and control women.

Clearly, a balance needs to be created. I believe *Loving Him without Losing You* can and will help create this balance by giving women another option—not to necessarily be more like men, but to be more their true selves.

Barnes & Noble Booksellers #2098
1600 Miller Trunk Highway
Duluth, MN 55811
218-786-0710

STR:2098 REG:001 TRN:7548 CSHR:Lawrence B

Loving Him without Losing You: How to St
  9780471409793   T1
  (1 @ 16.95)   16.95
Paleo Approach: Reverse Autoimmune Disea
  9781936608393   T1
  (1 @ 39.95)   39.95

Subtotal   56.90
Sales Tax T1 (8.375%)   4.77
TOTAL   61.67
VISA DEBIT   61.67
  Card#: XXXXXXXXXXXXX7814

A MEMBER WOULD HAVE SAVED   5.70

Thanks for shopping at
Barnes & Noble

101.37A   03/18/2016 03:37PM

CUSTOMER COPY

Barnes & Noble or Barnes & Noble.com.

Policy on receipt may appear in two sections.

Return Policy

With a sales receipt or Barnes & Noble.com packing slip, a full refund in the original form of payment will be issued from any Barnes & Noble Booksellers store for returns of undamaged NOOKs, new and unread books, and unopened and undamaged music CDs, DVDs, vinyl records, toys/games and audio books made within 14 days of purchase from a Barnes & Noble Booksellers store or Barnes & Noble.com with the below exceptions:

A store credit for the purchase price will be issued (i) for purchases made by check less than 7 days prior to the date of return, (ii) when a gift receipt is presented within 60 days of purchase, (iii) for textbooks, (iv) when the original tender is PayPal, or (v) for products purchased at Barnes & Noble College bookstores that are listed for sale in the Barnes & Noble Booksellers inventory management system.

Opened music CDs, DVDs, vinyl records, audio books may not be returned, and can be exchanged only for the same title and only if defective. NOOKs purchased from other retailers or sellers are returnable only to the retailer or seller from which they are purchased, pursuant to such retailer's or seller's return policy. Magazines, newspapers, eBooks, digital downloads, and used books are not returnable or exchangeable. Defective NOOKs may be exchanged at the store in accordance with the applicable warranty.

Returns or exchanges will not be permitted (i) after 14 days or without receipt or (ii) for product not carried by Barnes & Noble or Barnes & Noble.com.

Policy on receipt may appear in two sections.

Return Policy

With a sales receipt or Barnes & Noble.com packing slip, a full refund in the original form of payment will be issued from any Barnes & Noble Booksellers store for returns of

PART I

DISAPPEARING

N

YOU MAY ALSO LIKE...

Codependent No More: How to Stop Contr...
  by Beattie, Melody; Beattie, Melod...

Practical Paleo: A Customized Approach...
  by Sanfilippo, Diane; Staley, Bill...

Women Who Love Too Much: When You Keep...
  by Norwood, Robin

I

Are You a
Disappearing Woman?

*No partner in a love relationship . . . should feel that [she] has to give
up an essential part of [herself] to make it viable.*

MAY SARTON

I'm an artist and my work is very important to me. But I'd like to have a
relationship with a man, too. Unfortunately, I can't seem to do both. As
soon as I fall in love all my passion and focus go into the relationship. I can't
work. All I do is obsess about the man I'm in love with—wondering
whether he loves me, whether he's with someone else when he's not with me.

PRISCILLA, AGE TWENTY-EIGHT

I feel so ashamed. My friends would be horrified if they knew how
desperate and crazy I get when I'm in love. They all see me as a strong,
competent, successful woman who can handle any situation put before me.
But all that strength and confidence go out the window when I'm in love
and I become insecure and dependent, looking desperately to my lover for
any small sign of disapproval, any indication that he's losing interest in me.

LUCINDA, AGE THIRTY-FOUR

In an age when women are supposed to be strong, independent, and liberated,
it is embarrassing to admit that when it comes to relationships with men we
still tend to behave in ways that are far too reminiscent of our mothers and
grandmothers. Let's face it: it's just not politically correct for women to still be

losing themselves in relationships. We're supposed to have stopped all this foolishness years ago. Today women are expected to maintain a strong, independent, successful life while at the same time be a loving mate to their man.

But the truth is far different from the ideal picture some women wish to paint of their lives. *Women are still losing themselves in relationships as much as they ever were.* Many women have received enough information and support from the codependent movement to help them recognize their reasons for choosing unavailable, abusive, or alcoholic men. And due to public awareness and domestic violence programs fewer women tend to stay in abusive relationships, although the numbers are still alarmingly high. But while many women are now making better choices, many are surprised to find that they are sacrificing themselves for their man as much as they ever were. In fact, some of the women who are choosing more available and more loving men have found they are losing themselves in their relationships even more than before.

How to Determine if You Are a Disappearing Woman

No matter how successful, assertive, or powerful some women are, the moment they become involved with a man they begin to give up parts of themselves—their social life, their time alone, their spiritual practice, their beliefs and values. They begin to disappear. In time, these women find they have merged their lives with their partners' to the point where they have no life to go back to when and if the relationship ends. I call these women "Disappearing Women."

While Disappearing Women come in all ages, colors, and sizes and from all cultural, socioeconomic, and financial backgrounds, there are certain characteristics they all seem to share.

If you think you might be a Disappearing Woman but are uncertain, the following test will help you decide:

1. Do you tend to fall in love quickly and intensely and often feel as if you are out of control when it comes to the feelings you have for your lover?

2. Do you become less focused and therefore less effective on the job or in your career when you become involved with a man?

3. Do you tend to spend a great deal of your time daydreaming and fantasizing about your relationships?

4. Do you spend far more time thinking about the future than dealing with the present? Do you console yourself by telling yourself that things will soon get better instead of facing how bad things are today?

5. Do you neglect your friends to be with your lover? Or do you devalue your own friends in favor of your lover's friends, or drop your friends if your lover disapproves of them?

6. Do you drop your own interests and take on the interests of your lover in order to spend more time with him?

7. Do you tend to question or devalue your own feelings, opinions, beliefs, and knowledge whenever they differ from your lover's?

8. Do you become extremely depressed or anxious when you are unable to be with your lover for even short periods of time?

9. Do you tend to be distrustful, jealous, and possessive of your lover?

10. Do you need a great deal of assurance that your lover really cares about you?

11. Do you remain insecure in your relationships no matter how long you and your partner have been together?

12. Do you tend to feel invalidated, patronized, misunderstood, and unappreciated by those you are closest to?

13. Are you willing to change yourself to please your lover (including changing your physical appearance, buying new clothes, working on changing the way you speak, or trying hard to stop a particular behavior)?

14. Will you do practically anything to make the relationship work?

15. Are you usually not the one to end a relationship? If you are, is it because you have been forced to face the fact that your partner does not love you?

16. Do you feel so devastated when a relationship is over that you don't think you can survive the pain?

17. Have you ever had suicidal thoughts because of a breakup?

18. Have you ever entertained homicidal thoughts toward an ex-partner?

19. Do you take a much longer period of time to get over a relationship than other people you've known, even though you may get into a new one right away?

20. Have you ever avoided relationships altogether for a significant amount of time following a breakup because you were so emotionally devastated, even though you felt lonely and longed for an intimate relationship?

If you answered yes to more than five of these questions, you are a Disappearing Woman. While you may try to fool yourself into thinking that things will be different if you could just meet the right man, or if you could just lose some weight, etc., *the truth is you'd be the same no matter what kind of man you were with, or no matter how gorgeous you become; the truth is you have a problem when it comes to maintaining your sense of self in a relationship.*

If you are like most heterosexual women, you want an intimate, loving relationship with a man. You long for a committed relationship in which you can feel free to express your deepest emotions, where it is safe to be your most vulnerable and most loving. You want a relationship in which you can be yourself, drop the facades and pretense, and be real.

Unfortunately, like many other women, you may have begun to feel that your desires will never be fulfilled. Based on your past, and perhaps present, experiences, *you have come to believe that being yourself and being in a relationship are mutually exclusive.*

Ironically, you may have become afraid of the very thing you long for. Afraid because you realize you have a tendency to lose yourself each time you enter a relationship with a man, to give up important aspects of yourself or your life to please him. Afraid because loving a man has often meant sacrifice or pain.

You may have come to realize that for you, loving a man brings with it a tremendous risk—that you will once again put your career, your relationship with your friends, or your well-being in jeopardy to be with a man, that you will sacrifice your needs, your values, or your integrity to please and keep a man.

Some women have decided that no matter how much they want a relationship with a man, it isn't worth the price they end up paying. They've opted to stay alone rather than risk the loss of self they inevitably end up experiencing. Instead, they throw themselves into their careers and dedicate themselves to cultivating meaningful friendships. But most women keep trying, hoping they will find a way to do it right the next time, hoping they will learn how to achieve some sort of balance between loving a man and loving themselves.

If you are one of these women, if you still have even the slightest amount of hope in discovering this balance, *Loving Him without Losing You* will help you turn that hope into reality.

It's important to realize that you are not alone. As you read *Loving Him without Losing You* you'll meet many other women who struggle as you do to maintain their sense of self when in a relationship with a man. Today, millions of women such as yourself are suffering needlessly because they don't understand why they continue to sacrifice their individuality and their very souls when they enter a relationship. Far from feeling like an anomaly, you need to understand that your surprising and often shocking behavior is actually more the norm than the exception.

The next step will be for you to realize that there are valid reasons for your behavior. Losing yourself in a relationship is not a sign of weakness, stupidity, or incompetence on your part, as many women come to feel. By reading *Loving Him without Losing You* you will discover that women are actually culturally and genetically programmed to be nurturers and pleasers; this programming causes us to automatically set aside our own needs to take care of the needs of others. You'll learn that even today our culture encourages women to view the needs of the men in their lives as more important than their own needs. And you'll learn that women tend to have what are considered "thinner" boundaries that predispose them to have a tendency to lose themselves in relationships. Finally, you'll learn that women and men view relationships from different perspectives—men from the point of view of *separation,* women from the vantage point of *connection.*

Realizing that your behavior is not your fault—that it is part of your cultural and biological legacy—will help free you from the shame and embarrassment that have continually whittled away at your self-esteem and contributed to your behavior.

And it definitely will help you to know there is a way out. Next, you'll learn specific strategies that will help you curb your urge to merge, strategies that will help you no matter how extreme your problem is.

Last but not least, *Loving Him without Losing You* will help you transform yourself from what I call a Disappearing Woman to a Woman of Substance. It will teach you how to go deep inside and find your true inner voice and to discover the wisdom, integrity, and sense of balance that lie dormant within you.

By discovering your inner wisdom you'll learn when it is appropriate to give and when it is time for you to receive, when it is appropriate to ask for nurturing and when it is time to retreat and provide nurturing for yourself.

By discovering and developing your integrity you will refuse to stay with a man who doesn't appreciate and totally accept you the way you are.

By developing a sense of balance you'll learn that no one is all good or all bad, that there are many shades of gray. You'll come to understand that a healthy relationship has many ups and downs and is based on give-and-take, intimacy, and autonomy.

Loving Him without Losing You will:

- provide strategies to help you avoid getting involved too quickly with a man;
- show you how to stop idealizing the men you are involved with;
- offer suggestions for how you can stay out of fantasy and remain focused on the present;

- offer insight into why you tend to devalue your own opinions and beliefs and offer encouragement and strategies to help you begin to stand up for them;
- encourage you to value solitude and show you how to tolerate it better;
- show you how to develop a more substantial sense of self and create a life that you will be less willing to discard for a man;
- show you how to develop better relationships with the opposite sex, from dating to flourishing in a committed relationship;
- show you how to maintain your sense of self while in an intimate, committed relationship.

Who Will Benefit Most from This Book?

Those of you who've had a long history of losing yourself in relationships will probably benefit from this book the most. It will help you discover the reason why you have developed such a pattern and offer you strategies to help you break it once and for all.

This book will also be of particular interest to those who are currently in a relationship in which they have submerged their needs or given over their power or individuality. Some have lost so much of themselves in their relationship that they feel it is impossible to change or to leave the situation, even though they are desperately unhappy. This was my client Beth's predicament:

I realize I've allowed my husband to control our lives. When we married I was young and naive and I'd just left my parents' house, where my father completely dominated my mother. I ended up marrying a man just like my father and for many years I guess I thought it was normal to not have a say in decision-making, to center my life around my husband's needs. But as I've gotten older [she's now thirty-nine] I've come to realize that it isn't normal and it isn't healthy. I feel stifled. Sometimes it feels like I can't breathe and I just want to run away. But I'm afraid to venture out on my own, and besides, I love my husband. It's not entirely his fault. After all, I've allowed him to control me.

I'm the one who has to change. I'm the one who has to start acting different, and when I do, he actually responds fairly well. I just don't know if I have the strength and wherewithal to keep it up long enough to change the dynamics in our relationship. It just seems so much easier to give in and maintain the status quo.

This book will also benefit those of you who are so fearful of losing yourself in your relationships with men that it prevents you from experiencing true intimacy. This was the situation with Shawn, age twenty-three, one of the women I interviewed for the book:

> This is my first serious relationship. But instead of being happy because I'm in love, I began to feel myself becoming less and less my own self and more and more a part of him. Like I was gradually disappearing, like the Cheshire cat in *Alice's Adventures in Wonderland.*
>
> Even though I still love Mark I finally had to break up just to see if I'd feel better alone. We see each other now as friends but whenever he starts talking about getting back together I start to feel smothered. I love him but I just don't think I know how to have a relationship and be myself at the same time.

Loving Him without Losing You will also help those who have experienced so much pain because of their tendency to lose themselves in relationships that they are afraid to get involved in another one. This was the case with my client Jenny, age twenty-seven:

> There's this man at work who's very interested in me. We've had lunch together a few times and he seems like a really nice guy. But I'm afraid to risk it again. After my last relationship ended I couldn't sleep, I couldn't eat—I lost fifteen pounds in two weeks. I became so weak and so distracted I couldn't do my job and almost got fired. I'm just getting my life back on track and I don't want to mess it up again by getting involved in another relationship.

No matter what situation you are in, whether you are just beginning to date or have a lifetime of losing yourself in relationships, whether you are married or single, whether you still have hope of changing or feel your situation is hopeless, *Loving Him without Losing You* will help you understand your behavior and discover ways to begin changing it immediately.

One of the first steps will be for you to understand exactly *how* women lose themselves in relationships. This will be the focus of the next chapter.

2

How Women Lose Themselves
in Relationships

The Four Truths You
Need to Know

At thirty-four, Toni is a successful advertising director for a major firm. By devoting herself to her work she's been able to come a long way in only four years. However, she's had to sacrifice her desire for a loving relationship in order to maintain her success.

"You know how people keep telling us that women can have it all? How we can have a career and a family, too? Well, I couldn't even have a career and a *boyfriend,* much less a family."

Toni went on to explain how each time she'd become involved in a new relationship her career had suffered because she focused all her attention on the relationship. Not only that, but she became so emotionally distraught when she and a boyfriend were having problems that she could barely work at times.

> Eventually it got so bad that I lost a job because I couldn't concentrate on my work. I was constantly on the phone trying to reach my boyfriend or agonizing over an argument we had the night before. I got fired because I wasn't concentrating and made a major mistake, one that cost the company a lot of money. To make matters worse, my boyfriend wasn't the slightest bit supportive about my situation. He told me he was tired of hearing me agonize over my lost job. He finally kicked me out of our apartment because I couldn't pay my share of the rent.
>
> That was the most horrible time in my life. Not only was I devastated at the breakup of my relationship but I didn't even have a job or

enough money for the first and last month's rent required for a new apartment. I was forced to go back home for a while, and I do mean forced, since I'm not close to my parents and they really didn't want me there. My mother insisted I try to get a new job right away, even though I wasn't in any condition to be taking job interviews. I vowed then and there that if I ever got another job I wasn't ever going to risk being put in that situation again.

While Toni's solution to her problem leaves something to be desired, her predicament is all too common. Many women lose themselves in their relationships with men because they become so preoccupied with their partner and the drama of their relationship that they are unable to focus on the other important aspects in their life—their careers, their own needs, and their personal growth. In this chapter we'll discuss the various ways in which women lose themselves in relationships and the surprising truths about their situations.

The Ways Women Disappear

For many women the disappearing act begins slowly and subtly. They don't return their friends' phone calls because they're too busy with their new lover; they don't attend an office mate's wedding because their lover doesn't want to go; they stop going out to dinner with their girlfriends because they're afraid their lover will go out to bars that night and meet someone else.

Some women give up their power right away, allowing the man to determine the pace in which the relationship will develop, while others start out strong but gradually, over time, allow the man to control more and more of their lives.

Others maintain their sense of self until they marry, at which time they give over their identity to their husbands, merging with him to such an extent that they seldom ever think of their own individual needs and desires.

Some Disappearing Women choose men who are controlling or abusive, while others become controlling and abusive themselves in their attempts to hold on to a man.

Some sacrifice their voices and their wills to appease their mates, while others complain so much that their partner stops listening. There are women who feel they are disappearing because their partner doesn't pay attention to them, and others who feel invisible no matter how much attention they get from their partner.

For many Disappearing Women, relationships are painful because they are constantly fearful of being abandoned or rejected. They are so insecure that their jealousy and possessiveness cause them to become preoccupied with their relationship to the point that they lose all sense of proportion. They can't enjoy the present because they are so fearful of the future.

For others, relationships are painful because they feel so suffocating. They give up so much of themselves that they often feel relationships are to be endured rather than enjoyed.

Although women lose themselves in many different ways, some patterns emerge. The typical Disappearing Woman tends to lose herself by engaging in some or all of the following behaviors:

- getting involved too quickly;
- not being honest about who she is, what she likes and dislikes, what she wants in a relationship, and what she feels at any given time;
- not maintaining a separate life from her partner;
- letting herself be bought with expensive dinners, vacations, gifts, or promises of wealth;
- trying to change herself to please her partner;
- getting involved in unequal relationships;
- trying to get power/talent/accomplishments/wealth vicariously from her partner;
- not speaking up for what she believes in;
- allowing others, particularly her male partners, to make decisions for her.

EXERCISE: *How Do You Disappear?*

To begin the change process it is important to recognize exactly how you lose yourself in your relationships.

- Make a list of all the ways you disappear in your relationships with men. While your list will undoubtedly have some of the items I've listed above, after spending some time reviewing your past you'll likely be able to come up with some other ways as well.
- Keep your list handy as you continue reading this book. This will be particularly helpful if you run into resistance at some of my suggestions.

The Four Truths You Need to Know

Over the past twenty-four years I have worked with thousands of women who entered therapy with a variety of complaints. What has been surprising to me is that no matter what their initial complaint, most women eventually get around to dealing with the issue of losing themselves in relationships. Along with this awareness, I came to recognize four truths:

Truth 1: Women have a tendency to lose themselves in relationships with men no matter how old or how young the women are.

In my practice I've been appalled at the treatment very young women are willing to put up with from their boyfriends—everything from infidelity to emotional and physical abuse. On a recent *Oprah!* show on female teens who are being abused by their boyfriends, it was revealed that *one in four teenage girls will be victims of dating violence before they leave high school.* In fact, the rate of violence against teenage girls has escalated in the past ten years.

It seems that young women today who are just starting out in relationships with men are clueless when it comes to the most basic information concerning codependency, boundaries, self-esteem, and abuse. Many enter into relationships that resemble servitude. An example of this is the current trend among some young men to buy their girlfriends a pager to keep track of them and to make sure they aren't with another boy. No matter where the girl is or what she is doing, she is supposed to answer his page. If she doesn't, he becomes enraged and accuses her of being unfaithful.

Many of my young female clients tell me that they're afraid that if they don't allow their boyfriend free rein he'll leave them and they couldn't bear it. They say they'd rather put up with even the cruelest behavior than to be without a boyfriend.

The story of one of my clients was particularly poignant. Amber is seventeen years old and has already been in two serious relationships. She started having sex when she was fourteen with her first boyfriend, Charlie. They were together for two years, during which time Charlie had sex with at least four other girls. As Amber explained it:

"Each time I'd find out he'd been with another girl I'd get really hurt and really angry. I'd confront him with it and of course he denied it. The first time it happened he was so convincing I ended up believing him. But then several of my friends told me they saw him making out with another girl. After that I stopped confronting him. I knew he wouldn't tell me the truth and I figured that as long as he came back to me I'd better just keep my mouth shut."

When I asked Amber why she didn't break up with him and find another boyfriend she said, "What was the point? I figured they all do the same thing. All my girlfriends have the same experience. It's just how guys are."

As it turned out, Charlie left Amber for another girl and she was heartbroken. She remembers crying her eyes out for weeks. After that she became so seriously depressed that she missed several weeks of school and even contemplated suicide. She was convinced she'd never get over Charlie. Three months later, she got involved with Kevin.

She and Kevin were very happy for about six months. Then she found out that he, like Charlie, had been with another girl. She was devastated. Unlike Charlie, Kevin freely admitted his infidelity. He told her he'd done it because she wouldn't do the kind of things he wanted to do sexually. So to keep Kevin, Amber agreed to do whatever he wanted sexually, even though some of the acts were repulsive to her and some caused her tremendous physical pain.

This is finally what brought Amber into therapy. She wanted to know if there was something wrong with her because she couldn't enjoy the kinds of sex acts her boyfriend liked. It had never crossed her mind that Kevin was wrong to insist on her performing these acts or that she had a right to refuse him.

If you are young and have had similar experiences in your relationships with boyfriends, you have much to feel optimistic about. The younger you are when you begin addressing the problem of losing yourself in relationships, the better chance you have of overcoming it before it becomes too deeply ingrained and becomes a pattern.

Unfortunately, many of you reading this book have a long history of losing yourself in relationships. You've spent your entire life becoming involved with one man after another, losing parts of yourself in each relationship until you have little of yourself left.

This was the case with Marta. At fifty-two she had finally reached her limit. "I just can't continue on this way. I need some help. As soon as I get into a new relationship I start changing my life. In the past ten years I've moved twice, quit three jobs, and lost several friends. All because at the time I felt it was more important to please the man I loved. But I'm getting too old. I need some stability in my life."

Despite the women's movement, even older women, women we expect to have learned to maintain their sense of self in relationships, still tend to give their power to the men in their lives. If this applies to you, even though it will be more difficult for you to break this pattern of behavior after so many years, it certainly is possible if you are committed to change and to regaining your sense of self.

Truth 2: Even women who have never lost themselves in relationships before are at risk.

Some women are astonished to realize that they have a tendency to lose themselves with a man, since they never were this way before. Patsy, forty-two, a highly successful chiropractor who had been seeing me to clear up some issues with her childhood, shared with me how surprised she was at her own behavior ever since she started dating an accountant in her office building.

PATSY: LIKE A SCHOOLGIRL WITH A CRUSH

I haven't dated for more than ten years, since I got my divorce. I just didn't feel like it, what with the kids to raise and my business to establish. But Frank is so sweet and we've become good friends over the past several months. It just felt natural that we would begin dating. That's why I'm so surprised at how I've begun to act—like some schoolgirl with a crush!

It's so embarrassing. All day long I find myself looking out the window to see if his car is in the parking lot or waiting for him to pop in to say hello. When we do see each other I feel light-headed and silly and I say stupid things that I know puzzle him. And you know what I hate the most? I hate it that my mood is so affected by how he acts toward me. If he pops in to say hello and seems very happy to see me I'm set for the whole day. But if he doesn't stop by, or if we happen to pass in the hall and he seems uninterested, I feel crushed.

I can't stop thinking about what I might have done to turn him off or whether I'm coming on too strong, or whether he's decided he doesn't like me. I just hate it. I don't remember acting like this when I was younger. I remember always feeling like I could get any man I wanted and I didn't seem to feel so self-conscious. You'd think I would have gotten more self-confident as I've matured, not less.

Truth 3: It doesn't matter how confident, strong, or assertive you are, you can still lose yourself in a relationship with a man.

Time after time I've been struck by the fact that otherwise competent, confident, and assertive women give their wills and their lives over to men. Women who are independent, assertive, or even aggressive in other areas of their lives, women who don't hesitate to stand up for themselves and their needs in other areas suddenly begin to disappear into the woodwork and lose their voice when it comes to their private lives. This was the case with Stephanie, age thirty-five, one of the women I interviewed for the book, a highly successful, dynamic woman who put her husband through medical school.

STEPHANIE: THE DOCTOR'S WIFE

In the beginning of our relationship, I was considered the strong one. My husband was awkward and shy in public and I was very outgoing and charismatic. I was active in local politics and had a lucrative job as a sales representative for a major firm. I don't know if you know anything about sales, but let's just say I always knew how to close a deal.

But everything changed after my husband became a doctor. Suddenly he was the important one and I was just the doctor's wife. People who had merely tolerated him because of our friendship suddenly started asking him for advice and began kowtowing to him. And I was expected to view him in a different light as well. He suddenly became more demanding of me, expecting me to run errands for him and answer the phone, even if it was sitting right next to him. When I complained about it he explained that it didn't look good for a doctor to be answering his own phone, even at home.

I got so angry I told him he could hire a secretary. So he hired a housekeeper who also answered the phone! Before I knew it he and she set up an alliance and began treating me as if I were incompetent and a burden on him. It wasn't long before I felt displaced in my own home. Things just kept going downhill from there. I eventually bought into the belief that he was better than I was and started treating him like everyone else did. I gained a lot of weight and, of course, this made me feel even more invisible. By the time he asked me for a divorce (because he fell in love with a younger woman, of course) my self-esteem was so low and I was so depressed that I almost committed suicide.

Truth 4: Even extremely attractive, wealthy, and famous women can become Disappearing Women when it comes to relationships.

The problem goes beyond intellect, beyond self-esteem and self-confidence. It involves the very core of a woman's identity. Even some of the most beautiful, dynamic, famous, and talented women in the world have been known to lose themselves in relationships. This is particularly true of women who become involved with powerful or famous men.

FRIDA KAHLO: THE WOMAN WITHOUT A SELF

Frida Kahlo, one of the most popular female artists in history, had a flamboyant but intimate style that earned her an enthusiastic following worldwide. Her life, riddled with suffering and pain, has spoken strongly to women in particular.

On August 21, 1929, the petite twenty-two-year-old Frida married the overweight, middle-aged artist Diego Rivera—the most famous man in Mexico. From the beginning Frida was aware that Diego had numerous affairs, but she developed a defense system by pretending to others that she and Diego had an ideal union of unbroken devotion. This defense did not work when she discovered that Diego had begun a relationship with her younger sister, Cristina, who was her dearest family member and confidante. Frida was devastated and took an apartment alone in Mexico City for a time, trying in vain to find an independent life.

For all the strength of her personality, Frida felt insecure without Diego to praise her talents, cleverness, and beauty. When he withdrew from her, feelings of abandonment overwhelmed her. As she wrote Diego, she "loved him more than her own skin."

In desperation, Frida returned to Diego and put up with his numerous affairs. Even at the end of her life, after she had gained international recognition herself, Frida's love for Diego was still the major focus of her life, as evidenced by one of her diary entries:

Diego . . . beginning

Diego . . . builder

Diego . . . my child

Diego . . . my sweetheart

Diego . . . painter

Diego . . . my lover

Diego . . . my husband

Diego . . . my friend

Diego . . . my mother

Diego . . . my father

Diego . . . my son

Diego . . . I

Diego . . . universe

Diversity in unity

Why do I call him my Diego?

He never was and he never will be mine.

He belongs to himself.

Unfortunately, Frida, like so many other Disappearing Women, did not belong to herself. She did not have the sense of self necessary to walk away and make a life of her own.

As you will see throughout this book, developing and maintaining a sense of self is vital if you are going to stop losing yourself in relationships. By practicing the strategies outlined in this book you will be able to develop such a strong sense of self that you no longer *need* to look to anyone else for self-definition, self-expression, or self-esteem. This, in turn, will help you to stop disappearing in your relationships.

No matter how you lose yourself in your relationships with men, change is possible. Throughout this book you will experience changes in your beliefs about women and men, in your understanding of what a relationship is supposed to be, and in your self-image. All these changes will add up to the most profound change of all—you will no longer be a Disappearing Woman who gives up parts of herself because of her desire to be with a man.

3

Why Women Tend to Lose Themselves in Relationships

THE CULTURAL, BIOLOGICAL, AND PSYCHOLOGICAL INFLUENCES

Women are taught to enhance other people at the expense of the self;
men are taught to bolster the self, often at the expense of others.
It's hard to get it all in balance.

HARRIET LERNER, PH.D.,
THE DANCE OF INTIMACY

Why are women so much more likely to lose themselves in relationships than men? Are we genetically and emotionally weaker, more dependent, and less able to maintain our separate identities? Or is it because men are cut off from their emotions and less capable of true intimacy? The answer is far more complicated than these generalizations imply. Part of the answer lies in our cultural conditioning, part on biological factors, and still another part is based on psychological factors.

Cultural Conditioning

There are many cultural reasons why women are more susceptible to losing themselves in relationships than men. In this section I will focus on the most prevalent. Most of these influences exist in every culture throughout the world, among every race, religion, and socioeconomic segment of the world's population.

Girls Are Trained to Be Dependent, Boys to Be Independent

Even today families still tend to push boys toward independence far more than they do girls. Both in early childhood and in early adolescence boys are encouraged to be more independent in their thinking and in their actions and to be less dependent on their families than are girls. Parents still tend to comfort girls more than boys when they are frightened or injured, and boys are given greater freedom at an earlier age than girls are.

Girls Are Raised to Be Protected, Boys to Be Strong

Having a sense of competence means believing that we can make things happen for ourselves in the world, that we can master our environments. Unfortunately, the expectations that parents and our culture have for boys lead to far greater feelings of competence than the traditional expectations of girls. Parents often expect less of their female children and tend to place more demands on little boys, expecting them to be more responsible and to take more risks. This sends a subtle yet powerful message that girls are less competent. Moreover, the traditional "sugar and spice" view of girls—the idea that girls need to be protected and "done for" rather than learning to do for themselves—promotes feelings of insecurity and incompetence.

Girls Are Raised to Be Compliant

Parents continue to raise girls to be more passive and compliant than boys, and research shows that girls are far more likely to placate to keep the peace. While most boys are aggressive about getting their individual needs met, girls are raised to smooth things over in relationships rather than stand up for their own wishes and needs. They are much more likely to sacrifice their own needs if they think that doing so will benefit the relationship and to back down, apologize, or take the blame whenever there is a disagreement.

Girls are far more likely than boys to give in to what their date wants to do, have sex even if they aren't ready, and give up their social life to sit home waiting for him to call.

This is due in part to the fact that during adolescence girls experience a tremendous amount of social pressure to put aside their authentic selves and to display only a small portion of who they truly are. It is often in their adolescence when girls first come to realize that males have most of the power and when many come to believe that their only power comes from becoming submissive to male needs.

Girls Learn Helplessness

Girls and women are frequently the victims of inequality, prejudice, misogyny, and violence in our society, and socialization often supports this role. While boys are encouraged to fight back when others violate them, girls are encouraged to do nothing. The helplessness a girl learns in childhood is often carried over into adulthood, so that passivity may seem to be the only way to handle problems.

While girls and women are far more likely to be physically and sexually violated in our society, it is boys, not girls, who are most often encouraged to develop the skills with which to fight back. Boys' will to fight back is nurtured by their parents and the culture; girls are often robbed of their will to fight back (if they ever develop it). Girls are taught that it is "unladylike" to fight back and that they do not have the right to say no, especially to adults—messages that have a lasting effect. Even when women equip themselves with self-defense skills, it is still difficult for many to put these skills to use when needed because they lack the gut conviction that it is okay to stand up for and protect themselves.

In addition, if a girl was raised in a home where her mother was emotionally or physically abused by her husband or boyfriend, she may conclude that being a woman is synonymous with being a victim.

While boys also grow up in abusive households, because it is socially unacceptable for males to be seen as victims, generally speaking, male children tend to identify with the aggressor and to emulate the behavior of the abusive person rather than become victims themselves.

Girls Are Taught the Illusion of Inherent Inferiority

Unfortunately, even in these "enlightened times," men are still seen as inherently superior to women. In spite of the fact that we now expect men to be more emotional, "male" traits such as rationality, independence, and leadership ability are the traits most valued in our culture, whereas "female" traits such as emotionality, sensitivity, and cooperativeness are valued less.

Instead of men becoming more respectful of women, there is an alarming trend among many young men to devalue and denigrate women, as evidenced by the blatant way they refer to them as "bitches" and the way they treat them as sex objects and targets for their anger.

Women Look to a Man for Completion

Women, far more than men, tend to look to love to make themselves feel complete. It's not that women have any innate inclination toward searching for completion through love (as opposed to money, status, politics, or religion), it's that for women love is the most culturally sanctioned and encouraged form.

The idea that women need men to validate them is pervasive in our culture. One only need listen to popular music or read popular literature to find examples. In addition, biographies and autobiographies of famous women exalt those women who surrendered their identities, if not their very lives, to love.

Women who remain single past a certain age (usually thirty) are still viewed as "less than" those who are married and often seriously begin to believe that there is something wrong with them.

Women Buy Into the Romance and Fantasy Syndrome

Another factor contributing to the "Disappearing Woman" syndrome is that girls and women tend to get caught up in romance and romantic fantasy much more than boys and men, and this in itself encourages girls and women to lose themselves to the experience and the relationship.

Girls are raised to be in love with love. From the earliest age, many girls are still given the message that their life won't really begin until they meet that special man who will sweep them off their feet and transform their life. Even the smallest of girls still play "wedding," dressing up as a bride, walking down the aisle with a make-believe groom. When was the last time you saw a little boy playing "wedding" or dressing up as a groom?

Girls are given far more permission to fantasize than are boys, particularly when it comes to romantic fantasy. Boys have traditionally been given more permission to have sexual fantasies than are girls, who are encouraged to sublimate their sexual fantasies into more acceptable "romantic" ones.

Women Are Addicted to Male Approval

Women are taught from an early age that it is their duty to attract and please men and that their very survival is contingent on it. Because of this, by the time the average girl reaches adolescence, she is addicted to male approval. She primps, worries about her weight, wears uncomfortable clothes and crippling shoes, and waits patiently for the remark, look of approval, or telephone call that will inform her that she is worth something.

No amount of intelligence or feminist consciousness can completely obliterate the average woman's need for male approval, nor does the need for it get magically whisked away just because a woman reaches an intellectual understanding of it and decides she isn't going to "live like this anymore."

Even the most self-sufficient, successful, and intelligent women still fall prey to the need for it.

Several women I interviewed for the book spoke about their need for male approval, including Janice, thirty-three, a successful real estate broker.

"I hate to admit this, but nothing, absolutely nothing, makes me feel better about myself than when a man compliments me about my appearance. It's even better than the rush I get when I sell a house! Isn't that pathetic?"

Diane, a forty-two-year-old college professor, told me a similar story. "I've reached a point in my life where I take my intelligence and academic accomplishments for granted. But even when I was younger I never felt attractive enough to men. I've always paid a great deal of attention to my appearance and quite a lot of my paycheck as well. It's always been far too important to me. But when a man finds me attractive, it makes it all worthwhile. I suddenly feel validated and acceptable. I'm sorry to say that nothing else gives me that same feeling."

Women Are Trusting

With their less competitive natures and their stronger ability to share feelings, women have far less difficulty trusting others than men do. Women instinctively know that trust nurtures closeness and that distrust undermines it. However, some women trust too much and are easily impressed, duped, and deceived.

Biological Reasons for Disappearing

In addition to cultural conditioning, there are also biological differences between men and women that contribute to women losing themselves in relationships. Some of these include:

• *Males are, in fact, "less emotional" than females by nature.*

Many researchers believe that testosterone, the human sex and aggression hormone, is a major factor in cutting boys off from emotional development. By late adolescence, boys' testosterone levels are as much as twenty times that of girls.

In addition, according to Michael Gurian, author of *A Fine Young Man*, the male brain is wired to function much more mechanically than emotionally, to prefer action to ongoing intimate connection, and to display physical and social aggression toward others. This often prevents men from becoming as emotionally intimate with others and consequently from losing themselves in romantic relationships.

Gurian also claims that the female brain is better able to process emotive data, while the male brain is hardwired to be better at spatial relationships than emotional ones. There are many examples of this wiring, but one of the most important is that the corpus callosum, the bundle of nerves that connects the right and left hemispheres of the brain, is larger in the female brain. Because of this difference, women are better able to process emotional information that needs to cross between hemispheres to be processed and communicated.

- *It's harder for men to talk about their feelings because of the way their brains are constructed.*

While it is common knowledge that men don't access or verbally express their feelings as well as women, most people attribute this to cultural conditioning alone. But another factor at play is that from early on, the female brain is generally superior in terms of basic verbal ability.

According to Anne Moir and David Jessel, the authors of *Brain Sex,* women have a more efficient brain organization for speech, which is located in the front of the left hemisphere, while the same function in male brains is found both in the front and back—a less efficient distribution.

All through life, female verbal abilities, especially about emotive content, are on average superior to male verbal abilities. It has been observed during neural imaging scans that the male brain is less active and there is less cross talk between hemispheres, which, in turn, creates less verbal expression.

Testosterone also affects boys' ability to communicate emotionally. While some boys are readily able to put their feelings into words at age nine, by the time they reach sixteen many are less able to do so. While we can attribute some of this to the fact that boys are discouraged from being emotional as they grow older, the primary reason is that the amount of testosterone surging through the body and brain throughout adolescence causes adaptations in boys' emotional systems that cut down the emphasis on feelings in their speech.

- *Men are more independent than women.*

The way the male brain is structured, combined with higher levels of testosterone, propels boys and men toward independence-seeking activity. According to Anne Moir and David Jessel, both boys and girls whose mothers had taken extra male hormones during pregnancy were found to be more self-sufficient, self-assured, independent, and individualistic on a standard personality questionnaire. Those whose mothers had taken female hormones were more reliant on others.

- *Men do not need to be emotionally connected to a woman, nor even sexually attracted to her, to have intercourse.*

Even though the biological drive to reproduce is very strong, men must be sexually aroused in order to have intercourse. For this reason, the human brain is wired to make it possible, through the use of fantasy, for men to become sexually aroused even when they are not attracted to a woman or don't have enough energy for intercourse.

Conversely, for the average woman to become sexually involved she must lower her defenses and allow herself to become vulnerable. Most men are capable of having sex with someone without going through this process. Spurred on by their hormones, men can more easily have sex while their emotional walls are still up, so they usually don't have the problem of losing themselves.

Not only does the average woman need to become vulnerable to have sex, she also continues to open up each time she repeats the act with someone. The closer she becomes physically, the more involved she is emotionally. This is partly due to the fact that, contraception notwithstanding, with every act of sexual intercourse, a woman may be facing a potential new life.

Even those men who lower their emotional walls and fall in love tend to bounce back from lovemaking easier and faster and are able to maintain their separate identity better than women. We seldom see a man so lovesick that he can't do his work, so preoccupied with his lover that he talks about her all the time with his friends.

- *Boys and men are less likely to use pain as a bonding agent.*

Testosterone propels boys and men toward quick tension release, not only in the sex act but even in their response to physical pain. A boy is far less likely to cry when he is hurt, especially one who has reached puberty. Not only has the acculturation process taken hold by then ("big boys don't cry"), but also boys and men are hardwired to release tension quickly rather than engaging in an activity such as crying, which not only prolongs the release of tension (as compared to a quick curse or a physical act), but also extends the involvement of others (if a boy starts to cry, people come around to talk and help). While this involvement would no doubt benefit him emotionally, it is not hardwired into his system, as it is in girls and women.

A girl, on the other hand, tends to want to get help in releasing her stress and uses the stress as a way of creating emotional connectedness. Women tend to see their partners as potential givers of comfort when they are upset. When the comfort is not forthcoming, many are disappointed but continue to try to get it. This is what traps many women—their false hope that someday they'll get the comfort they need from their partner.

• *Women are literally more sensitive than men.*

The female brain is organized to respond more sensitively to all sensory stimuli, including tactile sensitivity. In a sample of young adults, women showed "overwhelmingly" greater sensitivity to pressure on the skin on every part of their bodies.

The Psychological Reasons

In addition to cultural conditioning and biological hardwiring, there are also psychological factors that contribute to women's tendency to lose themselves in relationships. While psychology *is* biology to a great extent, it is also greatly influenced by environment and warrants its own category.

The most significant psychological factor has been discovered by some fairly recent research on female psychology. Within the emerging body of literature on differences between women and men, several studies, including those of Gilligan and Miller, suggest that women value connectedness and relationship more than men do. In her study, Harvard professor Carol Gilligan dramatically demonstrated that in making moral decisions women value maintaining connections with others and not hurting others more than men, who base their moral decisions more on general principles. These findings were consistent with those found by Jean Baher Miller:

"Women's sense of self becomes very much organized around being able to maintain affiliations and relationships. Eventually for many women the threat of disruption of connection is perceived not just as loss of a relationship but as something closer to a total loss of self."

It is no wonder that most women will do nearly anything to maintain a relationship, including going along with things she doesn't believe in. To do otherwise is to risk the loss of connection, the very core of what makes her who she is.

Women Have Thinner Boundaries Than Men

Women also tend to have what Ernest Hartman, M.D., the author of *Boundaries in the Mind,* calls thinner boundaries than men. This is especially significant when it comes to personal relationships. Thin interpersonal boundaries cause a person to become involved in relationships rapidly and deeply and at times to lose one's sense of self in a relationship. Conversely, having thick boundaries implies not becoming overinvolved, being careful, and not becoming involved with anyone rapidly.

According to the results of Hartmann's boundary questionnaire, there are clear-cut differences between men and women in boundary scores. "Overall, women scored significantly thinner than men—thinner by about twenty points, or 8 percent of the overall score."

Although women scored thinner on almost all categories of boundaries, the differences in scores were especially pronounced on the first eight categories, what Hartmann referred to as the "Personal Total," describing personal experiences, feelings, sensitivities, and preferences.

Judith Bevis, a member of Hartmann's boundary research group, conducted a study in 1986 on groups of evening students at an urban university. Her most prominent finding was that the women in the study tended to value certain aspects of thin boundaries, such as interpersonal connectedness, and to feel comfortable with them, whereas they found certain aspects of thick boundaries, such as autonomy, to be uncomfortable. The men in the sample tended toward the opposite viewpoints, considering autonomy and self-sufficiency as comfortable but merging or connectedness as less comfortable or less desirable.

How a Woman's Childhood History Contributes to the Disappearing Woman Syndrome

A number of psychological influences contribute to the Disappearing Woman syndrome:

- an insufficient bonding experience with the primary caretaker, particularly the mother;
- the long-term absence of one or both parents;
- the loss of a parent either through death or divorce;
- an insufficient, inappropriate, or negative relationship with the father;
- parental neglect;
- emotional, physical, or sexual abuse;
- poor parental modeling (misogyny, domestic violence);
- rejection or ridicule from parents, siblings, or peers.

Any of these factors can cause an adult woman to feel insecure and inadequate in her relationships and to look to her male partners for the kinds of caring, support, and direction she did not receive from her parents. This makes her more vulnerable and dependent than she might otherwise be. And a history of having been emotionally or physically neglected or abandoned as a child or an adolescent can cause a woman to fear abandonment and cling to her partners even when she is not getting her needs met or is being mistreated. Having a history that includes any form of abuse also predisposes women to become attracted to men who are domineering and/or abusive and to allow the men in their lives to dictate their behavior.

Although males also suffer from such problems as childhood deprivation and abuse, females react to these experiences in a decidedly different way than males do, internalizing their anger versus acting it out, and building up different types of defenses against their pain. This in turn leads to different types of psychological problems, as we shall now explore.

Anger in versus Anger Out

When a boy or a man is hurt by another person, either physically or emotionally, he will tend to lash out at that individual, either verbally or physically. "You hurt me so I'll hurt you." When a girl or a woman is hurt, however, it is not so simple. By the time they have gone through the acculturation process, most women have long since given up the natural instinct to retaliate directly. (Some researchers believe that females are also biologically wired to avoid anger and to instead work toward peaceful solutions.) Instead, most women immediately shift into either the *diplomat mode*—asking themselves, "Did he mean to hurt me?"; the *victim mode*—when they try to elicit sympathy from the person who hurt them; or the *self-blame mode,* asking themselves, "What did I do to make him hurt me?" Instead of the simple and direct, "You hurt me so I'll hurt you back," girls and women tend to think, "You hurt me so I must have done something to deserve it."

While boys and men tend to act out their anger, girls and women internalize their anger and tend to become self-effacing or even self-destructive. (This phenomenon further explains why male victims of childhood sexual abuse tend to become abusers themselves, while female victims tend to continue to be victimized or mistreated during their lifetimes.)

If something goes wrong in his environment, a boy or a man tends to look outside himself first for the cause of the problem. This tendency is partly based on a male's biological tendency to take action (versus introspection) and partly on the male's ego, which encourages him to blame others versus taking responsibility for his actions.

Conversely, if something goes wrong in her environment, a girl or a woman will tend to look inside herself first for the cause of the problem. Most women are far more inclined to blame themselves for a problem than to blame someone else.

How does this "anger in, anger out" difference relate to a woman losing herself in her relationships? Because a woman is more inclined to question and blame herself when there is a conflict with another, she is more inclined to give in during an argument or to become confused as to exactly what her role was in the conflict. This, coupled with her need to keep the peace, will encourage her to compromise and sacrifice in relationships when she shouldn't, which, in turn, causes her to lose herself.

Because women tend to turn their anger inward and blame themselves for problems in their relationships, they tend to become depressed and their self-esteem is lowered. This, in turn, causes them to become more dependent and less willing to risk rejection or abandonment if they were to stand up for themselves by asserting their will, their opinions, or their needs.

Men often defend themselves against hurt by putting up a wall of nonchalant indifference. This appearance of independence often adds to a woman's fear of rejection, causing her to want to reach out to achieve comfort and reconciliation. Giving in, taking the blame, and thus losing herself more in the relationship seems to be a small price to pay for the acceptance and love of her partner.

While both extremes—anger in and anger out—create potential problems, this doesn't mean that either sex is wrong in the way they deal with their anger. But each could benefit from observing what the other sex does. Most men could benefit from learning to contain their anger more instead of automatically striking back, and could use the rather female ability to empathize with others and seek diplomatic resolutions to problems. Many women, on the other hand, could benefit from acknowledging their anger and giving themselves permission to act it out in constructive ways instead of automatically talking themselves out of it, blaming themselves, or allowing a man to blame them. Instead of always giving in to keep the peace, it would be far healthier for most women to stand up for their needs, their opinions, and their beliefs.

False Selves and Fragile Egos

We all learned as children to hide our real feelings and our real selves in our attempt to fit into society and to protect ourselves from the slings and arrows of others. We construct false selves in our attempt to appear more confident, more knowledgeable, and more independent than we actually are. But men and women tend to construct different types of facades.

The male ego is actually more delicate than the female ego, yet men are expected to be the stronger sex nevertheless. Most men are forced to submerge their weaknesses and vulnerability and hide them behind a mask of confidence, independence, and even bravado. A man's self-esteem is usually measured by how strong and confident he appears—the way he holds himself, the way he walks. While in some cultures this is more pronounced than in others, nearly every society requires boys and men to take on this facade in order to be accepted by others. (One only needs to be reminded of how "sensitive" boys are treated in our culture to realize this is true. At the very least they are called "effeminate" and at the worst they are beaten up and called "queers" and "faggots," whether they are actually gay or not.)

Often the less self-esteem a man has, the more pronounced his mask of bravado is. For example, many boys and men from ghettos have mastered the "gangsta" facade to compensate for their feelings of inadequacy caused by growing up in poverty, often without the love and guidance of a male father figure, and to armor themselves to face the constant threat of violence.

By reading *Reviving Ophelia* by Mary Pipher, many of you learned about the drop in self-esteem that young girls experience during middle-school years and soon after. But further research has suggested that in many circumstances, adolescent boys experience a *worse* self-esteem drop than girls do. In an independent study of nine thousand eighth-grade boys and girls conducted by Valerie E. Lee of the University of Michigan, it was concluded that in many academic categories where self-esteem might be measurable (engagement in school activities, study habits, grades), girls were doing better than boys. This study is consistent with similar research on eighth-graders and twelfth-graders by the U.S. Department of Education.

To relieve bad feelings about her self-image, a girl will often forgo self-assertion in real life and substitute the superficial "feeling good" that comes from clinging. Whereas boys tend to hide their feelings of inadequacy with an *inflated* sense of self, girls tend to produce what is called the *deflated false self*—deflated because the bad self-image reflects weakness and insecurity, and false because it is based on a fantasy. This fantasy, that people will provide support for clinging behavior, is then projected on the external world. The girl feels she will only feel good and actually "loved" when she is passive, compliant, and submissive to the person to whom she clings for emotional support.

To the deflated false self, "proof" of being loved is essential for feeling good. Therefore, by denial and rationalizations, a girl learns to successfully stave off the withdrawing or rejecting behavior of the people she loves. For example, if her boyfriend verbally attacks her, an adolescent girl will tend to rationalize, "He's attacking me because he's upset about his grades, not because he really feels this way about me."

Instead of standing up for herself and letting her boyfriend know she doesn't want to be talked to that way (and risking rejection), many girls will quietly take the attack, tell herself it really didn't bother her, and then be extra loving to her boyfriend, convinced that if she is patient and loving it will all blow over.

The Need for Separation and Individuation

Another psychologically based reason why women tend to lose themselves in relationships more than men is that, as many experts believe, the separation-individuation phase is more difficult for girls.

In an article in the *New Yorker* about successful businesswomen, Harvard professor Carol Gilligan suggested that "relationships, and particularly issues of dependency, are experienced differently by women and men." She argued that "males tend to have difficulty with relationships, while females tend to have problems with individuation."

Individuation is (1) the process of recognizing that one is becoming a unique, individual self, separate from one's parents and other authority figures, and (2) the process of developing that self. C. G. Jung spoke of individuation as the goal of psychic development, of allowing the unique individual personality to unfold. One of the reasons that has been cited for girls having difficulty individuating is that since girls are the same gender as their primary parent—their mother—they do not develop a full sense of their difference and separateness from her, and this extends to other relationships. Conversely, since boys are the opposite sex from their mother, they develop a strong sense of themselves as separate from others.

A child cannot find her own identity unless she frees herself first from her parents and other authority figures. We see this occurring in adolescence, when both boys and girls begin to question the values of their parents, school, and peers and begin to rebel against their parents and all other authority figures. This is a positive step toward achieving a full, adult identity.

However, boys are given much more latitude in this process than girls are. Parents tend to give male children later curfews than female children of the same age and to allow boys to attend more functions that are considered "risky," such as rock concerts, weekend trips, and spring break vacations. And boys are expected to act out, even to get into trouble. The old adage "boys will be boys" implies that it is within the boy's nature to act out and rebel, while girls are expected to conform to society's values.

Girls are often encouraged to remain enmeshed with and dependent on their families. While there certainly are some parents who become too enmeshed with their male children as well, causing them to remain dependent on them, far more tend to hold on to their female children, discouraging them from becoming independent, leaving home, and starting a life of their own.

What Losing a Father Does to Girls

Still another reason why girls may have a more difficult time individuating is that so many girls grow up without a father. Due to our high rate of divorce, many children, boys as well as girls, are having to grow up fatherless, but girls seem to be affected in different ways than boys.

According to Victoria Secunda in her book *Women and Their Fathers,* while it is true that boys living with single mothers tend to be more aggressive and have more behavioral problems in and out of school, some authorities believe that divorce is actually more harmful to girls. This is primarily because girls, raised to be more emotionally invested in relationships than boys, seem to suffer more from the loss of their father. In addition, not having a father can cause a girl to become and to remain far too dependent and enmeshed with her mother and can interfere with the natural individuation process necessary for true independence.

Perhaps the most important role a father plays in the lives of his children is that of helping his offspring develop a sense of their own competence and independence outside the powerful intimacy of the mother/child relationship. By providing an alternative to the mother's point of view, style, and temperament, he helps his children to separate from her emotionally.

The father is usually the most "significant other" in his child's life and, as such, helps his child learn about comings and goings, transitions, and separations. The child learns, through her father's in-and-out schedule, how to develop a mental image of something longed for and trusted, though not always actually present.

Because a child is accustomed to separations from the father, she often turns to him for help in differentiating herself from her mother. When the "terrible twos" arrive, a time when the child actively begins separating from her mother, the father is pursued by the child as the parent who is already seen as separate, novel, interesting, and a source of adventure.

When a father is not around to help a girl in the individuation process from her mother, some girls become overly dependent on their mothers. This is especially true when a mother, left alone with her child to deal with her own feelings of loss and abandonment, looks to her child for emotional support, making her into a confidante or even a parent.

The Differences between Male and Female Identities

For a person to develop a sense of herself as a unique individual she must first learn who she is separate from others.

Traditionally, while adolescent boys are encouraged to identify and sharpen their skills, clarify their interests and objectives, make important choices, and prepare for the future, adolescent girls are encouraged to focus on being attractive, fitting in, getting along with others, and being popular. In other words, males are encouraged to ask, "What are my needs and how can I fulfill them?" while females are encouraged to ask, "What are the needs of others and how can I fulfill them?" Similarly, women are not supposed to ask, "What is it I desire" but to ask, "Am I desirable?"

As Mary Pipher noted in *Reviving Ophelia,* a typical adolescent girl struggles with the following questions concerning her identity:

- How important is it to be attractive and well liked?
- How do I take care of my own needs and not be selfish?
- How can I be honest and still be loved?
- How can I achieve and not threaten others?
- How can I be sexual and not be a sex object?
- How can I be caring and yet not be responsible for everyone?

According to Michael Gurian in *A Fine Young Man,* adolescent boys are plagued by entirely different questions concerning core self-development, namely:

- Who am I?
- When will I be independent?
- What is right or wrong behavior for me?
- What is love, and how do I do it well?

Several things can be extrapolated from these two significantly different lists:

- The questions that girls grapple with all involve *their relationship to others, most significantly how they are viewed by others.* The only question boys ask themselves regarding their relationship with others is not about how they are *perceived* by others but about right and wrong *behavior.*
- The questions boys tend to struggle with are far more directed toward identity in general, not identity as related to others or the opposite sex. The issue of love does come into play but as you notice, Gurian put this item last on the list, which is surely not a coincidence.
- The issue of independence does not even come up for girls but is close to the top of the list for boys, second only to Who am I?
- Perhaps most significantly, instead of asking "Who am I?" female adolescents focus on "Can I be myself and still be accepted or loved?"

Interpersonal Relationships versus Achievement

Women, far more than men, tend to avoid their personal conflicts (such as their inability to individuate) by becoming absorbed in an "other" (most commonly a man). Men, on the other hand, tend to avoid conflict by engaging in activity—such as sports, career, and other achievements—which actually helps them develop more of a sense of self.

By looking to interpersonal relationships rather than achievement for a sense of self, women imbue their relationships with far too much importance and risk far more damage to themselves when a relationship doesn't work out.

Whether we want to admit it or not, men still hold most of the power in the world. Men still make more money and head most of the major corporations. Most politicians are male, as are most judges, legislators, attorneys, doctors, and ministers. Many women still believe the only way to gain power is through a man rather than by their own accomplishments. (Classic folktales such as *Snow White and the Seven Dwarfs* and *Cinderella* reinforce the idea that a girl can't resolve her problems on her own but must wait to be rescued by a handsome prince.)

Charlotte, age forty-nine, explained it to me like this:

I was raised to believe that the only way for a woman to obtain any real power or significance was to marry a wealthy or accomplished man. My family didn't have enough money to send both my brother and me to college, so I was sent to secretarial school, with the expectation that I would work a few years in a legal office and then marry a lawyer.

And that's exactly what I did. Robert is a very powerful man, and I guess I thought I could take on some of that power vicariously by being with him. And in some ways I did. People treated me with a great deal of respect when they learned I was Mrs. Robert Black. It opened a lot of doors. Unfortunately, it prevented me from remembering who Charlotte Baker was. My entire existence centered around pleasing my husband— maintaining a beautiful home for him to come home to, looking good so he could be proud of me, and keeping up the appearance that we had it all. As the years went by, Charlotte Baker began to disappear, and all that was left was Mrs. Robert Black. When we divorced I didn't have Charlotte Baker to go home to. She was gone.

Disappearing Women and Psychological Disorders

Another factor in determining why women tend to lose themselves in relationships more than men are the psychological disorders women tend to suffer from versus those experienced by men. Women tend to suffer from what are referred to in the psychological community as personality disorders far more than males, who, conversely, suffer from conduct and thought disorders.

A personality disorder is an exaggerated version of a personality trait. According to the *DSM-IV,* the diagnostic statistical manual used by clinicians to help determine psychological diagnosis, a personality disorder is an enduring pattern of inner experience and behavior that deviates markedly from the expectation of the individual's culture, is pervasive and inflexible (unlikely to change), is stable over time, and leads to distress or impairment in interpersonal relationships.

Of the personality disorders, Borderline Personality Disorder (BPD) is the one most commonly experienced by women. According to the *DSM-IV,* Borderline Personality Disorder is characterized by a pervasive pattern of instability of interpersonal relationships, self-image, and affects (moods), as well as a marked impulsivity beginning by early adulthood and present in a variety of contexts, as indicated by five or more of the following criteria:

1. Frantic efforts to avoid real or imagined abandonment. This does not include suicidal or self-mutilating behavior covered in no. 5, below.

2. A pattern of unstable and intense interpersonal relationships characterized by alternating between extremes of idealization and devaluation.

3. Identity disturbance: markedly and persistently unstable self-image or sense of self.

4. Impulsivity in at least two areas that are potentially self-damaging (e.g., spending, sex, substance abuse, shoplifting, reckless driving, binge eating). This does not include suicidal or self-mutilating behavior covered in no. 5, below.

5. Recurrent suicidal behavior, gestures, or threats, or self-mutilating behavior.

6. Affective instability due to a marked reactivity of mood (e.g., intense episodic dysphoria, irritability, or anxiety usually lasting a few hours and only rarely more than a few days). [Dysphoria is the opposite of euphoria and is a mixture of depression, anxiety, rage, and despair.]

7. Chronic feelings of emptiness.

8. Inappropriate, intense anger or difficulty controlling anger (e.g., frequent displays of temper, constant anger, recurrent physical fights).

9. Transient, stress-related paranoid ideation or severe dissociative symptoms.

Borderline Personality Disorder is often associated with symptoms such as eating disorders, other addictions, and self-mutilation, and is the common denominator of many of the syndromes of the 1980s, such as codependency and "women who love too much." It is considered primarily a "women's illness," since according to the *DSM-IV,* about 75 percent of those diagnosed with BPD are women. In fact, BPD is so pervasive among women that it has been referred to by the media as "the women's illness of the '90s."

Why is this so? Why would a particular personality disorder be more common in women than in men? There are several theories as to why this is true, including the following:

Of those men who do suffer from a personality disorder, more suffer from narcissistic personality disorder than Borderline Personality Disorder. On the surface the narcissist appears to be self-assured, exuding an aura of self-importance, success in his career and love relationships, and a strong sense of knowing what he wants and how to get it. He is often brash, exhibitionistic, and grandiose. In reality, the narcissist's personality is based on a defensive false self that he must keep inflated to hide his inadequate sense of self. While a man may suffer from the same sense of inadequacy as a woman, he is more likely to defend himself against it with a false facade than will a woman.

Some researchers believe that just as many men fulfill borderline criteria as women, but whereas women tend to become depressed, attempt suicide, or seek psychiatric care, some men tend to act out violently against the world. This leads some to believe that Antisocial Personality Disorder (APD) is the male equivalent of BPD, since most people diagnosed with APD are men. But although BPD and Antisocial Personality Disorder have some external similarities (i.e., difficulties with relationships, tendencies to blame others), their internal states are strikingly different. Those who suffer from BPD feel shame, guilt, emptiness, and emotional distress, while those with APD usually do not.

Other theorists point to the types of cultural conditioning women experience as the answer, such as:

• Women experience more inconsistent and invalidating messages in this society.

• Women are more vulnerable to BPD because they are socialized to be more dependent on others and more sensitive to rejection.

Some point to the fact that sexual abuse, which is common in childhood histories of borderline patients, occurs more often in women than in men. The problem with this theory is that not all women who were sexually abused become borderline.

The Borderline/Thin Boundary Connection

Those with very thin boundaries feel immediately attracted to someone, often sharing with others such comments as: "I knew right away he was the kind of person I could trust" or "He just felt right to me." They are the people who fall in love at first sight or who become fast friends with someone, and they are apt to open up and share even the most private aspects of themselves with perfect strangers "because it felt right."

People with thin boundaries tend to have intense but short-lived relationships in which they live only for the other person. Typically they then go through a traumatic breakup and experience pain that far outlasts the relationship. Suicidal thoughts during these painful separations are not uncommon.

Several of the women I interviewed for this book talked about how difficult it would be for them to leave their current relationships, even though in some cases they knew they would be better off if they did. One woman expressed it this way: "I can't even imagine my life without him—it's like he's become a part of me." This is not just a figure of speech for these women but a way of describing a very intense, painful feeling. Many women describe their feelings at the loss of a relationship with a man as the same sensation as losing a limb.

There is, in fact, a relationship between boundaries and mental disorders, although the cause of the relationship is unclear. It may be that having extremely thin boundaries predisposes one to personality disorders such as Borderline Personality Disorder, or it may be that this disorder actually "thins" the boundaries of these people.

While generally, stressful conditions tend to produce a thickening of boundaries in an attempt to defend oneself, trauma can tear boundaries and make them thinner. Patients with the diagnosis of Borderline Personality Disorder have often experienced sexual, physical, or extreme emotional abuse in childhood. According to Dr. Hartmann, these patients show evidence of thin or torn boundaries, such as a tendency to enter relationships quickly, an inability to control emotions and keep out stimuli, or an intolerance of being alone. But they also attempt to form thick defensive boundaries, such as projection, a tendency to be paranoid, and "splitting"—insisting on seeing others as totally good or totally bad. These defense mechanisms are characteristic of Borderline Personality Disorder.

Now that you have learned the reasons why you, like so many other women, lose yourself in relationships with men, you undoubtedly feel less confused by your behavior and less critical of it. You can stop blaming yourself for your behavior and begin to make the kind of changes that will enable you to live a healthier, more autonomous life.

In the next chapter you will learn where to focus your energies, depending on how mild or how extreme your problem is.

4

The Disappearing Woman Continuum

The way out is through the door you came in.

R. D. LAING

Something happens to me when I fall in love with a man. It's like I merge with him so strongly—sexually and emotionally—that I vacate my own body and soul. It's a weird, almost supernatural experience. When I was young I used to think that's what love was about but now I realize that most people don't experience it like I do. I know it's not healthy. There have been times when I've felt like I was losing my mind. And when the relationship is over I'm in so much pain I feel like I'm going to die.

MELINDA, AGE THIRTY-NINE

In this chapter I will describe the Disappearing Woman continuum, the spectrum of behaviors that make up the definition of "Disappearing Woman," as well as explain the likely cause for each position on the continuum. This continuum reflects my years of working as a psychotherapist, feedback from other colleagues, the results of the interviews I conducted for this book, and my extensive study.

Nearly all women suffer from some version of the Disappearing Woman syndrome. Those rare exceptions—women who have resisted their cultural conditioning and overcome their biological hardwiring and the effects of their childhood—make up only a small fraction of the total population.

If the only influences you experienced were cultural, biological, and those that are psychologically innate, you will likely suffer from only a mild version of this syndrome. This version is characterized by a tendency to seek male attention and male approval, including focusing too much time and attention on your physical appearance (especially your weight); a tendency to drop friends and social activities to be with your new lover; an inability to maintain a separate life from that of your lover; and a tendency to placate and to seek consensus to the point that you sometimes go along with things that are against your best interests. In addition, some women on this end of the continuum have difficulty bonding with female friends and see other women primarily as competition. Based on my clinical experience, I estimate that a little more than one-fourth of all women fall on this end of the continuum. This estimation was confirmed by my own informal survey. Of the forty-seven women I interviewed for this book, thirteen fit into this category.

Most of us don't get through childhood, however, without poor parental modeling, neglect, abuse, or the loss of a parent to divorce or death. These experiences, coupled with the cultural, biological, and psychological factors discussed earlier, push most women into the moderate category and to the middle of the continuum. By my estimation this comprises nearly half of all women. This estimate is based in part on the following criteria:

- Current estimates reveal that one in four women was sexually abused as a child.
- Fifty percent of American marriages end in divorce.
- Twenty-three of the forty-seven women I interviewed fit into this category.

As we move to the middle of the continuum we find women who have a tendency to become involved with men too quickly and too intensely. If you're one of these women, you may have other interests, but you may not be able to carry on a conversation for any length of time without focusing on the current man in your life, the man who just left you, or the man you wish you had. You may have a tendency to become obsessed with a particular man, even when he shows little or no interest, and you probably have a difficult time ending a relationship, even when you are being ignored or treated badly. You may be unable to fully bond with female friends, and if you do, you become dependent on them for advice.

You have consistently placed the needs and desires of the men in your life ahead of your own, to the point where you have forgotten what your needs and desires are. You don't speak up for yourself and don't take care of yourself in your relationships with men. Often, everything else is secondary to your relationship—your job, your social life, even your friends and family.

You may have had a mother who modeled this behavior or you may have had a neglectful or absent father. You may have a history of child abuse or neglect or come from a home where women were not respected or were abused.

Finally, slightly less than one-fourth of women fall into the extreme category. If you're one of these women, you did not have an adequate bonding experience with either parent, or your one significant connection was very unhealthy—either too smothering or too rejecting. You probably suffered from severe forms of deprivation, neglect, and abuse in childhood.

Unlike the average woman who may become emotionally involved too quickly or who may become too emotionally invested in a relationship that isn't mutual, if you're this type of Disappearing Woman, you tend to lose yourself whenever you are in any kind of relationship. While this happens most intensely and obviously when you are involved romantically with someone, it actually occurs whenever you are involved in any kind of close relationship, including with family members and friends. You begin to lose touch with how you feel, what you believe in, and what you like and dislike, and you tend to either take on the beliefs and preferences of those you are close to or become confused or disoriented when someone disagrees with your beliefs or has different preferences. In other words, your sense of self tends to be more amorphous than the average person's.

If you are at this end of the continuum, you tend to completely turn over your life to the men you are involved with. You put up with mistreatment, infidelity, or even abuse, and you tend to neglect your children to be with a man.

Often accused of being a chameleon or of being "spineless," you are the woman most likely to pack up and go off with a new lover, leaving everything behind; convert to the religion of your partner; or drop your friends if your partner doesn't approve of them.

Some women at this end of the continuum have been known to abandon their children, become estranged from their parents, or turn a blind eye to criminal behavior once they become caught up in another person's life. They tend to be desperate for attention and recognition from everyone—women as well as men—and are sometimes bisexual.

If you're at this end of the continuum, you may have decided to avoid intimate relationships with men altogether for fear of the tremendous chaos, confusion, and despair you experience each time you have a relationship, or you may go from relationship to relationship, desperately seeking the type of acceptance and love you fantasize about, continually being disappointed, constantly feeling abandoned.

Eleven of the forty-seven women I interviewed were at this end of the continuum.

Why the Continuum Is Important

Determining where you fit on the continuum is important for several reasons. First, it will help you have realistic expectations of yourself, as opposed to expecting yourself to be someone you can't be at present. Those of you who fall into the extreme category, for example, need to understand you are operating under an emotional handicap and need to go slowly. You should give yourself a tremendous amount of credit for even the smallest change.

Second, it will help you to know where you should focus your energies in order to make the kind of changes you desire. While this entire book will help you no matter where you are on the continuum, certain sections will help more than others, depending on where you fall.

Those women who suffer from a milder version of the problem brought on by the normal socialization process may find that this book is all you need to turn yourself around. Discovering the fact that you are not alone and the reasons for your behavior will help rid you of the shame you have carried about your tendency to lose yourself in relationships. And by applying the strategies outlined in part II, you will likely gain the confidence, skills, and determination needed to maintain your sense of identity in your relationships with men. For example, by changing overt behavior such as not having sex with a man right away and limiting the time you spend with a new partner, you can learn to maintain a separate identity and not be as inclined to merge with a partner.

Those in the middle of the continuum who have shaky boundaries due to such experiences as emotional, physical, and sexual abuse can learn from part II how to create healthier boundaries. But you also need to develop a stronger identity, and this can only be accomplished by focusing on the deeper work recommended in part III.

By reading this book, those of you who suffer from extreme versions of the problem will learn for the first time exactly what is wrong with you and how the problem was created. You likely suffer from the psychological disorder known as Borderline Personality Disorder, discussed in the previous chapter.

Many of you were raised by parents who were completely incapable of providing the necessary emotional and physical bonding, mirroring, and acceptance that a child needs to be emotionally healthy. Or you may have been raised by parents who merged with you in an unhealthy way, such as living vicariously through you or being overly possessive of you.

While some healing will inevitably take place just by understanding and naming the problem and by realizing you aren't alone and that you are not to blame for your tendency to lose yourself in relationships, you will probably find that you need to focus on the deeper work suggested in part III before you can successfully master the strategies listed in part II.

Third, knowing where you fall on the continuum will help you determine what direction you should take once you've completed this book. At the end of the book I offer three appendixes, one for each position on the continuum, in which I provide information and resources specific to the needs of each.

For example, those who fall at the mild end of the continuum will benefit from forming a women's circle. There you will find a way to counter the societal messages that discourage women from being as independent and successful as men. You will also be encouraged to embrace the feminine values I call the three c's: connection, cooperation, and compassion.

Those of you who fall within the moderate range may need to seek further help to heal the underlying cause of your problem, if you haven't already done so. You will likely benefit from individual therapy or a support group specifically designed to fit your particular problems. For example, those who were sexually abused can benefit greatly from the information and support gained by being in a group with other survivors. In addition, you may choose to form your own "Women of Substance" support group or to join an existing one where you will find the encouragement you may need to continue practicing the strategies outlined in this book.

Those of you who fall within the extreme range will need to seek professional help that goes beyond the scope of this book. In appendix III I help you further understand your problem, recommend treatment options, and help you locate a therapist specifically trained to work with this disorder.

Where Do You Fit on the Continuum?

While some of you may be able to determine where you fall on the continuum simply by reading the descriptions I have provided above, others will not be as certain. The following case examples will help, as will the questionnaires later on.

SUSAN: CHOOSING A MAN OVER A FRIEND ANYTIME

Susan is a very attractive and young-looking woman of forty-five. She is tall with long legs and a shapely body, and her hair, raven black with only hints of gray, cascades over her shoulders in thick curls. Extremely bright and with a charming, outgoing personality, she is the envy of many women half her age.

I met Susan shortly after I'd moved to a small town along the central coast of California. She, too, had recently moved from a big city, and we seemed to have a lot in common. Before long she was inviting me to meet several of her women friends in town, all of whom seemed to adore her. Even though she'd been in town only a short time, she was the focal point of their social activities, frequently hosting afternoon teas and organizing trips into the nearby city for dancing, skating, or the movies.

She called me several times a week asking to go to lunch or dinner, and when I could afford to take time away from my writing I would join her. She was highly intelligent and we often had stimulating conversations about art, literature, even psychology. But as time went by it seemed that more and more of our conversations were about men. It seemed that there was always a man occupying Susan's thoughts, either someone who was interested in her, someone from the past who still haunted her, or someone she was flirting with (she frequently looked around at men in the restaurant while we talked).

Several times she arrived more than thirty minutes late to meet me either because she had received a phone call from a man at the last minute or had run into a man on the street on her way to meet me. While she apologized for being late, she seemed to think that I should understand—after all, men were more important than arriving on time to meet a friend.

I'd known several women like this when I was younger. I was even guilty of the same behavior myself when I was young. But I was surprised to see a woman of forty-five still acting this way. Most women our age had come to value their women friends, understanding that in many cases they were more permanent than male-female relationships.

Later, on two separate occasions, Susan canceled our plans at the last minute because a former boyfriend had arrived in town unexpectedly. At this point my patience was wearing thin and I became reluctant to make plans with her in the future. It was becoming clearer and clearer to me that Susan put men before her friendships with women, and I felt the handwriting was on the wall—it was just a matter of time before she became involved with a man and she would dump her girlfriends altogether. I declined further invitations to lunch or dinner and saw her only when a group of women went out together.

Within months Susan called to tell me she was madly in love with a man she'd dated a few times. Her voice was higher than usual and she talked a mile a minute, describing how he looked, what he'd said to her, and what they did on their last date. She reminded me of a teenager with a crush. I listened patiently for a few minutes, then said I had to be going. At no time in our conversation did she ask how I was doing.

After a few weeks I heard from friends that Susan was involved with a man from out of town. I knew I wouldn't hear from her again, that she no longer had any reason to call me. At first her friends were happy and excited for her. But soon I began to hear how much they missed Susan because they hadn't seen her in a long time. After several months, missing her was replaced with complaints that she never called and never returned their calls. Several friends became very angry with her and shared with me how they felt abandoned and used by her.

Sure enough, she'd dropped her friends just as I had predicted. I felt sad for her, sad for her close friends, and grateful that I wasn't one of them.

It turned out that few people saw her anymore, even in passing. It seems she spent most of her time at her boyfriend's home, an hour and a half drive away from town. I often drove by her house on the way to town and was saddened to see her beautiful garden, the one she had worked so hard to create, slowly dying. I wondered what else she was allowing to die in order to maintain her relationship.

Two years later, when her relationship ended, I once again got a call from Susan. Sounding like the charming person I'd first met, she tried to engage me in a conversation and invited me to dinner at her house. I thanked her and courteously declined her invitation, telling her I simply didn't have time for socializing at the present time. It turned out that I wasn't the only one to turn her down. It seems her other friends had become so hurt and angry because of her disappearing act with them that they refused to speak to her again.

MICHELLE: A MAN JUST LIKE DADDY

Michelle entered therapy because she wanted help deciding whether she should leave her boyfriend.

> Carl and I don't have any friends and he never wants to go anywhere. I get bored staying home every night watching television, and I want to go out and have some fun. Carl says I'm afraid of intimacy, that's why I always want to be doing something or going somewhere instead of just being together. He says that when we do go out all I do is flirt with other guys—but I don't think I do. I'm just friendly.
>
> I don't know. Maybe I do flirt. I get so confused. I like being close to Carl, but I also like to do things. Does that mean I'm afraid of intimacy?
>
> If he just wouldn't criticize me so much. He's on me constantly for something. He doesn't like the way I dress, and he thinks I'm too skinny. I've tried to gain weight, and even though I'm more comfortable in

pants I wear dresses because he likes me in them, but he's still not happy.
He constantly complains about my son taking up too much of my time
and about me not wanting to have sex often enough. I tell him that if I'm
so horrible, why does he stay with me, and he always answers that he's
just so in love with me that he can't help himself. I'm totally confused.
I don't want to hurt him by leaving, but I'm just not happy with him.

It turns out that Michelle had broken up with Carl several times before,
but she always went back. When I asked her why, she explained, "I get lonely
and I'm afraid I won't find another man who loves me as much as Carl does.
I start thinking about the good times we've had and that maybe it is all my
fault—if I'd just do the things he asks of me we could be happy. I end up calling him up and we end up having great sex together and before I know it I'm
over there all the time again.

"I don't want to keep going back and forth. It isn't good for my son and
it makes me feel like an idiot to keep breaking up and going back together all
the time. My friends think I'm nuts. I want to figure out whether I want to be
with him once and for all."

ANNA: TRYING TO AVOID HER EMPTINESS

Anna had been married for twenty-six years when she finally got the strength
to leave her husband. Devastated, she packed up and moved to another state
in an attempt to get a new start. For four months she spent most of her time
in bed, either crying or sleeping. She was so severely depressed that she
would sometimes spend days without eating or seeing anyone.

Finally, after a visit from her twenty-two-year-old daughter, who was
horrified to see her mother in that condition, she was convinced to seek professional help.

Over the months that followed, Anna told me horror stories about what
she had put up with from her former husband—severe emotional abuse,
numerous extramarital affairs, and eventually, physical abuse when she finally
confronted him. And yet it was taking all her strength not to give in to her
desire to go back to him, back to the life that defined her for so many years.
"I don't know who I am now. I'm not a wife, I don't even feel like a mother
anymore (she had three grown children). I feel like just a lump sitting here
taking up space. I thought it was bad living with John, but this is worse. The
pain is unbearable."

As the weeks and the months progressed, I discovered that Anna had been
severely emotionally deprived as a child. Her mother, an extremely selfish

woman, refused to give in to what she considered Anna's "unreasonable demands" for attention. Only two weeks after Anna was born, she left her in her alcoholic father's care and returned to work. What occurred while her father cared for her was uncertain, because Anna had very little memory of him or of their time together. What was clear was the pervasive rejection she received from her mother her entire childhood.

Anna began dating boys when she was only thirteen and started having sex shortly afterward. She remembered that she loved the attention she got from boys, but she knew all they really wanted was sex. It wasn't until she started dating John during her senior year that she felt loved for the first time in her life. "John was different from all the other boys. He really cared about me, how I felt, what I was interested in." When he asked her to marry him after graduation, she confessed that she agreed partly because no one had ever been as kind to her and partly because her mother informed her she was no longer welcome to live at home once she turned eighteen.

Although she had done very well in school and could have gotten a scholarship to nearly any college she'd applied for, Anna didn't have the emotional strength to forge a life on her own. Instead, she married a man she didn't really love in exchange for the security of being loved. Predictably, John eventually discovered that Anna didn't really love him. Through the years his love turned into hate, and he started looking elsewhere for someone who could give him the affection and adoration he craved.

Still unwilling and unable to strike out on her own, Anna clung to the marriage, trying desperately to please John in any way she could. The more she put up with his philandering, the less he respected her, and eventually he began to emotionally abuse and verbally degrade her.

Now, all alone and with no one to cling to, Anna was having to confront her feelings of emptiness for the first time, feelings that had plagued her since infancy. Therapy with Anna was going to take the form of reparenting her, essentially providing for Anna what she had missed as a child—the sounding board, the unconditional regard, and the structure she so desperately needed to develop a true self.

The Real Differences

As you can see, there are some similarities among Susan, Michelle, and Anna. All three women focused far too much attention on attracting or keeping a man, making significant sacrifices along the way. Susan sacrificed her female friends, Michelle sacrificed her ability to achieve a healthy relationship by staying in an abusive one, and Anna sacrificed her entire identity.

The differences among them lie not only in the type of sacrifices they were willing to make but also in the extent to which their lives have been affected by their tendency to lose themselves in a relationship. Susan lost her friends by dumping them for a boyfriend, but she didn't lose herself entirely. By all reports she had a healthy enough relationship with the man she was involved with (although she continued to put the relationship ahead of everything else). And even though she held on way past the time when the relationship should have ended, they did end their relationship amiably. Unfortunately, when the relationship ended, she had no support system in place to help her recover from the pain and the loss since she had alienated all her friends.

Michelle, on the other hand, lost more than the few friends who tired of her vacillating with Carl. Each time she returned to Carl, she lost more of her self-respect. And by staying with Carl and allowing him to emotionally abuse her with his constant criticism, over time her self-esteem was slowly being eroded. Not only this, but also her sense of reality was progressively becoming more and more distorted until she wasn't certain when Carl was right and when he wasn't.

Anna lost even more. By marrying for security, she robbed herself of the experience of real love. And by staying in her marriage, she sacrificed her chance to develop a true self as opposed to living only through another person.

The biggest differences among the women lie in their backgrounds. Although Susan was not my client, she had shared with me a great deal about her family background. She grew up in a seemingly normal family as an only child. Her mother stayed home while her father worked. Her mother was a typical housewife of the times, keeping an immaculate house and preparing three full meals a day. While she was attentive and loving to Susan during the day, as soon as her father came home from work, her focus became directed primarily on her husband, whom she fawned over for the rest of the evening.

Not only did Susan learn early on that her father's needs were more important than her own, but she learned from her mother's example that men were more important than women. We can see why Susan grew up devaluing her female friends and placing the needs of men ahead of not only those of women but also those of her own. Since Susan received adequate bonding with her mother, and since the cause of her disappearing act was primarily cultural as opposed to psychological, she developed only a mild version of the Disappearing Woman syndrome.

Michelle came from a large family in the Midwest. She had three older brothers and two younger sisters. Although her mother was too busy to give her much individual attention, she appears to have bonded sufficiently with her, and Michelle always felt loved by her. Her father, on the other hand, was extremely critical and domineering. In his words, he ran a "tight ship," expecting the children to excel in school as well as to do extensive chores after school. No matter how well Michelle did, however, her father was never satisfied. He always insisted she could do better.

Her father was also extremely rigid when it came to socializing. As a young girl Michelle was never allowed to go to friends' houses, and the girls weren't allowed to date until they were eighteen. When she did begin to date, her father constantly accused her of being promiscuous.

While Michelle was saved from having a more extreme version of the problem by the fact that her mother had bonded with her, her father's dominance, hypercriticalness, and possessiveness could be categorized as emotional abuse. Emotional abuse eats away at people's self-esteem, causing them to doubt their perceptions and their ability to love and be loved. The fact that Michelle had chosen an emotionally abusive boyfriend and one who restricted her social interactions is by no means a coincidence. In essence, she had become involved with a man just like her father in her attempts to work out her unfinished business with him. She not only didn't have the confidence to break up with Carl for fear that no other man would love her, but she was neurotically attached to him in her attempts to work out her conflict with her father. This placed her in the middle of the continuum.

Anna clearly suffers from an extreme version of the problem due to the lack of bonding and severe neglect by her mother. This, coupled with the fact that she was essentially raised by her alcoholic father, who provided no structure, limits, or boundaries, prevented Anna from developing a true identity. Instead, she developed a "false self" designed to please others and hide her real feelings.

If you are still unclear where you fall on the continuum, the following questionnaire will help.

Childhood History Questionnaire

1. Did your mother tend to be distant or aloof toward you as a small child?
2. Was your mother unable to take care of you when you were an infant for any reason (illness, absence)?
3. As a young child were you adopted, placed in a foster home, or sent to live somewhere outside the family home?
4. Did either of your parents die when you were a child?

5. Did your parents divorce or separate when you were a child or adolescent?

6. Do you feel that you were deprived of physical affection as a child?

7. Do you feel that your emotional needs such as being listened to, being encouraged, or being complimented were not met as a child?

8. Did your parents neglect to provide you with adequate supervision, leaving you alone for long periods of time in your home or car?

9. Did your parents seem to be too busy to bother with you? To ask about your homework or talk to you about your feelings?

10. Was one or were both of your parents excessive drinkers or alcoholics, or did either of your parents use drugs?

11. Was one or were both of your parents extremely critical or domineering?

12. Did you find that it was difficult to please one or both of your parents, or did you get the impression that no matter what you did, your parent or parents would never approve of you?

13. Were either of your parents extremely possessive of you, not wanting you to have your own friends or activities outside the home?

14. Did either of your parents treat you as a confidante or seek emotional comfort from you?

15. Did either of your parents ever physically abuse you?

16. Were you ever sexually abused by a parent or other authority figure?

17. Were either of your parents emotionally incestuous with you—either by looking at you in a sexual way, asking you inappropriate sexual questions, walking around half dressed or naked in front of you, or expecting you to meet their emotional needs, such as taking the place of an absent partner?

18. Was a sibling ever emotionally incestuous or sexually abusive toward you?

19. Did you ever run away from home?

20. Did you ever feel so enraged with one of your parents or siblings that you seriously wanted to kill him or her?

Give yourself five points each for answering yes to questions 1 to 5, and 15 to 20. Give yourself three points each for answering yes to questions 6 to 14.

If you answered yes to *any* of the above questions, the cause of your problem is not confined to cultural conditioning and biological factors. You may, however, score as many as eight points and be on the border between a milder version of the problem and a moderate version.

If you scored more than eight points, your life experiences have differentiated you from those women who suffer from a milder version of the Disappearing Woman syndrome brought on by cultural and biological factors. This means that you will have to work a bit harder to overcome your tendency to lose yourself in relationships with men by doing the work suggested in part III. It also means that unless you have already done so, you need to focus on healing the damage caused by the loss, neglect, or abuse you suffered as a child by joining a group such as those offered for adult children of alcoholics or survivors of sexual abuse.

If you scored more than twenty points total or if you answered yes to more than two of questions 1 to 5 or 15 to 20, it is probable, but not absolutely certain, that you suffer from a more extreme version of the problem and therefore fall at the extreme end of the continuum.

How to Distinguish between Moderate and Extreme

By far the most significant factor in determining whether you fall at the moderate or the extreme end of the continuum is whether you had an adequate bonding experience with your primary caretaker and whether you received what is referred to as "good enough" parenting. Basically, good enough parenting means that as an infant and toddler your emotional and physical needs were adequately met, your primary caretakers were reasonably consistent and available, and you were given adequate supervision, protection, and nutrition. Without these important stepping-stones a child cannot develop the necessary foundation to develop into a healthy adult. A child who is neglected in this way doesn't develop a coherent, enduring sense of self. She is filled with a feeling of emptiness that can only be filled with external sources of support.

For example, those whose mothers had several other small children to take care of or who became pregnant again while still caring for another infant are often shortchanged when it comes to nurturing and attention. This is the case with Roni:

"When I was born my sister Carrie was only a year old and my mother had three other kids to take care of. She just didn't have time for me. My older brother Mark told me he remembered me lying in my crib crying all the time. He said he'd come in and put a pacifier in my mouth and try to soothe me but Mama would just let me cry myself to sleep."

As it was in Roni's situation, it generally isn't only the fact that the mother is too busy to care for each child adequately, it is also the attitude the mother has toward her children that determines whether they feel loved and cared for:

Roni said: "I don't ever remember my mother holding me when I was little. All I remember is following her around, tugging on her skirt, trying to get her to pick me up or pay attention to me. It was as if I was invisible to her."

Even if you did indeed receive adequate bonding and parenting as an infant and small child, suffering from the loss of your primary caretaker, particularly in early childhood, due to illness, divorce, death, or other factors, can cause problems serious enough to place you on the extreme end of the continuum. Finally, severe and/or prolonged emotional, physical, or sexual abuse can also cause you to suffer from an extreme version of the problem.

In most instances there are multiple factors contributing to an extreme version of the problem—an inadequate bonding experience with at least one primary caretaker, the long-term absence or loss of one or both parents, severe neglect, a pervasive feeling of being rejected by a parent, and an experience of some form of abuse during the early years of development.

This means that some of you who suffered from neglect and abuse in childhood will fall within the moderate range on the continuum, while others will fall in the extreme range. The reason is that it is not the neglect or the abuse alone, whether it be physical, emotional, or sexual, that determines how damaged you were as a child. Some people who experienced especially traumatic abuse are less affected than those who suffered less abuse. For this reason, knowledgeable therapists emphasize the entire context of the experience of childhood trauma rather than isolated actual events.

Despite the impact of abuse on a child's psychological development, other contributing factors are of equal or more importance, namely whether you got off to a good start developmentally, the environment in which the abuse occurred, and the support or lack of support you received from others following the abuse experience.

While it is often a neglectful family environment that allows sexual abuse to occur, those victims who were also neglected will inevitably suffer more adverse effects from the abuse than those who were nurtured both before and after the abuse experience.

For example, if your mother was unable to emotionally bond with you when you were an infant and you were then sexually abused by your father from ages five to ten, you not only were traumatized by the abuse experience but you also did not have the emotional foundation to help you cope with the experience. In addition, because you were not emotionally close to your mother, you would be less inclined to tell her about the abuse and feel that you were on your own without any hope for rescue.

FRIDA KAHLO: AN EXTREME CASE OF A DISAPPEARING WOMAN

Strongly influenced by the effects of an inadequate attachment to a primary caregiver, Kahlo was a needy, depressive woman who was intolerant of aloneness and had a constant feeling of being a misfit. Born to a mother who was too ill to care for or even feed her newborn daughter, Frida never had the opportunity to have a bonding experience with her mother. No doubt still grieving for the newborn son she had just lost, Frida's mother had her breastfed by an Indian wet nurse. When her mother discovered that the nanny was drinking alcohol she fired her and hired a second nursemaid, causing Frida to break the bond with the only mother figure she'd known, though this relationship lacked the sense of attachment, tenderness, and intimacy one usually associates with "mother and child."

In her painting *My Nurse and I,* Frida depicts herself in the arms of an Indian wet nurse. Salomon Grimberg, the author of *Frida Kahlo,* wrote:

> There is no eye contact between the nanny and Frida. No cuddling, not even a sense of attachment; the nanny's face is covered by a mask, and her transparent left breast reveals swollen milk ducts; drops of milk spill onto Frida's unresponsive lips. Frida is listless, self-absorbed, and to the viewer it is not clear whether she is living or dead. The nursemaid holds Frida's small body as if offering her to the viewer. . . .

But there were other factors adding to Frida's already shaky sense of self. When she was six years old her older half sister Margarita told her she was not the daughter of her parents (a lie), but was picked out of the trash. As an adult Kahlo recalled that those words had such an impact on her that she "immediately became an introverted creature." These words would no doubt have affected any child, but since she already felt that there was something horribly wrong with her, they affected her more profoundly by confirming what she already believed.

Contracting polio in the same year, being an invalid for nearly a year, and coming out of it all with a thinner right leg reinforced her feeling that she was defective even further.

What Your Adult Behavior Can Tell You

In addition to looking at your history to help you determine the severity of your problem, examining your adult behavior can give you even more significant clues. The following questions will help you determine whether the experiences of neglect, loss, or abuse you suffered likely pushed you into the extreme category.

Adult Behavior Questionnaire

1. Have you been unable to experience a long-term relationship that lasted longer than a year? (This question applies only to those over twenty-five.)

2. Do you need almost daily reassurance that your partner loves you?

3. Are there times in your relationships when for no apparent reason you feel very loved, only to be followed by times when you are certain your lover doesn't love you at all?

4. Do you constantly question your partner's love based on criteria such as how considerate or inconsiderate he is, how often he is affectionate or wants to make love with you, or how much attention he pays to other people?

5. Do you constantly accuse your partner of being unfaithful even though there is no evidence that he is?

6. Do you often drive by a man's house to check on whether he is with someone else or if he's at home as he said he'd be?

7. Have you ever exploded in a jealous rage and then regretted what you'd said or what you'd done while in the rage?

8. Are you often shocked by your own behavior when you are in a relationship?

9. Have you ever felt so frustrated or angry in a relationship that you damaged the property of your lover?

10. Have you ever become so frustrated or desperate in a relationship that you became emotionally or physically abusive?

11. Have you allowed a partner to emotionally, physically, or sexually abuse you?

12. Are you ashamed to admit that you've taken a lover back because you can't bear to live without him, even after he's beaten you severely?

13. Have you ever stayed with a lover even though he is repeatedly unfaithful to you?

14. Have you ever stayed in a relationship that you know was damaging to you because you were afraid of being alone?

15. Have you ever had such a difficult time accepting the ending of a relationship that you continuously called your ex-lover on the telephone or mailed him letters even after he asked you to stop?

16. After a relationship is over, have you ever parked outside his house for hours just to be near him?

17. Even long after a relationship is over, do you call your ex-lover on the phone and then hang up just to make him mad or hear his voice?

18. Have you ever stayed with a man who emotionally, physically, or sexually abused your child?

19. Have you ever seriously feared that a relationship or a man was going to drive you insane?

20. Have you ever engaged in behavior (such as stealing, prostituting yourself, or selling drugs) that you were strongly opposed to or behavior that is completely uncharacteristic of you to please or to keep a man?

21. When a relationship is over, do you suffer from severe, debilitating depression that lasts for more than two weeks?

22. Have you ever attempted suicide or seriously considered it because you were so distraught about a relationship ending?

23. Have you retaliated against an ex-lover by damaging his property or getting him in trouble with his job or with the law?

24. Do you still feel enraged with an ex-lover every time you think of him or hear his name mentioned, even though you've been apart for several months or even years?

25. Have you ever seriously considered killing an ex-lover?

If you answered yes to more than five of the above questions, the likelihood is very strong that you are suffering from a more extreme version of the Disappearing Woman syndrome. In addition, if you answered yes to more than two of questions 18 to 25, you most certainly fall on the extreme end of the continuum.

There is no shame and should not be any self-blame in being at the extreme end of the continuum. It just means you didn't get some of the breaks some women got. And always remember: healing can only begin with honesty and self-awareness. In addition to suffering from the same cultural conditioning and biological hardwiring other girls received, you either didn't receive good enough parenting to prepare you for an autonomous life, you had an overly possessive, consuming parent who did not allow individuation, and/or you experienced severe emotional, physical, or sexual abuse.

No matter where you fall on the Disappearing Woman continuum, there is hope for a change. In the next part you'll learn strategies you can begin using immediately, whether you are single or currently in a relationship. These strategies will help you begin to reverse the cultural conditioning that has encouraged you to lose yourself in relationships. Even more important, they will enable you to trade in your unhealthy behavior patterns for those that strengthen rather than diminish your sense of self. And while they won't heal the damage from your childhood, they will help you stop causing yourself more harm by continually repeating the cycle of neglect, abuse, or rejection in your current relationships. As you come to realize you have options and begin to take better care of yourself in relationships, you'll also find that both your self-esteem and your self-respect are increased.

How to Maintain Your Sense of Self while Flourishing in a Relationship

The Seven Commitments

In this part I will provide specific strategies to help you flourish in a relationship while learning how to maintain your individuality and your identity. By following these strategies, those of you who are currently single will learn to behave differently in your next relationship. By learning to go slowly, maintain a separate life, stay in the present and in reality, not change yourself to please your partner, have equal relationships, and speak your mind—all the strategies suggested in the next several chapters—you'll discover you will not only be able to maintain your sense of self better but also tend to attract men who respect you more and treat you as an equal.

These same suggestions can also work for those of you who wish to "start over" in your current relationship and can be especially beneficial for those who are reconciling after a separation. Once you have shown by your behavior that you will no longer place the relationship or your partner ahead of your own needs, you will likely demand a newfound respect from your partner.

You'll also learn how to apply the information you've already learned, particularly the differences between women and men, to help you relate to men in a way that is less threatening to them and more fulfilling for you.

Instead of thinking of these strategies as rules you must follow in order to stop losing yourself in relationships, I encourage you to think of them as commitments to yourself. By making and keeping these seven commitments you'll find you will not only stop losing yourself in your relationships with men but also begin to attract more of the type of men who are willing to make a commitment to you.

5

Commitment 1

LEARN TO GO SLOWLY

True love is not a feeling by which we are overwhelmed.
It is a committed, thoughtful decision.

M. SCOTT PECK

Love is a process, not a destination . . . a holy interpersonal environment for
the evolution of two souls.

DAPHNE ROSE KINGMA

The moment I met him I knew he was the one for me.

TAWNY, AGE TWENTY-FOUR

Earlier, you learned that men tend to have thicker boundaries and are more
defended against intimacy than women. Because of this it makes sense that
men tend to go more slowly in a relationship than women. This is a constant
source of frustration for many women who accuse men of being afraid of
commitment. While some men do have problems with commitment, it's also
true that many women become emotionally involved too quickly and scare
away those men who are willing and able to commit. And many women
become involved with men without taking the time to discover whether they
are able and willing to commit, setting themselves up for disappointment and
rejection.

One of the most important things you can do to ensure that you will not
lose yourself in a relationship, as well as not scare off men, is to go slowly.

In this chapter you will learn exactly why it is important to take plenty of time when it comes to getting involved in a relationship with a man. You will also learn specific strategies to slow yourself down and to discourage a partner who is pushing too hard and too fast.

Disappearing Women tend to fall in love at first sight or become instantly infatuated far more than other women. But this is a surefire way to lose yourself. *Getting involved in "instant" relationships—relationships that begin with very little preparation, little or no information, and based on little or no reality—is one of the most common ways women lose themselves in relationships.* If you identified with the information from chapter 3 on thin boundaries, there is even more reason for you to slow down in your relationships with men.

While we often read and hear romantic stories about "love at first sight" and see them constantly depicted in films, this portrayal only encourages women's tendency to fantasize and reinforces the myth of the white knight on the shining horse. *The fact is, you cannot truly love someone you do not know.* You can be in love with a fantasy or with who you *think* the person is, but not with the real person.

To establish a healthy, lasting relationship, one based on mutual interests and complementary personalities, you need time—time to get to know the other person, and time for him to know you. Not the superficial, beginning-of-the-relationship persona that we all initially present, but the *real* person. This true self is revealed only through time, as layer after layer of defensiveness is stripped away and as our false self slowly melts.

Dating used to be a time when two people would get to know one another, to determine whether they were compatible enough to begin a love affair. Today, people seldom even date in the true sense of the word. As the comedienne Roseanne joked, "I don't date, I get married." While this is good for a laugh, the consequences can be quite sad.

Back in our grandparents' and great-grandparents' time, a young woman tended to date several men at the same time. This gave her the opportunity to compare one man with another and to learn which type of man she preferred. Since the rules of social and sexual behavior were far different then, the couple would spend their time socializing with other young people, attending dances, picnics, and parties. There was plenty of time for a woman to observe her suitor in various social situations and to determine whether they enjoyed the same activities. While I'm sure their hormones were as active as ours, because of social mores, they seldom acted on their impulses, at least in the beginning of the relationship, which allowed them to remain far more objective as they got to know one another.

You owe it to yourself to take the time to get to know a man before embarking on a romantic relationship. Nowadays it is hard enough to make a relationship work because of the stresses of modern living. Why risk a broken heart unnecessarily just because you jumped in too fast?

The Consequences of Instant Romance

1. One of the biggest problems with "instant romance" is that by the time you finally get to really know the man you've become involved with, you are already emotionally and sexually involved and can no longer be objective. This makes it nearly impossible for you to perceive the man for who he really is.

In addition, Disappearing Women tend to perceive people as either all good or all bad. If they find themselves instantly attracted to a man, they tend to idealize him, put him on a pedestal where he can do no wrong, or justify any wrong he does. If you have someone on a pedestal, your view of him is obstructed and distorted—you're simply not seeing the real person.

Some men are very charismatic and very good at casting a spell over women. These men know women—they have studied them carefully and know exactly what women want and what they want to hear. Disappearing Women are particularly susceptible to such charmers, partly because they are hungry for attention and affirmation and partly because they tend to live in fantasy so much.

By the same token, Disappearing Women tend to cast a pretty good spell themselves. They tend to present an idealized image of themselves to a man, appearing far more understanding, hip, flexible, or whatever, than they really are. When these two spellbinders get together it's hard to tell who's fooling whom.

2. If you don't take your time to really get to know someone, you run the risk of being disappointed later, when you discover who he really is. Since you have probably idealized him in the first place, he'll come tumbling down from his pedestal as soon as you get to know him, causing you to feel devastated. And you'll no doubt resent him because you'll feel he fooled you so much. Unfortunately, you're probably so hooked into him by then or so emotionally dependent that you'll find it difficult to leave.

3. Conversely, when he gets to know you, he may also be disappointed. He may feel that you've tricked him, that you "caught him" by presenting a false version of yourself. You'll try even harder to please him, but since

you really aren't what he wanted in the first place, you'll never be able to, *even if you make yourself into someone else.*

If this scenario sounds all too familiar, you have even more reason to get to know a man before getting involved. Don't continue to set yourself up by rushing blindly into even one more relationship. Determine that this time you are going to do it differently.

4. Another problem with instant romance is that instead of taking the time to get to know a man and determining whether they have much in common and are compatible, many Disappearing Women base their decision on appearances (i.e., how he looks and how successful or powerful he appears to be) and/or on their immediate reaction toward him. Unfortunately, appearances can be deceiving, as can initial impressions.

While it is certainly important for women to trust their feelings and initial instincts to a certain degree, we can't always trust them when it comes to a man. First of all, our instincts or intuition can be clouded by our hormones, overshadowed by negative patterns of attraction based on childhood experiences, or distorted by feelings of insecurity or inadequacy.

In addition, many a woman has overridden her gut instincts when a man is particularly attractive, charismatic, sexy, or powerful. This was the case with my client Allison. Although she intuitively knew that she was going too fast and had too little information about the man, she found herself embarking on a whirlwind romance that ended very badly:

"Deep inside I knew I was taking a big risk with Hank. He was too smooth and too evasive about his background. But he was so handsome and so charming I guess I just got swept off my feet.

"I've always been insecure about my looks, so having a man as handsome as Hank fawning all over me was such a boost to my ego. He seemed devoted to me, calling me up every day, sending me flowers. And he didn't stare at other women the way a lot of men do. When we were together his entire attention was on me."

Unfortunately, Hank turned out to be a con artist who swindled Allison and her friends out of a great deal of money. A so-called entrepreneur and inventor, he managed to get them to invest in what he convinced them was a sound business deal, only to skip town with all the investment money.

"When I found out that Hank's attraction to me was based on the fact that I had connections with some wealthy people, I felt like such a fool. How could I have been so naive?"

Overriding your instincts and not listening to your inner voice is the first and most significant sign that you have begun to disappear in a relationship.

When a woman becomes invested in a relationship, whether it is because she has been lonely for a long time, because, like Allison, she feels unattractive or unlovable, because a man is particularly attractive or powerful, or because she has already had sex with him, she is far more likely to ignore her intuition and her better judgment.

"Love at First Sight" with Clearer Eyes

Instead of misinterpreting your feelings of instant attraction as the real thing, begin to view them with a more realistic, skeptical eye. If you are like most Disappearing Women, you can afford to be a bit skeptical when it comes to men and instant romance, and you certainly can't afford to maintain a naive stance.

More often than not, love at first sight is actually symptomatic of one or more of the following:

1. *Being caught up in an illusion or fantasy.*

Since you don't really know this man, your feelings of "love" are no doubt based more on fantasy than reality, more on the illusion of who you want him to be than on who he really is. When you are caught up in this fantasy world, you tend to view everything that happens as "magical" and "special," and this blinds you to the reality of what is actually happening.

2. *Unfinished business from the past.*

Those who come from homes where their emotional needs were not met will often "fall in love" right away with a man who seems to offer the unconditional love they are so hungry for. In actuality these women are looking for the "all good" parent, the parent they didn't have but fantasized about having. However, no one is "all good," no one loves unconditionally, and no one can give you now what you didn't get as a child.

3. *Evidence that you're repeating a pattern.*

One of the reasons many women give for becoming involved so quickly with a man is that they feel so comfortable with him, like they've known him for years. The reason they feel this way is that they have known him for years, just in another form. They've been getting involved with people just like him all their lives.

There is a story that is often told at Alcoholics Anonymous meetings: "If there is only one practicing alcoholic in a roomful of people at a party, a woman whose parents were alcoholic, who is codependent, or who is an alcoholic herself will walk into that party, take a look around, and make a bee-line for that one man, bypassing all the healthy men as she does so."

This is but one of the typical patterns that women repeat every day, mis-taking comfort or intense attraction for love when it is actually an unconscious attempt to rewrite the past. Examples of other common patterns are:

- becoming attracted to someone because he reminds you of one or both of your parents;
- becoming attracted to someone because he reminds you of another sig-nificant authority figure;
- becoming attracted to someone who reminds you of an abuser.

These patterns are based on our futile attempt to master and change what has already happened—that is, if you couldn't get your parents to love you in the way you wanted or needed, you become involved with those who are very much like your parents and try to make *them* love you.

4. *Avoidance of the pain of separation from parents (inability to individuate).*

Earlier I mentioned the process called individuation, in which a child grows up to develop a separate identity from her parents and other authority figures. Unfortunately, for many children, especially those who did not receive "good enough" parenting and those who were abused, this process becomes arrested at a certain age and they do not complete the individuation process. Since they have not developed a fully actualized, separate self, they have a tendency to merge with those they become emotionally involved with, seeking the connectedness they longed for as a child.

Those who had parents who were too enmeshed with them, who did not encourage them to individuate but instead to remain dependent on them, also grow up having difficulties with individuation and they, too, can become attracted to men who are very much like their parent—in essence, replacing one parental figure for another.

5. *Avoidance of the pain of separation or rejection from a previous lover.*

Sometimes a woman will become instantly attracted to a man because he reminds her of a past lover, in terms of the way he looks or behaves. In this way she not only "replaces" her lost love but also can avoid the pain of end-ing the previous relationship.

6. *Your fear of being alone.*

Many women allow themselves to get swept up by a man who declares he's fallen in love with them even though they don't initially feel the same way. These women are often so afraid of being alone that they rationalize to themselves that it feels good to have a man be so crazy about them for a change and that his love will be contagious. In essence, these women are merely settling for what they can get instead of holding out for what they desire and deserve.

7. *The desire to achieve power, talent, or wealth vicariously through someone else.*

Women, who still have to work much harder to achieve the kind of wealth, fame, and recognition that men do, tend to do the next-best thing: they become satellites to brighter stars, hoping that some of the brightness will shine on them.

In addition, many women have disowned their own power and therefore tend to envy the power that men so easily embrace and wield. This envy often manifests itself in a strange love/hate type of relationship wherein the woman is attracted to a man's power but at the same time hates him for it.

Look Before You Leap

When you base your decision to get involved with a man on attraction only, you rob yourself of the benefit of vital information. As good as it may *feel* to be with a man, if you don't know who he really is, you are essentially entering into a relationship with a stranger.

Unfortunately, most women don't give their love life as much respect as they do their money. Women who wouldn't think of investing money without seriously investigating the situation will give their hearts away to a complete stranger.

An even better analogy might be that of buying a house. While you may "fall in love" with a house, you hopefully wouldn't buy it without finding out more about it. You'd want to know all of the following: How old is the house? Are there any major problems with the roof? the plumbing? the electrical system? In fact, you'd hire a home inspector to rule out any major problems. You'd investigate what the neighborhood is like and whether homes in the area have gone up or down in value in the past several years.

The same should hold true for a relationship. Don't allow the fact that you've "fallen in love" (or, more accurately, in lust) with a man blind you to finding out more about him—his family background, his relationship history, his work history, his plans for the future. For example, if having children is very important to you, find out if he eventually plans on having children.

While you don't need to view every potential partner as a potential spouse or a major risk, you do want to find out as much about him as you can to determine if you and he are compatible and to rule out any potential problems.

Why take on a problem unnecessarily? For example, why would you want to allow your attraction to blind you to the fact that a man seems to drink too much, especially if you come from an alcoholic family? Maybe he's just nervous around you, but why not share your own family background concerning alcoholism and check out his reaction? For example, you might say something like, "If you notice, I don't drink. It's because my father was an alcoholic, and I know it runs in the family." If he ignores your comment completely, you may be in trouble. Follow up your comment with some relevant questions about his family and his feelings about drinking, such as, "What about your family? Are there any heavy drinkers or alcoholics?" If there are, ask him how he's coped with the problem and whether he worries about becoming an alcoholic himself.

If you have a pattern of getting involved with men who are unfaithful, wouldn't it seem like a smart thing to ask some questions concerning his dating and relationship history? Asking questions such as, "What was the reason for the breakup?" can provide vital information and can be asked in such a way as not to make a man feel like he's being interrogated. Start out slowly if he isn't much of a talker by prefacing your questions with, "Do you mind talking about your relationships?" or "I hope I'm not being too forward, but I'm interested in getting to know you."

Many women fool themselves into thinking that it doesn't matter what a man's background is. They tell themselves it's just an affair—they are just in it for the sex or the companionship. But in reality, casual sex leaves most women feeling sad and unfulfilled, and they simply cannot separate sex from love as easily as men can. Women tend to get emotionally involved when they have sex, partly because a woman's body releases hormones during intercourse that create a bond with her partner and partly because the more often a woman has sex with a man the more emotionally involved she becomes with him.

How to Slow Down

The following strategies will help you slow down instead of immediately merging with a new man:

• *No matter how wonderful you feel with a man, go slowly.*

In the beginning of the relationship, do not go out with a man more than two times in one week and do not have long phone conversations (over twenty minutes) more than twice a week. Immediate intimacy is a warning sign that either or both of you have a tendency to lose yourself in a relationship or are caught up in fantasy. To reconnect with yourself and maintain your sense of separateness, give yourself time between dates and evenings when you don't talk to one another on the phone. (In addition, he'll want to see you in person more if you don't talk too much on the phone.)

Even though you may feel like calling him the next morning after a date to tell him what a wonderful time you had, save it for the next time you meet. You probably already told him the night before, and you both need space to allow yourself to *process* the date—which means thinking about what occurred, how you felt about what occurred, and whether you really want to see each other again.

Even though you may feel like faxing him a cute note or leaving him a little gift at his office or front door, restrain yourself. In *The Rules* by Ellen Fein and Sherrie Schneider, you may have read similar advice, since the authors warned you that this kind of activity sends the message that you were "too easy" or too desperate. While I agree, I am more concerned that you will send the message that your life is so empty that a date with him is a very big deal; this not only gives a man too much power but also sets a precedent for the rest of your relationship.

- *Don't be blinded by your attraction or your need to be accepted to such an extent that you don't take time to get to know a man.*

Just because you find a man attractive and just because he seems to like you doesn't mean he is the right person for you. Only time will tell whether you are truly compatible. Force yourself to take the time to get to know him by observing him in a variety of situations and in various moods. Arrange for several platonic dates in which you share your likes and dislikes. You can start out by sharing your passions in life (which, by the way, is nearly always a turn-on to people), and notice his reactions to what you are saying (i.e., does he share your interests, or does he make comments that lead you to believe that he has absolutely no interest in what you find exciting?). Then ask him what he likes to do in his spare time or what his hopes and dreams are for the future. Notice such things as how he treats other people, what he says about other people, and how much of himself he shares with you.

- *Don't immediately jump into bed with a man just because you are attracted or because you think you are "in love."*

No matter how strong the chemistry between you, remember that you do not know this person. Sex should only be engaged in with someone you have found you can trust, and this will take time. Engaging in sex too early makes you extremely vulnerable and will cause you to lose your objectivity. Remember—this is what has gotten you into trouble in the past.

Recent studies have shown that most couples have four dates before having sex, and this sounds fairly appropriate. You need at least this much time to get to know one another, to develop emotional intimacy, and to build up to the sex act step by step (a good-night kiss on the first date; holding hands, embracing, and more kisses on the second; deeper, more passionate kissing and fondling on the third). Later in this chapter, I'll share more about how to establish emotional intimacy.

• *Make a conscious decision to have sex.*

Instead of just getting carried away and letting your hormones dictate your behavior, make a conscious decision about whether you are ready to have sex. This decision should be based on how much trust has been established, whether you feel you are ready for emotional intimacy, and a clear understanding of just what type of relationship you are going to have. This can only be determined by discussing with him whether you are each going to continue to date other people or be monogamous, and whether each of you is interested in pursuing a committed relationship.

• *Don't have sex until you have the "sex talk."*

You should *never* have sex with someone without first discussing protection. This doesn't just mean asking a man at the last minute whether he's wearing a condom or not. It means sitting down beforehand and stating loudly and clearly that you are concerned about all types of venereal diseases, including herpes, and that therefore you expect him to wear a condom each and every time. I also recommend that you ask him whether he has herpes or any other venereal disease. Another by-product of the sex talk is that it can be very revealing: How responsive is he to the idea of *always* wearing a condom? Does he seem equally concerned about not contracting or passing on a disease? Is he willing to be tested for AIDS?

• *Give yourself permission to be discriminating.*

Just because a man is interested in you doesn't mean you have to get involved with him. Just because he's handsome doesn't mean he has anything else going for him. And just because he's powerful or successful doesn't mean he'd make a good partner for you.

1. Spend time thinking about what you want in a man and in a relationship, and then set your standards.

2. Make a list of the qualities you want in a man. Be realistic, but include those qualities that you feel are essential to a good relationship.

3. Go over your list from time to time to remind yourself of what qualities are important to you. Do this especially just before you go on a date.

Then when you are on a date, instead of getting lost in his gorgeous eyes or becoming mesmerized by his tales of success and power, concentrate on determining whether he meets your standards. Instead of listening to him talk all night, ask some questions about his history and about his beliefs and values. For example: if it's important to you that a man have ambition, ask what his long-term goals are.

• *Don't tell a new man your life history when you first meet, including all your present and past affairs.*

While it is important to be open and honest about who you are, it isn't safe or healthy to bare your soul and tell a man your deepest, darkest secrets when you first meet. First of all, it opens you up emotionally and causes you to be far too vulnerable. Second, you don't know him well enough to trust him with that much of yourself (i.e., you don't know yet whether he is the type of person who will use the information against you later). Finally, men often get scared off by women who divulge too much about themselves, especially if they open up too soon about all their past and present problems. They perceive this as neediness. There will be plenty of time for confessions once you have developed a more lasting, trusting relationship.

Neither should you go into detail about how many affairs you've had, how many men have dumped you, or how you've felt so deeply depressed after a breakup that you've been practically immobilized for weeks. There is a subtle but distinct difference between presenting a true picture of yourself in terms of what you want in a relationship and dumping all the past garbage of your relationships on his doorstep. You can talk honestly about what kind of man you think would be most compatible with you and what type of relationship you're looking for without bringing up all your past mistakes and heartbreaks. Save this until you've been together for a while (at least six months) and are talking about long-term commitment.

Questions You Need to Ask Yourself

If you or your partner seem to be pushing things, ask yourself the following questions:

1. What's the hurry? Is it fear that is motivating me? Fear that I'll lose him?

Fear that he'll change his mind? Fear that I'll never meet another man who cares about me?

A lot of women rush into a relationship out of fear. They're afraid if they don't get a commitment from a man while he's "hot," so to speak, he'll lose interest and go elsewhere. This prompts women to do everything from having sex with a man before they're ready to pushing for marriage before they or their lover is ready.

The sad truth is that a lot of men (and women as well) are addicted to the excitement and passion that comes at the beginning of a relationship. When the heat begins to fade, they begin to lose interest. If you feel pushed to get a guy while he's hot, the chances are high that he's the kind who'll cool off very quickly, whether you have sex with him or not, whether you get a commitment from him or not.

Some of the women I interviewed for this book told me they rushed into marriage because they were afraid that if the man had time to really get to know them he wouldn't want to be with them. This is a common belief for women who have low self-esteem, but I've found it to be most typical in women who were abused as children and who came to believe, as a result of the abuse, that there is something inherently wrong with them that others would discover in time.

Others fear that if too much time goes by before they get a commitment from a man they risk rejection because of the emotional problems they suffer from. Based on their past experiences in relationships, they know they have a tendency to become jealous, clinging, or demanding, and this behavior has turned men off in the past. Fearful of risking rejection, they push for commitment.

Still others fear they will never meet another man who cares about them the way this one does, or another man who has the qualities this man has. This was my client Lauren's situation. Lauren had been married two times, and with a four-year-old daughter, she feared her marriage days were over:

> Every time I told a guy that I had a kid I could see him mentally packing up to go, you know what I mean? That is, until I met Ben.
>
> Ben seemed to love my daughter; in fact, that's how we met. We were at the park one day when Maggie walked right up to him and started talking to him. I scolded her for talking to strangers, but Ben was so nice about it and he seemed to enjoy talking to her.
>
> We began dating, and he always thought to bring Maggie a little gift. Sometimes he'd come by on Saturday and we'd all go to the park

together. No guy had ever wanted to take my kid along on a date before.

Before long, Ben was talking about getting married and becoming a family. Even though it all happened so fast, he was so kind and considerate, especially to my daughter, that I just fell in love with him.

Lauren and Ben were married after knowing each other for only two months. Unfortunately, it turned out that Ben was much more interested in her daughter Maggie than he ever was in Lauren. He began molesting Maggie shortly after the marriage and continued for nearly six months before Lauren began to suspect that something was going on.

While there is no guarantee that if Lauren had taken more time to get to know Ben she would have discovered he was a child molester, the chances were certainly higher than they were by rushing into marriage.

"Now, looking back on it, I realize that I loved the idea of being a *family*, of having a father for my daughter more than I really loved Ben. And I was so convinced that I wasn't going to get another chance at marriage that I jumped at Ben's proposal without really considering the consequences. It was one thing to take a chance with myself but something else entirely for me to take a chance with my daughter like that."

2. By the same token, if your partner is the one who is rushing things, ask yourself the same questions. What's his hurry? What is he afraid of? What is he hiding? Why isn't he willing to take the time for us to really get to know one another?

If you're getting the distinct message, either through his words or his actions, that the man you are dating is threatening to leave if you don't have sex, if you don't see him more often, or if you don't commit, *proceed with caution!* First of all, threatening to leave for these reasons is unreasonable, manipulative, and controlling, and you don't want to be involved with anyone who is going to resort to such tactics to get his way. The chances are very high that this man is either controlling or incapable of developing the type of intimacy that is necessary for a healthy long-term commitment.

And just as some women push for intimacy and commitment out of fear that once a man gets to know them they won't want to be with them, many men have the same concern. In my client Rosie's case, both she and her partner were operating out of the same fear.

After my father molested me I always felt like damaged goods, like I was rotten inside. I believed no man would ever want me if he found out what had happened. I became very promiscuous when I was a teenager and all through my twenties because I figured I might as well, I was already a slut, and that was all men would ever want from me.

When I met Jacob I noticed right away that he treated me differently from all the other men I'd known. At the end of our first date I invited him up to my apartment and just assumed he'd want to have sex with me. But instead of making a play for me we just sat and talked for a while and then he excused himself and said good night. I assumed he just didn't like me until he called me the next day and asked me out for that night.

We dated for more than a month before we finally slept together, and that night he proposed to me. I was completely overwhelmed. Usually after a guy had sex with me I hardly ever saw him again, and here was this guy asking me to marry him!

Even though I knew we were rushing things, that we really didn't know each other very well, I figured I'd better grab this guy before he got to know me any better and changed his mind. I figured that this was my chance to start all over. I'd make myself into the woman he thought I was.

Unfortunately, there was much that Rosie didn't know about Jacob either. It turned out that Jacob was gay and that he desperately wanted a heterosexual life. Since Rosie didn't push him for sex, he felt that he could perform for her when necessary and that they might even be able to have a child together. He could continue having sexual relationships with men, and Rosie wouldn't have to know.

But eventually Rosie did find out and was deeply hurt. She once again felt used and betrayed by a man, just the way she had with her father. In addition, she began to doubt her own sexuality, fearing that somehow she'd attracted a homosexual man because she was really a lesbian. All in all, the marriage to Jacob was devastating to her self-esteem.

Once again, while there is no guarantee that she would have discovered Jacob's homosexuality had she waited, the chances are fairly high that she might have and even higher that given more time, she would have realized that she and Jacob weren't really in love.

3. If either one of you is pushing for sex or commitment, ask yourself: If it really is true love, can't it wait? Won't it merely deepen as time goes by rather than diminishing?

One of the women I interviewed for this book, Holly, told me that since she'd had a history of making bad choices and of losing herself in relationships, she vowed that from that point on, she'd take her time getting to know a man.

> Am I ever glad I made myself that promise. Right after that I met a guy I'll call Harry. We went out on one date and suddenly he was "in love" with me. Now, in the past I would have felt flattered, but this time I was much more cautious. I told myself, "If he really loves me, he'll wait for me."
>
> He started calling me every morning before I left for work and showing up at my job to take me to lunch every day. It all just felt like too much, and I told him so.
>
> He backed off for a while, and this made me feel more comfortable. Then things started getting hot and heavy and we had sex. After that I really had to work to slow things down because the sex was so good and I was beginning to have strong feelings for him. He wanted to get married, but something told me to wait and see what happened.
>
> But Harry kept pushing me to marry him. He became very insecure and started accusing me of seeing other men. One night after work I even saw him watching me from his car across the street. He really started to creep me out. I told him I thought we should give it a rest for a while, let things cool off.
>
> That's when he really got weird on me. He started leaving notes on my doorstep about how he couldn't live without me. He sounded so pathetic and desperate that my feelings for him started to really change. Then I started getting phone calls at all times of the night and day. The person would always hang up, but I knew it was Harry. By that time I'd lost so much respect for him that I didn't want to see him again, much less get married. I'm so glad I restrained myself for a change. I saved myself from making a *huge* mistake.

4. Ask yourself: Why treat my relationship as if it is temporary if I really want it to be permanent?

There are certain personality types who tend to gobble up anything new in their lives, anything they have developed a taste for. Unfortunately, by overdoing whatever they are into at the moment they also tend to get burned out easily. This was the case with my client Sandra:

> I've always gone to extremes. When I was younger I'd get a tape I liked and play it over and over. I just couldn't get enough of it. Eventually I'd get tired of it and wouldn't want to hear it at all. I do the same thing with food. When I find something I like I'll eat it for days until I get so sick of it I don't want it again for a long time.
>
> Unfortunately, I tend to do the same thing with men. When I first start to like a guy I want to see him all the time. I'm just crazy about him. Everything he does seems to be adorable to me. I buy him gifts and take them by his house and I go crazy if we don't at least talk on the phone every day. I can't stop telling my friends how wonderful he is. It's like I live and breathe him. I become obsessed with him.
>
> If I don't scare the guy off with my behavior I end up getting tired of him eventually. I want to learn to go slowly so I can have a real relationship, one that will last instead of just becoming another flavor of the month for me.

5. Ask yourself: Do I really want to risk rushing into a relationship when I don't know him? What if there are things about him that will eventually turn me off in time, or worse yet, that might be damaging to me? Don't you owe it to yourself to take the time to discover who he really is before committing yourself to him? Don't you want to know the whole person before you move in together or get married?

Only time will tell if a particular man is someone whose habits, values, and attitudes are compatible with yours and someone you'll feel comfortable with on a daily basis. We all have an ideal self we present to new partners in order to impress them. Only by being around each other over time will you each drop your facades and begin to show your real selves. Make sure you aren't already locked into a commitment by the time this happens.

A Healthy Progression

Learning to be truly intimate with another person takes time. Time to get to know one another. Time to discover whether you have compatible interests, beliefs, and values. Time to develop trust. Time to discover whether you are capable of resolving conflicts and disagreements.

True intimacy is established one step at a time by taking a risk, then stepping back and giving yourself some time before taking another. The following list, adapted from my book *Raising Your Sexual Self-Esteem,* is an example of the kind of continuum a healthy sexual relationship might follow:

1. Holding hands and kissing as you get to know one another by sharing your likes, dislikes, goals, desires, and dreams.

2. Deep kissing and petting as you begin to learn more about each other's moods over time.

3. More and more intimate sexual sharing as your sense of safety with the other person grows.

4. Sexual intercourse and/or oral sex following a discussion of one another's romantic and sexual histories, including the important issues of protection against AIDS, and sexual fidelity.

5. Mutual exploration of each other's bodies as you continue to share one another's histories, including the sharing of sexual and other secrets.

6. A commitment to one another that may include an agreement to be monogamous as each discovers that he or she does not wish to be with any other person and as each discovers that he or she can indeed trust the other with his or her body, history, secrets, and most important, emotions.

These steps should be taken slowly and carefully. You should take an emotional or sexual risk only when it is appropriate to how vulnerable it makes you feel at that stage in the relationship.

For some of you, proceeding this slowly and cautiously may seem ridiculous. Many Disappearing Women like to be spontaneous, and few like to constrain themselves when it comes to feelings of attraction and passion.

But for many other people, including those who don't have the problem of losing themselves in relationships that you do, it takes weeks or even months to work their way down the list to step 6—making a commitment—especially if they are honoring their feelings and if they are consciously working to curb their urge to merge. Unfortunately, many of you reading this book have been known to make it to step 4—sexual intercourse (minus the discussion)—on your first date and to reach step 6—making a commitment (without the trust or conscious thought)—within a few days.

Just because you have entered a sexual relationship with a man does not mean the relationship will end up being a permanent one. Not every sexual relationship has the capacity for intimacy. Ask yourself the following questions concerning your sexual partner to help you determine whether it is wise to take the risk of true intimacy.

- Do I truly respect this person, and does he seem to respect me?
- Is he a person I can communicate openly with, and does he seem to be able to communicate openly with me?
- Am I able to be honest with him, or am I pretending, covering up, or putting up a facade?
- Do I believe he is able to be honest with me?
- Do I feel safe enough to show my real feelings with him?
- Are we able to compromise with one another?
- Do we work through conflicts well?
- Do we both take responsibility for the problems in the relationship, or does one of us continually blame the other?
- Can I talk to him about my childhood experiences, no matter how embarrassing they are?
- Can I talk to him about my former relationships?
- Am I willing to talk about how I feel my past is affecting our relationship, and is he willing to do the same?
- Is it possible for me to be my authentic self in this relationship? Or am I more concerned with trying to become the person I think he wants me to be?
- Is there room for me to grow and change in this relationship?

If your relationship continues to develop and to deepen, you can then take greater risks that require still more vulnerability. By carefully and systematically taking risks, one step at a time, and then sitting back to assess your level of trust and openness, you can create a healthy, conscious relationship instead of one driven by fear, compulsion, or unfulfilled childhood needs.

Allow a new relationship to unfold in its own time instead of pushing to make it happen. Instead of becoming invested in how a relationship will turn out, view it with a sense of curiosity. Ask yourself: What does this relationship hold for me? Is this person someone I might consider as a life mate, or is he merely in my life to show me what I *don't* want in a relationship?

View each new person you date as a gift, a lesson. Be open to what he and this relationship can teach you about life, relationships, and yourself.

Remember that no matter how instantaneously you may have connected with another person, the fact is you are strangers, two separate people who may or may not have much in common, who may or may not be compatible. Two separate people with separate histories—family histories, sexual histories, relationship histories, career histories. Two separate people with separate belief systems, values, hopes, and fears.

A good relationship doesn't simply materialize out of thin air. It must be nurtured, given time to develop. Sometimes our first impression is right, but more often it is inaccurate and we look back regretting that we didn't let the relationship evolve over time. Your relationship should be built slowly and systematically, as you would a house, not quickly and haphazardly.

Your foundation will be constructed as you experience one another in various situations and with different people, as you compare your belief systems and values, and eventually as you share your histories with one another.

The walls of your relationship will be created as you develop trust, determine your boundaries, and develop the parameters of the relationship.

Finally, the roof of your relationship is created as you develop stronger bonds and stronger feelings and as you experience a history together.

Starting out slowly will not guarantee that you won't make the mistakes some of the women discussed in this chapter made, nor will it guarantee that you will not lose yourself in the relationship later. It will, however, get your relationships off to a good start by reinforcing the idea that you can be the one to set the tone and the timeline for a relationship and by sending the message that you are not desperate but have a full life that is worth holding on to, helping you attract men who will respect your separateness.

Loving Him

One of the most loving things you can do for a man is to allow *him* to go slowly. By allowing a relationship to unfold naturally, not by pushing or prodding a man into a commitment, he will be more willing to open up and experience the joys of intimacy. By giving men the space they need they will be more likely to come forward, not at our insistence but of their own free will.

6

Commitment 2

BE YOURSELF AND TELL THE
TRUTH ABOUT YOURSELF

When one is pretending the entire body revolts.
ANAÏS NIN

*To know what you prefer instead of humbly saying Amen to what the
world tells you you ought to prefer, is to have kept your soul alive.*
ROBERT LOUIS STEVENSON

As painful as it is to admit, I act like a bimbo around men. I just smile and
go along with whatever they want to do, like I don't have an opinion or an
idea in my head. But I have a dialogue going on in my head all the time—
all the things I wish I could say but can't. And inside I'm seething, mostly at
myself for not saying something, anything, about how I feel, about what I
want, about what I need."

RHONDA, AGE TWENTY-FIVE

One of the most effective ways of ensuring that you will not lose yourself in
a relationship is for you to be yourself. This may sound like an obvious solution, but it is surprising to discover just how many women believe that not
being themselves is the best way to capture and keep a man's affections.

To find out if this applies to you, answer the following questions:

1. How many times in the beginning of a relationship have you pretended to be someone you are not?

2. How many times have you given the impression that you are more understanding or accepting than you really are?

3. How many times have you pretended to like something you don't really like just so you won't hurt his feelings?

4. How many times have you sat through a date with a man smiling sweetly as he told one story after another about his life, feigning interest yet being bored out of your mind?

5. How many times have you nodded in agreement as a man passionately stated his opinion about a political or current issue, all the while disagreeing adamantly about what he is saying?

6. Most important, how many times have you pretended that what a man says he wants in a relationship is exactly what you want when it isn't at all?

What's the harm in doing these things? you might ask. Everyone does it. It's all a part of being polite, of being social. While it's true that we all pretend to some extent, *these acts of pretending to be someone you aren't, of feigning agreement when you strongly disagree, can be among the first steps you take toward losing yourself in a relationship.* Not only does it create a false impression so that a man doesn't really know who you are, it also sets a precedent for you to put up with behavior you find boring or unacceptable in the future.

Unfortunately, it is often women who do most of the pretending. Since women are innately more compassionate, they often pretend in order to protect the feelings of others. In addition, girls are trained to be more "agreeable" and diplomatic than are boys.

Even today women are being encouraged to pretend their way into a relationship. For example, in *The Rules,* the authors tell women *not* to be themselves for the first three dates but to instead present a facade of being sweet, illusive, and nonchalant. They even go as far as to encourage women to "pretend you're an actress making a cameo appearance in a movie."

But pretending is just another way of lying, as Alice Koller, in her wonderful book *An Unknown Woman: A Journey of Self-Discovery,* so poignantly states:

But think of the ways there are to lie, and I'll have done every one of them. Pretending to like something because someone in authority does. Evading a question. Saying only part of what I believe. Not saying anything at all. Shaping my words to fit what I know will be acceptable. Smiling when someone intends to be funny. Looking serious when my thoughts are elsewhere. Agreeing when I haven't even thought over the matter. Drawing someone out just because I know he wants to talk. Trying to amuse in order to avoid talking about something I'm not sure of.

Acting. For the dear love of God, how could I have not understood it before! Those are all pieces of acting. And I don't know where it ends. I have to try to think of one thing I've done that was for free.

Risk Exposing Your Real Self

Men as well as women want to put their best foot forward when they first meet someone. And it is natural when you like or admire a man to want to impress him. You want him to like you, to be impressed with you in return. You want him to think you are kind, generous, loving, smart, beautiful, talented, energetic, or whatever qualities or values you feel are most important.

Both men and women have a "public self" that they present when they first meet someone. While men try to appear to be more competent and less insecure than they truly are, women tend to appear more agreeable, tolerant, and flexible than they really are. Men tend to present false impressions concerning their achievements, their wealth, and their experiences, while women tend to either portray themselves as sexier and more open to sexual experimentation than they really are, or the reverse—less experienced sexually than they really are.

But if you are going to have a healthy relationship, one in which you are accepted for your true self, you will need to set aside your public self and risk exposing your real self. Instead of "putting your best foot forward," you will need to show your partner your so-called negative qualities as well as your positive ones.

Our public self is created very early on when we learn as children that there is "acceptable" and "unacceptable" behavior. Our parents and other authority figures socialize us by rewarding acceptable behavior and punishing unacceptable behavior. Unfortunately, this can lead us to believe that others will not like us if we are ourselves and that we must suppress (ignore) or even repress (deny or "forget") the unacceptable parts of ourselves. Those who were raised in families where they were severely criticized, expected to be perfect, or physically abused are particularly susceptible to believing that they must be perfect to be acceptable.

My Good Girl Act

This was my situation. Raised by an extremely critical, disapproving mother, I grew up believing I was acceptable only if I was a "good girl"—which meant always obeying my mother, never questioning authority, and always being polite and kind to others. When I was "bad" my mother would verbally humiliate me and often stop speaking to me for days at a time. In addition, my mother's public image was extremely important to her, and since I was an extension of her, so was mine. That meant that no matter how I felt about people I was supposed to be cordial to them and at least *pretend* that I liked them.

When I started dating I continued my good girl act. I assumed the only way I could get men to like me was to passively and compliantly go along with whatever they wanted. I smiled sweetly, listened attentively, was kind, caring, and generous. The men who fell in love with me thought they were getting an angel. Unfortunately, they weren't seeing the entire Beverly, just a facade.

Although there certainly was a side of me that was all those things, there was another side that men never got to know—that is, until we were in the midst of an intense relationship. Then they got to see the entire me, the side that was fearful and jealous and needed constant reassurance of their love, the side that felt so needy for love that I became selfishly demanding and unable to see their point of view or recognize their needs.

Looking for Daddy's Love

In addition to believing that men will not accept us unless we are perfect, many girls and women develop a pattern of pretending they are someone they are not from their experience of trying to capture their father's attention. This is especially prevalent among daughters who had neglectful or absent fathers. Carmen, age twenty-four, told me about her experience:

> My father was very distant and preoccupied. I remember anxiously waiting on the front porch for him to return from work each night only to be terribly disappointed with his cool greeting. At dinner I tried to get his attention by telling funny stories about school, but he would listen patiently for a few minutes and then turn to talk to my mother. The rest of the evening I would try desperately to get his attention by singing little songs or by dancing around the room while he read his newspaper.

This belief that she must entertain her father or earn her father's attention often carries forward into a girl's adult life, causing her to work too hard to gain and keep the attention of men, setting her up to lose herself in relationships.

In Carmen's case, she tries so hard to impress men that they seldom ever get to know the real Carmen. As she explained to me:

> I always feel like I have to entertain a man to keep his attention. I put on a real show, acting silly and trying to get him to laugh at my jokes. But the real me is a fairly quiet person who loves to read and be close to nature. Most men never get a chance to see this side of me. I'm too afraid to show it, since I've already convinced them I'm this happy-go-lucky person and it seems to be the only way I can continue getting their attention.

Many women whose fathers have left the home due to a divorce also feel they must be perfect or they must work extra hard to achieve or maintain their father's love. Many divorced fathers try to remain close to their children; unfortunately, once a marriage ends, many drift away, seeing less and less of their children and eventually not seeing them at all. According to published findings in a nationwide study conducted by researchers at the University of Pennsylvania—which from 1976 to 1987 tracked more than one thousand children of divorced parents from all socioeconomic levels—nearly half of these children had not seen their fathers in the previous year.

It is often those fathers who were closest to and the most involved with their children who disengage from their children. After being with their children every day it is just too painful for these men to see their children at designated times—in essence, to become a "visitor" to their children.

The problem of getting and keeping their absent father's attention when they do see him is overwhelming to many girls. For many, each visit with her father can feel like a first date in which she feels she must put her best foot forward each time. This was the situation with Amy, age forty-one:

> I saw my father sporadically, all through my childhood, but he never seemed to be all that happy to see me. I assumed it was because he was disappointed in how I'd turned out. After only about an hour together he'd say he had to go and I always thought it was because of something I'd done or said. So I was always on my best behavior with him, afraid

that if I was ever my real self with him he'd go away and never come back.

These experiences with her father left Amy hungry for male attention. When she began dating she continued the same pattern of behavior, always being on her best behavior with men, doing whatever they wanted so they wouldn't leave her.

Making Him Fall in Love

Many women learn early in their dating careers how to make a man fall in love with them by playing down who they really are and playing up who they think the man wants them to be.

By presenting a false picture of who you are you may "catch" a man and make him fall in love with you. But the sad thing about it is that he will not be in love with the real you. He'll be in love with an illusion, and you'll need to keep up the illusion if you are to keep him. That means you will have to continue to pretend to be someone you are not.

Unfortunately, you hurt both yourself and others whenever you attempt to become what you think others want you to be instead of who you really are. *By attempting to be someone else, you run the risk of losing yourself.*

Sooner or later, when what is left of the real you begins to emerge, your partner will feel tricked and angry, as well he should. This only adds to men's fears of being manipulated by women and the impression some men already have about women being dishonest.

Clear Up False Impressions

In addition to putting up a false front, some Disappearing Women don't clear up false impressions, or set a man straight who has created an illusion about them. This was the case with Janette:

When I first met Paul he somehow got the idea that I was practically a virgin—that I had only had sex with a few men. I am kind of shy and I do tend to dress a bit conservatively so I guess that might have been what gave him that impression. But I also think he had some kind of fantasy going on about me. He started calling me his "little princess" right away and he'd say things like, "Of course, you're not anything like *that*," referring to women who'd been around. He seemed to pride himself on treating me like a lady and protecting me from what he called "the ways of the world." If we went to a movie where there was overt sexuality he'd always apologize and tell me he didn't know the movie was going to have scenes like that.

I have to admit that in a way, I liked being treated like that, but in another way it made me feel strange, like he wasn't seeing the real me. He waited a long time before trying to have sex with me, and I liked that, too. It was so different from other men. But by the time we finally did have sex I was afraid to respond very much. I didn't want to disappoint him by letting him know I'd been around.

He wasn't a very good lover and there were lots of things I could have shown him that would have made our sexual relationship a lot better, but by then I was stuck playing the part of the innocent, naive woman.

Had she cleared up the misunderstanding right away, she and Paul might have been able to enjoy a wonderful sex life. As it was, Janette merely tolerated their sex life and grew more unhappy year after year.

By clearing up false impressions you not only present yourself more honestly to the other person but also set a precedent for honesty in the relationship.

The Chameleon Syndrome

The biggest price you pay for pretending is that *when you pretend you are someone you are not, you begin to disappear.* The real you begins to fade away behind the shadow of your facade. To make matters even worse, you may begin to lose track of who you really are. This is especially true of those women who have thin boundaries.

Thin-boundaried people are much more likely to take on the values, beliefs, and interests of others. Unlike those with thicker boundaries, their values and beliefs are not set but are flexible and malleable depending on who they are with, partly because they want to please others and partly because they are so easily influenced.

This is why some Disappearing Women are compared to chameleons, the reptiles that take on the colors and patterns of their environment. These women can be gregarious or shy, conservative or radical, depending on who they are around. They are so bent on fitting in and being accepted that they simply take on the actions, opinions, beliefs, and values of those around them.

Some women are such emotional chameleons that they unconsciously end up changing themselves to be more like their partners without realizing it. They take on their mannerisms, their way of speaking, their attitudes, ideas, and behavior. This was the experience with my client Lexi:

> Several years ago a good friend of mine told me that I take on the personality of whatever man I'm dating, but for the longest time I just couldn't see it. But lately, since I've been working with you, I've begun to notice how I do it. It's subtle at first. I start talking like them, you know, using their expressions, that kind of thing. I noticed that with one guy I started laughing the way he does. It's like I'm some kind of mime or something. But the scariest part is that I take on their ideas. I mean, I heard myself spouting off at a party the other day, saying things my boyfriend had just told me the night before, as if they were my ideas. My boyfriend just stared at me in disbelief. He probably thinks I'm really weird.

If you are like many Disappearing Women you've been trying to be someone else all your life and it hasn't been working very well. You've lost your true self in the process and have probably continually felt like a fraud and a phony, just waiting for someone to expose you.

Being yourself may be painful at first. We are, after all, all flawed, and you, like many Disappearing Women, may have a need to be perfect. But accepting that your imperfections and so-called negative attributes are part of what make you unique will help you to stop continually trying to be someone or something you are not. Embracing your imperfections will give them less power, and this will empower you to move past them.

Tell the Truth about Who You Are

In addition to being yourself, it is also important to tell the truth about yourself. This includes telling the truth about the following:

- what you like and don't like;
- what you're looking for in a relationship;
- how you feel at any given time.

This is important at any stage of a relationship, but particularly when you first begin to date a man.

Everyone wants to be loved for who they really are. This is a deep and abiding human need. Unfortunately, many people, especially women, believe that if they are completely honest about who they are or if people really get to know them, they won't like them. Some even believe they are basically unlovable. This is especially true for women who were emotionally, physically, or sexually abused as children.

Sexual abuse in particular makes a person feel like "used property" or "damaged goods." Survivors of sexual abuse feel tremendous guilt and shame, and they often blame themselves for their abuse, as well as for harmful things they have done to themselves and others as a result of the abuse.

In addition, those who were emotionally abused as children and have unfortunately taken on some of their parent's abusive qualities often scoff at the idea of telling the truth about who they are to a man, as did my client Tanya:

"I can't imagine telling a man who I really am and him wanting to ever see me again! I mean, on the outside I'm friendly and courteous to people, but inside I'm critical and very judgmental. I compliment people on what they've accomplished, but inside I'm full of envy toward those who have more than I have."

Although you run the risk of turning some men off by telling them who you really are, you will find that the rewards far outweigh the negatives.

As we discussed in chapter 5, true intimacy is gained by taking one risk at a time. *Risking being yourself is the most important risk you can take.* Since we all have aspects of ourselves we dislike or feel ashamed of, sharing these with a partner can engender a poignant sense of intimacy. It is extremely refreshing to hear someone tell the truth about themselves, and it encourages the other person to be honest as well. Telling the truth about your weaknesses and faults also lets a man know that you are not just a superficial person who is trying to impress him, but someone who has the depth and honesty to look at and own up to her darker side as well.

Of course, I'm not suggesting you dump all your negative qualities on a man on your first date but rather, during the course of time, as you are getting to know each other. For example, if during a conversation a man says he doesn't like aggressive women, instead of agreeing with him or pretending to be passive, share with him that at times you can be quite aggressive and ask him what it is about aggressive women he doesn't like. Then tell him why you like (or dislike) that quality in yourself.

If a man tells you he has a difficult time with women who are jealous, don't sit there and agree with him and pretend you are not one of those women. You may *want* to be the kind of person who isn't jealous or possessive, but if you are, it's important to tell the truth about it. If he knows up front who you really are, he is now in the position to make an *informed* decision about whether he wants to go forward with you. If he doesn't know the real you, he is being deceived, and this is bound to backfire on you. Even more important, if *you* know up front that this man will not be able to tolerate your jealousy, why choose to go forward yourself? You'll only end up feeling bad about yourself each time you have an episode of jealousy, and the relationship is not likely to last long anyway.

Why not be honest about your tendency to be jealous? Explain to him where these feelings come from and tell him that you are working on yourself so you won't become as jealous. Then turn the tables and ask him if he ever becomes jealous. If he says yes, ask him to explain the circumstances. If he says no, ask him how he is able to avoid these feelings. You're likely to discover a great deal about this man during your conversation, including whether he can be trusted, and whether he is able to commit to one woman.

Please note: While it is important to be honest about who you are, if a man is not opening up and being equally honest, curb your urge to bare all. It is only safe to share those aspects of yourself that are especially vulnerable (such as the fact that you have a tremendous fear of abandonment caused by the fact that your mother left you to be raised by your grandparents, or by the fact that your father left when you were six years old and you never heard from him again) if a man is *also* being vulnerable and sharing *his* history.

Unfortunately, some men employ a double standard of honesty, especially in the early stages of a relationship. They urge a woman to be open and honest but secretly become critical of much of what she says. If a man feels that a woman's boundaries are not stable, he may become frightened—even if he's opening up about himself.

Never, *never* allow a situation to develop where you are seen as the "wounded" soul while he is the "together," well-adjusted teacher or counselor. If this situation seems to be developing, back off and turn the tables, as I suggested earlier. You can be honest without telling all, and you want to establish an equal relationship from the beginning, not one where you are seen as the weak, neurotic, or needy one.

The Benefits of Telling the Truth about Who You Are

1. By telling the truth about who you are, you will attract those who genuinely like and appreciate the *real* you, not those who are merely

impressed by a false facade. This will make it more possible for you to find someone you are truly compatible with.

2. This in turn will help raise your self-esteem, since being accepted and appreciated for who you really are will make you feel more accepting and appreciative of yourself.

3. By exposing your true self you are likely to discourage those men who are looking for someone they can manipulate or control, or men who are looking for the "perfect" woman.

4. Most important, by taking the risk of telling the truth about who you are you'll find that you feel stronger and more self-assured. Earlier in this book I presented information on individuation—the process of becoming whole and unique. One of the best ways to complete the individuation process is to put yourself out there in the world, to make a statement, or to take some action that defines you, that separates you from everyone else. *By exposing your true self you also create a stronger self.*

5. Finally, by being honest about who you are you'll decrease your chances of losing yourself in a relationship. Since you've set a precedent by being honest about who you are and how you feel, it will make it a lot easier for you to ask that your needs be met or to speak up when you don't like something.

Become Aware of Your Preferences and State Them Loudly and Clearly!

Many Disappearing Women are raised to be such placators, pleasers, and caretakers that usually they are not in tune with what they need and what they prefer. They often don't make the decision about where to go because they are so afraid the other person won't have a good time, and many truly believe they don't have a preference as long as everyone else is happy.

To many women, compromising and making concessions is a way of life. The preferences of others take precedence over their own on a routine, daily basis. For example, even if she is hungry for fish, if her partner wants to eat barbecue, a Disappearing Woman will likely give in to his desires, telling herself it really isn't all that important to her what she eats.

If your date suggests a place or a type of food that you dislike, *say so.* Most men would prefer that a woman be honest about her preferences rather than pretending. They want their date to have a good time and don't want to spend money on a meal she doesn't enjoy.

Don't pretend to be enjoying yourself when you aren't. If he has taken you to a place that makes you uncomfortable, *say so* instead of silently suffering for the rest of the evening. Many men are sensitive enough to sense your discomfort, and they will probably assume you are uncomfortable with them for some reason. Why let your discomfort get in the way of your getting to know one another and having a good time?

The Benefits of Being Honest about Your Likes and Dislikes

• *Being honest about your likes and dislikes will save you from having to put up with activities and behavior you really don't like in the future.*

For example, let's say the man you are dating is a science fiction buff. He tells you he practically lives and breathes science fiction. They are his favorite kind of movies, the only books he likes to read, and he regularly attends *Star Trek* conventions. Now let's suppose that you *hate* science fiction. Not only are you not interested in it, but much of it scares you. Whenever you've seen a science fiction movie you've ended up having nightmares for weeks.

Sure, by telling the truth about your preferences you might disappoint him. He may wish you had more of an interest and regret that you aren't compatible in this area, but it isn't likely to turn him off completely (unless he's a real fanatic, in which case the relationship probably wouldn't work out anyway). But by your stating up front that you don't like science fiction movies, your partner won't be as likely to expect you to go to them, and you won't be as likely to agree to go even if he does.

Here's another, more common example: By telling a man right away that you don't like being with someone who has had too much to drink, you will not only eliminate men with a drinking problem but discourage those who only overdo it from time to time.

• *Another benefit of being honest about your preferences is that it will make it more possible for you to find a man who has similar interests, beliefs, and values.*

Think of how exciting it would be to express your opinions and preferences about everything from religion to your favorite pastime and find that the man you are talking to has similar opinions and preferences. Contrast this with what a waste of time it is to pretend to have the same opinions and preferences as his.

EXERCISE: *Personal Ads Before and After*

The following exercise will help you become clearer about what your preferences really are.

1. Describe yourself as you'd do if you were placing a personals ad. Include as many of your likes and dislikes as you can think of.

2. Read your ad carefully to determine just how honest you really were in describing your preferences and what you are looking for in a man. Now go back and rewrite your ad, being *completely* honest. Make sure you've included those preferences that are most important to you, and that you describe the kind of man you really want.

Sexual Honesty Leads to Better Loving

Many women have a particularly difficult time stating their preferences when it comes to sex. Some become so confused between what they *should* do and what they really want to do that they can't tell the difference.

During the first stages of passion or the honeymoon phase of a relationship, both partners tend to focus on trying to please their partner more than on being honest about their real desires, preferences, and needs. In addition, many people are not clear about what their own sexual preferences and needs are.

Also, in new relationships people usually make love to their new partner by doing what turns them on, by doing what pleased a previous partner, or by doing what they have read women or men like. During the honeymoon period everything tends to feel good, but people become more discriminating as time goes by. At that point, if you don't let your partner know what turns you on or off, you will reinforce the belief that what is being done is okay, encouraging your partner to continue as he has.

Many women believe that their partner should be sensitive enough to know their needs without being told. How often have you heard someone say, "If I have to ask for it, I don't want it"? When you think about it, doesn't this seem rather silly? Don't allow this kind of misguided thinking to get in the way of your receiving the kind of touching and stimulation you really desire. No one is a mind reader, and no matter how well your partner knows you, there is really no way for him to know what you want sexually at any given time.

Some women are afraid to ask for what they want sexually for fear of being rejected. If they are able to ask at all, they couch their requests in indirect language, hoping their wishes will be understood but protecting themselves in case they're not. Unfortunately, the fear of not getting what they want can create a self-fulfilling prophecy. If you don't ask for what you want directly, your partner may never know what you really desire. And if you interpret not getting what you want as a confirmation that you were right not to ask because you wouldn't have gotten what you wanted anyway, then you won't make your needs known the next time either. Although it is difficult, being vulnerable with your partner by openly communicating your sexual preferences is an excellent way of building trust in him.

Many women also have the erroneous belief that the best way to communicate their desires to their partner is to do to him what they would like their partner to do to them. Unfortunately, this method of communication leaves just too much room for miscommunication. The main drawback to nonverbal communication is that it can be misunderstood. Often verbal communication is necessary to straighten out confusion created by nonverbal communication.

In a survey conducted by Philip and Lorna Sarrel, sex therapists at Yale University, it was found that among women who told their partners exactly how they like to be touched, seven out of ten indicated they have orgasms "every time" or "almost every time" they make love. The Sarrels concluded that the ability to share thoughts and feelings about sex with your partner is the single most important factor in a good sexual relationship. They also found that the good communicators had intercourse more often and were more likely to be satisfied with its frequency.

How to Talk to Your Partner about Sex

Many sex experts feel that the best time to talk about sexual matters is not when you're ready to have sex, or during sex, but at some other time. Then you and your partner will both be less likely to perceive suggestions and information as criticism. Make sure you don't bring up the subject during an argument or a disagreement.

Your first attempts at communication are likely to be somewhat awkward, but picking a time when you and your partner are both relaxed and when you feel close to one another will enhance the possibility of good communication and make it a little less uncomfortable. You may want to begin the conversation on a long walk or drive or use a book or television program to initiate the discussion. Just make sure you won't be distracted or interrupted and that one or both of you are not preoccupied with something else.

If you have been in a relationship for a while but have been unable to be honest about your preferences, open the conversation by reassuring your partner that you wish to continue the relationship or by expressing your love for him. You may want to say that you don't believe you've adequately communicated your needs in the past, or reassure your partner that you are not blaming him. Then begin to discuss your concerns about your sexual relationship, which of your needs are not being met, and the changes you wish to occur in the relationship. Finally, encourage your partner to share his feelings and any suggestions that might make lovemaking more satisfying to both of you.

Tell the Truth about How You Feel

It is especially important to tell the truth about how you feel. Although women are far more in touch with their emotions than men and can easily communicate about their feelings with women friends, many hold back emotionally from the men they date, especially in the beginning. Some hold back because they don't want to turn a man off, or in an attempt to be "fair," "open-minded," or caring.

What do I mean by telling a man how you feel? Certainly I don't mean that you go into a long diatribe about the argument you had with your best friend or that you share your deepest feelings about your mother, at least in the beginning of the relationship. But it is important to be honest about how you *generally* feel that night. For example, if you have had a very rough day, don't put on a happy face and pretend that everything is great. Without necessarily going into details, mention that you've had a rough day and that you're looking forward to a relaxing evening in his company.

The following guidelines will help you decide when it is appropriate to tell a man exactly how you feel:

• If a man does something on a date that offends you, *tell him about it.* Don't put up with behavior that is irritating, offensive, or insulting out of politeness. By not telling a man how you feel about behavior that is bothering you, you give the impression that the behavior is acceptable to you. Worse yet, you may send the message that you are passive and can be easily dominated or controlled.

There are certainly men who are more attracted to passive women, women they can dominate and control, women who will do whatever they desire. But by making the commitment to reading this book, you've declared that this is not the kind of woman you choose to be. You've either learned your lesson from being too passive in the past, or you know instinctively that this is not the path you wish to take in life.

Believe it or not, there are just as many men who are attracted to assertive, outgoing, independent women. These men are truly confident in their own ability to maintain *their* sense of self in a relationship and are looking for a woman who is the same. When they sense that a woman is overly dependent they think, "This woman is going to suck the life out of me," and they run the other way. They want a woman who will meet them face-to-face, who will take the risk of showing them *exactly* how they feel about any given situation, who will take the risk of truly being themselves. They want a woman who will stand toe-to-toe with them and debate the issues because they find this kind of woman stimulating and exciting. And finally, they want a woman who will meet with them heart-to-heart. They want a woman who isn't afraid to share her deepest feelings because they want to be able to do the same.

- If he asks you how you are feeling about him, *tell the truth.* Don't pretend you like him if you don't. Many women pretend to like a man because they are lonely and want to be taken out on dates, but it is terribly unfair to do this, and is a waste of your time and his. If you sense he likes you a lot more than you like him, be honest about how you feel. *Don't lead him on.* You hate it when a man leads you on, so don't do this to a man. Treating others the way you want to be treated will make you feel good about yourself and will pay off in the end.

- If you really like him and had a fabulous time, *tell him!* Playing hard to get doesn't get you anywhere, but honesty might. Most men feel complimented when a woman likes them. Since you're working on going slowly, you won't be vowing your undying love, just the fact that you like him and that you enjoyed yourself.

The Benefits of Telling the Truth about How You Feel

1. Men are socialized to express only a narrow range of emotions. Expressing feelings of confusion, fear, weakness, vulnerability, tenderness, and compassion are considered "unmanly," and so most men develop powerful denial systems that allow them to block out these feelings. Therefore, many men look to the women in their lives to encourage them to feel and express their emotions. They welcome a woman who is in touch with her emotions—they find it attractive.

There are, of course, men who are afraid of strong women, afraid that if a strong woman gets hold of them they will lose themselves. And, of course, there are men who are afraid of women who show their emotions because their own emotions are so frightening to them. If you scare this kind of man away, it is probably for the best.

2. If he enjoyed himself, too, he'll feel much more like asking you out again, knowing you had a good time.

3. Another side benefit of being honest about how you feel about him is that you will encourage him to be honest. Wouldn't you rather know how he's feeling about you, one way or another, than waiting around not knowing whether he's going to ask you out again? If you're met with silence when you tell him you had a great time, you've probably got your answer. While this may hurt at the moment, it will save you the agony of waiting for him to call and the disappointment when he doesn't.

4. Telling the truth about how you feel will improve your chances of continuing your relationship.

As your relationship progresses it will be even more important to continue telling the truth. Not telling the truth in a relationship is like not watering a garden. It doesn't matter how carefully you till the soil or how many seeds you plant, if you don't water it regularly, your garden will wither and die. The same is true of a relationship. It doesn't matter how good a start you got off to by telling the truth about who you are, what you like and dislike, and how you feel—if you don't continue telling the truth about these things, your relationship will slowly wither and die.

When you begin to hold back the truth from someone you care about, you end up holding back your love as well. The love and magic you once felt together gets buried underneath a pile of uncommunicated emotions. Each time you suppress a feeling you don't want to deal with, you destroy a little more of the passion you once felt for your partner.

Unfortunately, some women can't tell the truth about what they feel because they really don't know. They are so out of touch with their emotions that they can't tell when they are feeling angry or sad. If this is your situation, you will need to connect more with yourself and your emotions. We'll work on doing this in part III.

If you don't tell the truth about who you are, what you prefer, and how you feel, how can you expect a man to really know you? And if a man doesn't know you, he can't really love you.

No one wants to be with someone who loves only an idealized image of themselves. No one wants to have to be on their best behavior all the time. And most important, no one wants to have to submerge their real desires and feelings to the point that they forget who they really are. Don't set yourself up for this kind of life by pretending to be someone you aren't, by going along with things you don't really want to do, or by hiding your feelings to the point that you lose track of them.

Loving Him

Dishonesty, whether in the form of pretending or out-and-out lies, is unloving. One of the most loving things you can do for a man is to present an honest picture of who you are and what you want in a relationship so he can make an educated decision as to whether he wants to be with you. By the same token, it is very unloving to pretend to agree with a man or to like what he likes when you don't. A relationship must be based on honesty if it is to flourish and grow.

7

⚜

Commitment 3

MAINTAIN A SEPARATE LIFE

*Once the realization is accepted that even between the closest people
infinite distances exist, a marvelous living side by side can grow up
for them, if they succeed in loving the expanse between them.*

RAINER MARIA RILKE

*Respect . . . is appreciation of the separateness of the other person,
of the ways in which he or she is unique.*

ANNIE GOTTLIEB

Relationships are all-consuming for me. I become so caught up with my
emotions that I become nearly immobilized. I can't think of anyone or
anything else. I stop doing all the things that make me who I am—my
journaling, walking, nature, even my spiritual practice. I become so absorbed
in the relationship and in my partner's life that I forget who I am.

ADRIENNE, AGE THIRTY-ONE

A woman's initial dating behavior will set the tone for the entire relationship.
If you drop everything you are involved with to be with a man, this sends a
strong message. Not only does it say that the life you have established is not
that important to you, it also says that you will place a man and a relationship
above all else, including your own needs.

In addition, throughout history women have traditionally relinquished their separate identity when they marry. This begins with giving up their last names, and until very recently, a woman was always expected to leave her own or her family's home to join a man in his home. Moreover, until a couple of decades ago women were expected to give up their occupation, whether it be a teacher, an executive, or a sales clerk, to become a full-time housekeeper.

Even though most women today continue to work, since men still tend to make more money than women, in most relationships the man's job is still considered more important. If a man's job transfers him to another city or town, a woman is usually expected to quit her job, no matter how successful, and go along.

And while most women keep their jobs, women today still find that others view and treat them differently after marriage. This is how Cynthia, age thirty-five, explained it:

> Adam and I had lived together for two years, so I didn't think marriage would really change anything, especially in terms of how we treated one another and how others perceived us. But I was wrong. I didn't change my name because I wanted to keep my identity, but right away people started calling me "Mrs." and I immediately felt diminished. When we went to parties, especially those hosted by my husband's work colleagues, I noticed that men in particular stopped treating me like an individual and more like an appendage to my husband.
>
> And even though I kept my job, there's this assumption that I'll only continue to work until I start to have kids, and this attitude has affected how some of my colleagues at work treat me. Some of them don't take me as seriously.

Whether you are single, married, or in a relationship, in this chapter I will help you begin to make the distinction between rigidity and healthy boundaries and offer strategies for maintaining a separate life and a separate self instead of becoming enmeshed with your partner. These strategies are:

- Maintain your usual schedule.
- Maintain time for yourself and time to take care of yourself.
- Maintain your own friends and social life.
- Do not allow yourself to become isolated.
- Pay your own way.
- Maintain your own separate space.

Maintain Your Usual Schedule

Maintaining your usual schedule, whether it be your work schedule or your daily exercise routine, is vitally important to maintaining your sense of self. For example, if it is important that you return clients' calls in the evening, don't sabotage your career by ignoring them to spend time with your partner. If you have made it a habit of running every morning before work, don't put this aside to stay in bed longer with your lover. While many men, especially those who are workaholics or exercise fanatics, need to slow down and focus on relationships more, most Disappearing Women need to focus and remain focused on other aspects of their lives in order to maintain their identity.

As soon as they become involved in a relationship, many women tend to stop doing things that give them pleasure or a sense of accomplishment. Instead, they take on the task of pleasing their partners.

We all need structure in our lives; the weaker our sense of self, the more structure we need. A good analogy is that those with a weak sense of self are like wet cement. Wet cement has all the properties that are necessary to form a solid foundation, but it needs structure to give it shape. When wet cement is poured on the ground it will ooze and run all over the place unless a structure is built to contain it. Your schedule or daily routine is the container that gives your life structure and stability. Take this away and you risk losing yourself.

CLAIRE BLOOM: A WOMAN WHO SACRIFICED HER NEEDS AND LIVED TO REGRET IT

By putting aside her career and previous life to be with author Philip Roth, Claire Bloom, the beautiful actress of stage and screen, set herself up for a relationship that robbed her of her very self.

In her 1996 memoir *Leaving a Doll's House,* Bloom recounts how, during a business trip to New York (she lived in London), she and Philip became very close (within a few days, of course) and admitted they were in love with one another. When she overheard him talking on the telephone with a close male friend confirming plans to leave together in a few days for a vacation in the Caribbean, she became very hurt. She had planned on spending the time she had left in New York with him and couldn't understand why he didn't cancel his previous plans with his friend. Instead of recognizing the sensibility in maintaining his separate life since they were, after all, a new couple, she experienced this as rigidity.

This is typical of Disappearing Women who tend to rearrange their lives to accommodate a new lover and then resent the fact that he is unwilling to do the same.

On the other hand, by maintaining your usual routine you send the message that you are not desperate for a man, that your life and your needs are important to you, and that they will continue to be important even after you are in a relationship. This, in turn, will attract healthier men who are more capable of equal relationships.

It is equally important for women who are already in a serious relationship to maintain their separate identity by continuing to have interests and friends of their own and by spending time alone to reconnect with themselves.

Unfortunately, once a woman is married or in a serious relationship, she tends to drop her previous interests and even her friends unless they are people who can become friends of both her and her mate. Men, on the other hand, tend to hold on to their friends and fight for their right to maintain their previous interests (golf on Saturday, boys' night out, tinkering in the garage).

During Claire's and Philip's relationship, even during the first few months, when their love was new, Philip maintained his daily routine of going into his studio each day to work on his novels. Claire not only put her career on hold but also patiently waited for him all day to return.

> The sweetness and simplicity of the life we led there in those early days more than compensated for any sense that my other life, that of an actress, was in danger of getting lost. I was happy and cheerful in the mornings, until Philip left to go to his studio; then I began to wonder how I was going to get through the day. I took long walks, planned elaborate menus, I read; but my time was really passed in waiting until Philip came back in the afternoon.

You can see how putting her life on hold left Bloom feeling restless and at loose ends. Without a structure to help define her she was in grave danger of getting lost, which is, in fact, what happened.

Your interests and activities are partly what define you, make you the unique person you are. When you start giving these things up to be with your lover, you are giving up important aspects of yourself, aspects that will be difficult to recapture if your relationship doesn't continue. Even if your relationship continues, why be less than a full person?

It is also important to note that your hobbies and activities are what make you an interesting person and what made you attractive to your new lover in the first place. Remember this whenever you are tempted to cancel previous plans or set aside your obligations, interests, or hobbies to be with him.

Most men, with the exception of those who are insecure or need to control their partners, do not want them to give up their interests to spend more time with them. This is what my client Vincent told me:

> The reason I was attracted to Natalie in the first place was that she was so vibrant and exciting. She was involved in so many interesting organizations and activities. She always had so much to talk about. Then once we got involved she seemed to drop them all, one by one. Sure, I wanted to spend time with her, but I never asked her to give up the things she loved.
>
> After a while Natalie stopped having anything interesting to talk about. I tried to keep up the conversation, but frankly, I was getting bored. We became like an old married couple eating our dinner in silence! It just wasn't fun anymore.

You've no doubt heard this story before. Don't let yourself fall into this trap! Continue taking your night classes, continue your weekly tennis game with the girls, keep up your charity work. All these things add to the depth and breadth of who you are.

As my client Hayley told me:

> When Dylan broke our engagement he complained to me that one of the reasons he fell in love with me was because I was so socially conscious, so involved with helping the homeless and cleaning up the environment. But once we started getting serious I stopped those activities and concentrated on the relationship. My priority became making him happy and spending time with him. He said it all became too much—that focusing all my energy on him made him feel smothered. It made him wonder whether I'd been that committed to the homeless and the environment in the first place if I'd drop them like that. He even began to worry whether I could really be committed to him. I wish I'd known then what I know now. And I want to warn other women not to make the same mistake.

Unfortunately, some of you reading this book don't have any other activities or hobbies besides looking for a man. If this is your situation, my advice to you is to start to develop some now. If you don't, you won't have much to offer a man in the first place. And you won't have a buffer to protect you from losing yourself in a relationship once you are in one. (In part III I'll help those of you who are unaware of your interests to discover them.)

Maintain Time for Yourself and Time to Take Care of Yourself

While it's perfectly natural to want to spend as much time as you possibly can with your partner, you must never do so at the expense of taking care of yourself. Canceling a doctor's appointment to spend the day with your new lover may seem like an innocuous thing to do, but it symbolizes a lack of commitment to taking care of yourself above all else, and it is a subtle yet significant step toward losing yourself in the relationship. If you have a weekly ritual of spending a quiet night at home, taking a leisurely bath, and catching up with friends on the phone, don't sacrifice this important time to be with your partner.

Unfortunately, many women tend to take better care of themselves when they are not in a relationship, as was the case with Joey, thirty-two. Before Joey met Patrick she worked out regularly and took a weekly meditation class to help reduce the stress of her high-powered job. But once she began to date Patrick she dropped the class to spend more time with him, and before long she also stopped working out as often.

> I just didn't have time enough to do all the things I did before and still have time for Patrick. But gradually I noticed that I started getting sick more often and I started gaining weight. I told myself I needed to get back to my meditation class and my workouts, but somehow it always seemed more important to be with Patrick.
>
> After we'd been together for about seven months Patrick started telling me we should spend less time together, that he felt smothered. And he started telling me I was getting too fat and encouraged me to go back to the gym. I felt so stupid. Here I'd sacrificed my health to be with him and he not only didn't appreciate it, he felt *smothered*. I vowed I'd never do that again.

Not only does maintaining time for yourself help prevent you from losing yourself in a relationship, it also can improve an existing relationship and help a new one remain fresh and exciting. Most men have more of a need for distance and space in a relationship than women, and most can handle only a certain amount of closeness before they begin to feel smothered or engulfed and begin to pull away. Unfortunately, many men don't know how to tell their partners when they need distance. Instead, they grow silent, work late, or go out with the boys, which in turn usually causes women to feel abandoned. But when a woman maintains time for herself, she also gives her partner needed space, thereby eliminating or at the very least minimizing his need for space. This will make the time they spend together valued time for both of them.

Maintain Your Own Friends and Social Life

While it is tempting to want to spend all of your free time with your partner, it is very important to maintain the friendships and social life you had before you met him. Although it may not seem the case, you need your social life and friendships now as much as ever—they are part of what makes you who you are. Equally important, you will need to have your social life intact in case the relationship doesn't work.

MARCI: FORCED TO CHOOSE BETWEEN HER FRIEND AND HER LOVER

Marci, twenty-five, one of the women I interviewed for this book, told me the story of how she put her boyfriend ahead of her friend and ended up regretting it:

> When I first got involved with Todd I have to admit I neglected my friendship with Loretta for a while. You know how it is in the beginning of a love affair. You get so wrapped up in each other it's hard to tear yourself away. But before long I started to miss her—Loretta's been my best friend since grammar school, and we've always been there for each other. And I felt guilty about neglecting her. So I told Todd she and I were going to spend all day the following Sunday together.
>
> Well, I could never have anticipated his reaction! He was so hurt that I would be willing to give up one of our days together. We went around and around about it and finally, in desperation, I called Loretta and asked if Todd could come, too. I could tell by her voice that she was hurt, but she agreed.
>
> That Sunday was one of the worst days I ever spent. I was *so* uncomfortable. Loretta and Todd had absolutely nothing in common, and you

could tell that they didn't like each other. You could have cut the tension with a knife. I vowed to never try that again.

That meant I also didn't see Loretta very much after that. I just didn't want to have to hassle with Todd each and every time. I hoped Loretta would understand.

Todd and I were involved for only six months. I just got to the place where I couldn't take his possessiveness and his temper. When we broke up, the first thing I wanted to do was get together with Loretta. I'd missed her so much, and I wanted to tell her all about our breakup and how she'd been right about Todd all along. But I could tell by her voice that she wasn't eager to get together—that she was hurt. She told me she was too busy—that she didn't have time to see me. I knew she was just getting back at me for not seeing her, so I kept trying. But she was really hurt and she wasn't budging.

I felt pretty lonely without Todd, but I was amazed to discover that I felt even more lonely without Loretta. I guess I never realized just how much she meant to me, and the thought of losing our friendship was devastating. It took a lot of apologizing and a lot of reassurance from me that I would never do that again before Loretta finally agreed to resume our friendship, and in some ways I don't think she'll ever trust me fully again. But believe me, I'm never going to let her down again. I've learned my lesson.

Many Disappearing Women are too quick to put their friendships aside to be with their new lover, but it is important to remember that up until now (and possibly in the future) your friendships have been the most stable relationships you've had. Your friends have probably been there for you through all your ups and downs, good times and bad. They've probably grown to accept you for who you are. And they've probably seen you through many a crisis.

Don't underestimate how important this history together has been and will continue to be. Many women, especially by the time they reach their thirties and forties, realize that while their relationships with men come and go, their friends have been a constant in their life, a very important constant.

While it's great if your partner likes your friends and vice versa, it isn't necessary, so don't try to force them to socialize together. In fact, it's important to maintain your friendships separate from your romantic relationships.

Many couples I've worked with who insisted on bringing their friends and lovers together have suffered because of it.

It is natural for you to feel a bit territorial about your friends and not to want to share them with your partner. If your friends become buddy-buddy with your new partner, you may end up feeling a bit abandoned. After all, they were your friends first.

Also, if you have an argument with your partner, you may not feel as comfortable talking to your friends about it if they, too, have become close to him.

Even after marriage, each individual in the relationship should feel free to maintain and seek out separate friends. No one person can satisfy all our needs, and yet some couples take the words "forsaking all others" a little too seriously. Those women who are able to successfully maintain their sense of self in a relationship are those who view the relationship as only one of many ways in which they are connected to other people.

Do Not Allow Yourself to Become Isolated

Once in a relationship, do not allow yourself to become isolated from others. Becoming isolated can cause you to derive too much of your self-esteem from your partner. It makes you especially sensitive to rejection and causes you to become emotionally dependent on him. This was the case with Summer, a twenty-three-year-old client:

SUMMER: FROM OUTGOING AND FUN-LOVING
TO ISOLATED AND INSECURE

When Summer first met Matthew, who was six years older, she had many friends. Being an outgoing, fun-loving, attractive young woman, people gravitated to her. But Matthew was a very insecure man who was extremely threatened by Summer's popularity. Before long he was telling her that she was too friendly to strangers, that her friends were too important to her, and that if she really loved him, she wouldn't need anyone else.

Summer loved Matthew and wanted to make him happy, so she tried being less friendly to people when they went out and stopped seeing her friends as often. After work, instead of going out for a drink with her coworkers, as was her habit before she met Matthew, she went right home. And when her friends called to ask her out for the weekend, she turned them down. She even cut her phone conversations short if a friend called in the evening because Matthew would stare at her or motion for her to get off the phone.

As time went by, Summer became more and more dependent on Matthew. When he had to go to an out-of-state training program for his job, she begged him to take her along because she didn't want to be alone.

> Looking back on it now, I realize that it was a warning sign for me that I'd become too isolated and too dependent. I'd cut myself off from so many people that I actually didn't think I could *survive* without Matthew, even for a week.
>
> Instead of taking advantage of the fact that he was gone and I could finally go out with my friends again, I stayed home waiting by the phone for his nightly phone call. As soon as he hung up I started roaming around the house, crying like an abandoned child. I couldn't sleep because I missed him so much and because I was deathly afraid someone was going to break in the house. I was a mess.

Summer, who had been an easygoing, confident young woman, had turned into a nervous, insecure person who had grown dependent on her boyfriend for her very security.

Equally important is the fact that when your contact with others is limited, your suggestibility is greatly increased. Since you have little contact with the outside world, you not only tend to become too emotionally dependent on your partner but also are likely to become more easily influenced by your partner's beliefs, values, and perceptions. As experts in brainwashing will confirm, when a person is receiving very little information, what she does receive makes a more powerful impression.

MIA FARROW: WHY DID SHE STAY?

Even highly successful women can become emotionally dependent and blinded to what is really going on when they become too isolated in a relationship. In her autobiography *What Falls Away,* Mia Farrow laments:

> Why did I stay with Woody Allen when so much was wrong? How can I explain it to my children, when even to me it is incomprehensible and unforgivable?
>
> I could protest that I didn't know—how could I have known—what he was capable of. How could I believe it. I could argue that the world I had occupied with him for a quarter of my life was so utterly removed

from any other that it was impossible for me to envision a life for myself
beyond it. Every aspect of my existence was interwoven with his.

Mia had, in fact, isolated herself from her friends during her relationship
with Woody. It was only after she was able to break away from him that she
was able to reconnect with them.

I connected with my old friends and slowly, piece by piece, I began to
reclaim my *self*, the identity that had somehow, over the years, slipped
almost out of existence.

In addition to isolating herself with Woody, Mia also made another mistake. She agreed to work for him, making her not only emotionally but financially dependent as well.

When Woody first asked her if she'd like to be in his upcoming movie, her
initial instincts told her not to. Like most actors, she'd been hoping to work
with him, but it felt strange to be offered the role because she was "the girlfriend." And she was concerned that she wouldn't measure up. Besides, life
was complicated enough. What would it be like doing scenes with him and
having him be the director-boss *and* her boyfriend all at once?

Needless to say, Mia didn't heed her own internal warnings and began the
first of thirteen movies they would do together. By the time she became
painfully aware that he was not the man she had envisioned him to be and that
she needed to get out of the relationship, she felt stuck, partly because she had
become financially, as well as emotionally, dependent on him:

I felt I should end the relationship, but I didn't know if I would be able
to do that. Emotionally I was dependent on him, and the possibility that
he would not want to work with me anymore was frightening. I seemed
to have lost whatever definition I had once had of myself as an independent working woman, and in the process I had also lost confidence
in my ability to survive without him.

Pay Your Own Way

Money is power. There is no way around it. *One of the most obvious ways that
a woman loses herself in relationships is by allowing a man to buy her, by letting him have complete control over her finances, or by becoming dependent
on him for her livelihood.*

Certainly this does not mean you don't allow a man to pay for your dinner or take you out on a big night on the town. But it does mean you shouldn't expect him to pay each time and that you should sometimes reciprocate by cooking him dinner or taking him on a picnic you've prepared. And it especially means that at the beginning of a relationship you don't allow a man to buy you expensive gifts, pay your rent, or support you. Even after marriage, you will retain a lot more personal power and will not risk losing yourself in the relationship if you continue to contribute to your own support and the running of the household.

Even married women or women who live with their partner need to maintain a separate bank account with enough savings in it so that you are not dependent on your partner to take care of you or constantly bail you out of financial trouble. Many women end up staying with men they are unhappy with or men who are abusive just because they don't have enough money to pay their own way or enough money to leave.

Because women's salaries are often still less than men's, many women continue to enter relationships with men partly or primarily for financial security. Although things have changed considerably, many women still believe they can't survive without the support of a man, especially women with children.

But this economic dependency can greatly increase a woman's chances of losing herself in a relationship by encouraging her to be overly accommodating toward her partner. This is how Angie, forty-one, explained it:

> When I married Rick I felt pretty good about myself. I knew who I was, and I was proud of the things I'd accomplished. But after only a few years of marriage I noticed that my feelings of self-confidence had greatly diminished. I realize now that because Rick was so wealthy and because I was completely dependent on him financially, I tended to give into his every whim. In many ways I began to think of Rick as my employer—that I had to do whatever he wanted. If he wanted to do something, I'd go along, even if I had no interest in it, including having sex.

Paying your own way also means not working for your partner. Like Mia Farrow, several of the women I interviewed for this book shared with me how they had ended up working for their partners in some capacity—one became her boyfriend's secretary, another the office manager in her lover's business, another her husband's dental assistant. All regretted doing so.

"It just blurred the lines too much. How could we have an equal relationship at home when he was my boss at work?" Dana, fifty-two, shared with me:

"Since Carson told me what to do at work he started feeling like he had the right to do it at home. And I slipped right into obeying whatever he told me to do because I was used to doing it at work."

Maintain Your Own Separate Space

For those who are still single, maintaining your own separate space can mean resisting the temptation to move in together right away (even if you are spending most of your time at his house).

Your home should not just be a place where you live while you wait to meet the man of your dreams and move into your dream house. It is an extension of your identity, a reflection of who you are.

Maintaining your own separate space is similar to maintaining your usual schedule in that it helps provide you with needed structure and identity. It is a place where you keep your most precious belongings, reminders of places you've been and people you've known. It is a place where you can go to find solitude, a place where you can connect with yourself and your deepest feelings.

While many single women experience their homes as a lonely place instead of a warm, welcoming one, it nevertheless provides a space where they can let down their facades, kick off their shoes, and be who they really are without worrying about what someone else is thinking about them. This is essential for Disappearing Women, who are all too often preoccupied with their image and with gaining the approval or recognition of others.

The first months of a new relationship are especially stressful. While it can be a time of great joy and excitement, it is also a period when most people are still intent on presenting their best side to their partner, a time when we are still being careful about what we say and how we act for fear of turning the other person off. Having a sanctuary to come home to, a place where you can let your hair down, relieves some of the stress, helps ground you and reminds you of who you were before you met your partner.

The beginning of a relationship is also a time of great passion, especially when you first begin to have sex together. This is the time when many women are tempted to start spending several nights a week at a man's house or spending all weekend there. While all this closeness can feel incredibly exciting and fulfilling, it can also feel frightening. This is because during this time women are especially prone to merging with their sexual partner and losing track of how they feel. Getting up out of bed and returning home after a passionate night or morning together may be the last thing you want to do, but it is exactly what you need.

You need to go home where you are surrounded by reminders of who you are—pictures of the important people in your life, souvenirs of places you've traveled to, gifts and objects of art you love. You need to take the time to read books and return phone calls, take your clothes to the cleaners, and clean your house.

EXERCISE: *How Much Structure Do You Need?*

To test how important maintaining your separate space is in terms of helping to provide you needed structure, answer the following questions:

1. Do you tend to become depressed after returning home from a vacation or from a visit with a relative or a friend? Is this a feeling similar to the one you get when you return home after spending several nights at your boyfriend's house?

   This depression is what clinicians call *abandonment depression.* While you may convince yourself that you are depressed because you miss your lover so much, the truth is you are depressed because you are once again facing your aloneness. This in turn triggers unconscious memories of times when you felt alone and abandoned as a child.

   The more time you spend with your lover, the more likely it is that you will feel this abandonment depression when you are alone, especially in the beginning of a relationship. You need time to structure a life that leaves room for autonomy in addition to the intimacy of a relationship. Maintaining a separate space where you can go to integrate your new relationship into your present life will provide you this structure.

2. Is traveling especially stressful for you? Are you often relieved to return home from a vacation, no matter how pleasurable it was?

   Starting a new relationship is like going on a journey. It is new and exciting, but it is also stressful. Because you are in unfamiliar territory, you have to be especially alert. You may feel a little disoriented since you probably aren't doing things on your own time schedule and you are away from your familiar surroundings.

   Often what makes a vacation so wonderful is that it takes us away from the responsibilities and stresses of our regular life, with its work pressures, bills, and daily chores. Our mind is freed, and we tend to fantasize about what it would be like to live in this place, to change our whole life. But all the while, in the back of our mind, we have the memory of our real life back home to ground us. This memory helps make our vacation as pleasurable as it is, making every day we are away from our typical stresses that much more precious. However, no matter how much we may regret it when our vacation is over, if we are honest with ourselves there is a small part of us that is looking forward to coming home, where we can relax from the stresses of our vacation and check back in with our real lives.

The same is true of a new relationship. The very things that make it exciting and new are the things that make it stressful. You are on unfamiliar territory, not quite knowing where you are going from moment to moment. Because of this you may tend to become a little disoriented and be especially mindful of your actions.

You also tend to fantasize about what it would be like if you two were to join your lives together, how it would feel to give up your old way of life for an entirely new one with your new lover. Knowing you have to go home or to work makes the time you spend together that much more precious. But deep down inside, if you are honest with yourself, there is a part of you that welcomes those times when you can relax from the stress of the new relationship and check in with the rest of your life.

3. Do you often have arguments with those you are traveling with, especially in the beginning of the trip, en route to your destination, and when you first arrive?

   This is most likely because you are anxious and disoriented about being away from your home and your usual routine, which tends to ground you.

   But it also may be because you are anxious about spending a concentrated amount of time with your partner. We'll discuss the fear of entrapment later on in this chapter.

For those who are married or living together, maintaining your separate space can mean setting up a room in the house that is just yours, a space where you can go to get away, to gather your thoughts, to write in your journal, to pursue creative outlets.

Decorate this space with pictures and memorabilia that remind you of your life before the relationship and that remind you of who you are *separate* from the relationship. Even if space is limited, you can create a space for yourself in an existing room by placing a few meaningful objects there and by taking time alone there from time to time.

TURNING THINGS AROUND FRIDA KAHLO-STYLE

Frida Kahlo was a woman who turned things around in an existing relationship by establishing a separate space for herself and by maintaining certain boundaries.

On December 8, 1940, Frida and Diego Rivera remarried. But it was not the same Frida going back into the marriage. Perhaps it was the fact that she had survived the devastation of the divorce, perhaps it was the reality of her thirty-three years that confronted her. According to biographer Martha Zamora, this time Frida rejoined Diego with her eyes open, accepting the complexities of her own personality as well as his. She began to craft her own ambience, a personal world apart from the one she shared with her husband.

When she returned in 1941 to make the family home her residence, she set about arranging its decor to suit her unique personality. On the walls and in cupboards she arranged her distinctive figurines, pieces of folk art, and an array of toys and dolls. Larger-than-life Judas figures dominated patios and rooms and a skeleton hung next to her bed. The Judas figures, along with her exotic plants and animals, which were her constant companions, appear in many of her paintings.

The headboard to her bed, often her world for long periods of time, was completely covered with photographs of people dear to her, and alongside hung portraits of Marx, Engels, Lenin, Stalin, and Mao. Paintbrushes, pencils, and her diary completed the decoration.

In addition, according to Martha Zamora, Frida made two stipulations governing their reconciliation: She would pay half of the household expenses with earnings from her work as a painter, and they would not resume sexual relations, since for her the mere memory of Diego's infidelities prevented it. While neither of these conditions stood for very long, they represented a strong statement on Frida's part and a move in the direction of independence.

In spite of her poor health, the five years following Frida and Diego's second wedding were the most serene of their married life, a time when they seemed to come to terms with one another. This was more than likely due at least partly to the fact that Frida was determined to carve out a life separate from Diego.

According to Martha Zamora in her book on Frida called *Frida Kahlo: The Brush of Anguish,* by the end of her life Frida had built for herself a personal world separate from that of her famous husband.

> With strength and patient dedication, she created her own work, distinct from the art movements of her time. She demonstrated that she could flourish beneath the shade of a tree as prominent as Diego.

Coping with Your Fear of Engulfment

While many Disappearing Women have a fear of abandonment, many have an equal fear of engulfment. When they spend too much time with a partner, especially in the beginning of a relationship, many begin to feel smothered. This is a sign that you are losing yourself in the relationship and need some time apart.

Most women don't recognize this need when it comes up. Instead, they find they are irritable and critical of their partner. They suddenly discover things about him they don't like and begin to see him as all bad. Some pick a fight in an unconscious attempt to get some distance from their partner, while others withdraw in silence.

Instead of falling into this familiar pattern, recognize your irritability, criticalness, and withdrawal for what they are—indications that you need some time and distance from the relationship. Tell your partner you need a few days to yourself. Unless he's terribly insecure himself or a control freak, he'll respect you for it and you'll get a chance to regain your sense of self before going deeper into the relationship.

Even getting away from your partner for a few minutes can help when you feel suffocated. For example, if you are on a trip with your partner, a solitary walk can help give you the necessary space.

If you have a fear of being smothered in a relationship, it is important that you communicate your need for separate space early in the relationship, or at the first sign that your partner may tend to be a bit suffocating.

HANNAH: THE WONDERFUL GIFT

Hannah, a long-term client of mine, recently became engaged. Although she loves her fiancé, Stephen, very much, she had some reservations about getting married, since too much closeness felt threatening—even suffocating—to her.

I suggested she communicate her concerns to Stephen and make it clear that she would need space in the relationship.

Several weeks went by without Hannah speaking about this again, but one day she came into my office with a huge smile on her face:

Well, I guess I successfully communicated to Stephen how important having my own space is. Last week Stephen surprised me over dinner with the blueprints to a cottage—a cottage just for me, my own private sanctuary—he'd had designed to be built in the backyard of our new home.

I can't tell you what a wonderful gift this is to me. Not only the cottage, but the fact that he really heard how important my space is to me and that he didn't take it personally or become offended. I really feel that now I can get married knowing that I can truly be myself without having to apologize for it. That I can be connected to someone else and still maintain my connection with myself.

You can have a connection with a man without losing the connection with yourself.

In systems theory, a branch of family therapy, a relationship is viewed as a third entity. The goal of a healthy relationship is for each individual to remain intact as two separate beings, while a third entity—the relationship—is created.

When you merge with another person you don't create a true relationship but simply piggyback yourself onto the life of another person, losing part of yourself in the process. Not only have you not created a third entity, but you have lost part of one—yourself.

Allow yourself the space to continue growing, and give your partner the same space.

Loving Him

Since men generally need more space in a relationship than women, maintaining a separate life is a very loving thing for you to do for your man. The more of a life you can maintain outside the relationship, the more you will bring to the relationship and the less tendency you will have to be needy and to demand of your partner things he is incapable of or unwilling to give to you.

If you truly love a man, give him his space by practicing the following:

1. Don't always try to fill in the silences during conversations. Give him the time and space to think and to maintain *his* self. Constant talking can make

a man feel overwhelmed, and it is often just a way for you to avoid connecting with yourself and your feelings.

2. Don't come on too strongly when you first see him (i.e., at the beginning of a date or when he comes home from work), either by talking a mile a minute, or with demands for emotional closeness. Give him some time and space to come down from his hectic day.

3. When your partner begins to send out messages that he needs space, give it to him instead of taking it personally or asking for connection or comfort. Once he has had enough space, he'll return for more intimacy.

8

Commitment 4

STAY IN THE PRESENT
AND IN REALITY

In real love you want the other person's good.
In romantic love you want the other person.
MARGARET ANDERSON

You can never plan the future by the past.
EDMUND BURKE

I live most of my life in fantasy. Reality is just too painful for me. In my fantasy world my lovers are always loving and romantic and kind. They're never impatient and they never get angry with me like the men I date. And they never take me for granted. If I've had a fight with my boyfriend I just go home and go to bed and live in my fantasy world until it all blows over. That's how I get past the pain.

MARJORIE, AGE THIRTY-SIX

In this chapter I offer specific strategies for staying in the present and in reality, another important way for you to stop losing yourself in a relationship.

There are three ways women avoid staying in the present and in reality:

1. living in fantasy and not facing the truth;

2. trying to rewrite the past;

3. not differentiating the past from the present.

Be Aware of Your Tendency to Fantasize

Let's begin with fantasy. As mentioned earlier in this book, Disappearing Women tend to lapse into fantasy when they first meet a man, and many Disappearing Women continue to live in a fantasy world throughout the relationship. They create an elaborate fantasy about who the man is, how he will treat them, what they will do together, and ultimately, how he will change their lives.

Many women weave such a web of fantasy in the very beginning of the relationship that they never get to know the real person. This was the case with Tia, a thirty-five-year-old client of mine:

> I met Hunter while taking a walk along a beach in Malibu. He was tall and tan and good-looking, in that rugged kind of way. We talked casually for only a few minutes, during which time he told me he was in real estate. Then I had to go, so we said good-bye.
>
> I couldn't help thinking about him after that. He seemed to be just the kind of man I had been looking for—athletic, established in his career, but not so status-oriented that he couldn't take time off to enjoy life. I knew he must have money because he'd said he lived nearby, and Malibu is a very exclusive area.
>
> I went back to that stretch of beach several more times hoping to run into him again, and sure enough, I did. From the moment our eyes met I knew he'd been thinking about me, too. We started walking together, and it was just magic. We didn't talk much, we just enjoyed each other's company and held hands.
>
> He asked me out for that Saturday night, and we became a couple from that time on. I didn't find out for a long time that he wasn't at all like the man I'd fantasized about. He lived in Malibu, all right, but in the servant's cottage in back of someone else's house. And he was in real estate, but not as a top selling agent, as I'd imagined. In fact, he didn't even have his broker's license yet.

Just like Tia, many women fall in love with men they make up. Whether they create an illusion about a man's career, his personality, or his feelings about them, these women never really give the relationship a chance to develop. Instead, they weave a web of fantasy that impedes their ability to get to know the real person.

Many of the fantasies women weave have to do with the future, such as what they and their boyfriend are going to do next summer, what kind of a honeymoon they are going to have, and what it will be like when they get married. By allowing themselves to do this they are not perceiving the man or the situation through clear eyes. In addition, by lapsing into fantasies of the future they are probably avoiding dealing with issues in the present and are setting themselves up for disappointment.

This is what Vicki, age thirty-two, shared with me about her tendency to fantasize about the future:

"When I meet a man I'm interested in I immediately begin to fantasize about our future together. My fantasies are very detailed, down to what kind of dress I'm wearing when he asks me to marry him, who I will invite to the wedding, and what our honeymoon suite will look like. I have it all worked out in my mind before he even asks me out on a second date."

Women like Vicki are so ahead of themselves they can't appreciate the moment, and they are far too invested in a man before they have even gotten to know him.

When a woman spends too much time fantasizing about a man in the beginning of a relationship he becomes larger than life, and the relationship itself becomes unreal. The next time she sees him she will tend to feel off-center and awkward, since her emotions will be far more intense than the situation warrants. In this state she is vulnerable to losing herself.

Some women create such unrealistic fantasies they can't help but become disappointed. This was the case with my client Emily, who created elaborate, dramatic fantasies about the men in her life. Here is an example of the kind of fantasy she entertained:

The man I'm dating drives an older car and doesn't dress very well so I pretend he's secretly very wealthy. He wants to make sure I love him for who he really is, not for his money. He falls madly in love with me, and after a few months he decides I really love him, too. He tells me we're going to a party at a friend's house and we drive up to this gorgeous mansion in the hills overlooking the city. When we get there all the servants line up to greet us. We walk in the house and I notice there's no one else inside. He leads me to the back patio, where there's a beautiful table set for two with flowers and candles. We sit down, and he confesses to me that it's his home. I'm so shocked I don't know what to say. A servant pours some champagne and then goes back into the house. He makes a toast to me and looks deeply into my eyes. Then he gets down on his knees and asks me to marry him.

Since Emily's boyfriend is more than likely *not* a secret millionaire, if and when he ever does ask Emily to marry him, she will probably feel let down. Real life just can't compete with her fantasies.

Fantasy as Comfort

Many Disappearing Women have essentially lived their lives in fantasy, some spending more time in fantasy than in reality. They use fantasy as a coping mechanism to help them get through everything from the commute to work to serious illnesses. Some use fantasy to help them get to sleep at night, while others use it to help them get through their lonely weekends alone. Having found no other way to soothe and comfort themselves, they spend hours in bed weaving one elaborate fantasy after another in a desperate attempt to avoid their aloneness.

Women who did not receive appropriate bonding and nurturing when they were babies and toddlers are the ones who are most likely to use fantasy as comfort in this way. Since as infants and toddlers they didn't receive the comfort and soothing they needed when they were distressed, they do not have the memory of this comfort to call on in times of need. Instead, they use fantasies to soothe and comfort themselves.

Other Disappearing Women use fantasy as a way of comforting themselves when they are in unhealthy relationships with men who are unavailable or inappropriate. Several of the women I interviewed for the book told me how the use of fantasy kept them in relationships with married men. Sharon's story was typical:

> I was involved with a married man for five years. All during that time, except for the very end, I convinced myself that he was going to leave his wife to be with me. After he'd leave to go home to his wife I'd lie in bed crying my eyes out, feeling so lonely I thought I would die. Then I'd comfort myself with fantasies about what it was going to be like once we were together and soon I'd feel better and forget all about the pain.

The Two Kinds of Rescue Fantasies

The most common type of fantasy Disappearing Women have is the rescue fantasy—the hope and sometimes the belief that eventually a man will come to rescue them from their loneliness and unhappiness. Rescue fantasies have been encouraged by literature and film, teaching women that they must wait, like Cinderella, to be rescued by the prince. This tendency to live in a fantasy world and to hope that someone will rescue them also comes, as we discussed earlier in the book, from the socialization process that encourages women to feel "less than," incompetent, and helpless. In addition, those who fall on the more extreme end of the continuum may suffer from an intense desire for validation and an idealistic belief that saviors will rescue and transform them, a belief created by the severe neglect and/or abuse they experienced as a child. They hope that they will receive now what they didn't receive as children— protection, nurturing, and unconditional love.

This is the case with my client Maria. Raised in a very chaotic household by a mother who was emotionally, verbally, and physically abusive, Maria reported to me that from the time she was a little girl the only pleasure she remembers having was her fantasies. She couldn't wait to go to bed so she could daydream about a boy she liked or about the man she would eventually marry.

Unfortunately, Maria still lives her life in fantasy a great deal of the time. No matter what the actual circumstances are, whether a man is married, uninterested, or out-and-out abusive, she convinces herself through her fantasies that he really loves her and that soon they will be together and all her problems will be solved. As long as she continues to fantasize this way she doesn't have to face the pain of her childhood or the reality of her present life.

And there is another type of rescue fantasy that women get caught up in. This is the fantasy that through your love a man will be transformed, a fantasy that is common among those typically called "codependent" women— women who have a pattern of getting involved with men they try to rescue or take care of. Codependent women live their life for others, anticipating others' needs, and doing things for others they are actually capable of doing themselves. Often brought up in homes where one or both parents are addicted to alcohol, drugs, food, gambling, shopping, or sex, causing the children to feel out of control, they often gain a false sense of control as adults by becoming involved with men who have major problems such as addictions and who seem to need to be rescued.

Remember Tia and Hunter, the hunk on the beach? Right after they started dating, Hunter told Tia he was down on his luck financially. As she got to know him a little better she discovered that he couldn't seem to keep a job. He told her he didn't like his current job and was looking for something that was more interesting, something he could feel excited about doing. Tia, who had a long history of being with men who had problems making commitments, didn't recognize this as a warning sign but instead told Hunter that she understood and that he didn't have to worry about taking her out to expensive dinners. She told him she'd be just as happy ordering pizza and renting a video. She even offered to cook for him so he could save money.

When I pointed out to her that it sounded like Hunter had some serious problems since at thirty-five he still hadn't found his life's work, she became very defensive.

"Maybe he's never had anyone believe in him before," she countered. "Maybe with my support he'll be able to get his act together. He probably just needs to be motivated."

Tia's comments reflected the fact that she was already lost in a rescue fantasy about Hunter.

The Fantasy of Romance

The fantasy of romance is the idea that by meeting your "soul mate," the one true love meant for you, you will become complete or whole. This belief is based on the idea that we can, seemingly by osmosis, gain those qualities we lack by joining with someone who has these very qualities.

This fantasy has partly been created and made stronger by the fact that there is such a split in most societies between "male" and "female" qualities. Instead of recognizing that we all have within us both male and female characteristics, men are supposed to embody all the so-called male qualities of autonomous thinking, clear decision-making, aggressiveness, competence, and responsible action, and women are supposed to embody the so-called female qualities of passivity, vulnerability, empathy, and compassion.

In addition, if we have repressed or suppressed certain qualities in ourselves because they are "unacceptable" or "inappropriate"—such as aggressiveness in women and passivity in men—we are that much more likely to want to own or possess someone on whom we can project all our missing qualities. So women continually fall in love with men who are doing the kind of work they long to do themselves or living the kind of life they wish they could live. And men often fall in love with women who embody all the emotions they are unable to express.

In reality, the reason romance creates such an intense feeling of melting, merging, and losing boundaries is that, in essence, we are making love to those aspects of ourselves we have repressed, suppressed, or rejected, or that we have not developed in ourselves, as was the case with Justine.

JUSTINE: A LONGING FOR EXCITEMENT

Justine and Brett hit it off right away. Justine admired Brett's enthusiasm and spontaneity. Although she liked her job and had some very good friends,

Justine's life felt very empty to her, and she longed to break out of what she considered a mundane life and to discover more meaning and more excitement. Brett seemed to offer her just that. He introduced her to a lot of new people, people who were involved in the kinds of activities she'd always wanted to do—artists and writers and other types of creative people. Soon she was spending every weekend with Brett and his friends, attending concerts and lectures. Her own friends and the area where she lived began to seem boring to her by comparison.

Unlike Justine, Brett didn't hold a steady job but instead freelanced as a writer for various magazines throughout the United States. Because his work didn't require him to live in one area, he tended to move often, going wherever his spirit led him. Justine had always been afraid to take the kind of risks in life that Brett did. Because of her need for security, she tended to stay at the same job and live in the same area for many years.

After dating for only a few months, Brett started talking to Justine about moving to Oregon, where many of his friends had recently moved. He constantly told Justine about how much more beautiful it was there and how culturally active the area was. Soon Justine began talking about moving up to Oregon, even though she hadn't explored job opportunities there.

When Brett announced he was going to Oregon in a few months and wanted Justine to go with him, Justine hesitated. She didn't want to give up the security of her job and leave the area she'd lived in for so long, but at the same time she chastised herself for being afraid and told herself that this was her chance to finally change her life.

"All I could think of was I didn't want my life to go back to the way it was before I met Brett. I knew I was taking a chance, but at the time it felt worth it to be with Brett and to get a chance at living a more exciting life like he did."

Within a month after moving to Oregon, Justine realized she'd made a huge mistake. The qualities she'd initially admired so much in Brett and had tried to emulate—his free spirit and spontaneity—soon grew old when it came to living with him daily. He refused to make plans and this felt far too chaotic for Justine, who preferred to know what to expect. And although she was having trouble finding a job, all she ever heard from Brett was that she was worrying too much and that the right job was going to turn up anytime now. All she had to do was stay positive. While Brett was generous enough about sharing what little money he had, Justine soon grew tired of living in the small cottage they rented in the back of a friend's house and having no money to spend.

Justine had merged with Brett because she wanted what he had—spontaneity and the willingness to create. But instead of merging with someone who had the qualities she admired, Justine needed to develop them in herself.

In real love we truly appreciate the other person for who he is. In romantic love we merely covet what the other person has.

Real love is expansive, open, and trusting, not restrictive, withholding, and possessive. It is not based on need but on a desire to give the person we love the space and the encouragement to be the best he can be, and in the process we become the best we can be. It is based on caring, trust, and mutual respect.

True love brings out the best in us. Romantic, needy love often brings out the worst. When we genuinely love someone and feel loved, we become the best version of ourselves that is possible, and so does our partner.

How Fantasy Can Lead to Obsessive Love

Often those women who are prone to constant fantasizing are also prone to becoming obsessive. Some become obsessive about a man they hardly know and are not even dating, while others become obsessive about men they are actually involved with.

One of the indicators of obsessive love is having an all-consuming preoccupation with a lover or wished-for lover. Often this preoccupation is painful, since the more you allow yourself to fantasize about a man, the more you want him. The more you want him, the more likely you are to act in ways that drive him away.

We've all had the experience of thinking about a man constantly, wondering whether he is going to call, replaying in our mind everything he said to us or everything that happened the last time we saw him. But some people never outgrow this initial state of preoccupation and instead become driven by obsession.

Just as our culture has encouraged fantasy, it has also cultivated a romantic fascination for obsessive love. We see this fascination played out in everything from ads for popular perfumes to movies such as *Fatal Attraction* and the classic *Play Misty for Me*. We are led to believe by movies, television, advertisements, and popular songs that love is not real unless it is all-consuming.

Fantasy can turn to obsession under the following conditions:

- When your relationship is not mutual—if you don't even know a man or have only dated him once or twice but begin to fantasize about him continuously.

- When the man you are interested in is not available (he is married, involved with another woman, much older, or gay).

- When a man has shown you, either by word or action, that he is not interested in you or not *as* interested in you as you are in him, and this does not diminish your preoccupation with him but, in fact, *increases* it.

No matter how promising a relationship may be at first, the insatiable needs of the obsessive person will drive away most partners. Because she is driven by her own unmet needs and desires, she places these needs and desires ahead of those of her partner and ahead of everything else—including reason.

Although rejection is the obsessor's biggest fear, when confronted with the growing lack of interest or the loss of a lover, obsessors don't let go. Instead, they become even more desperate for their target's love.

While obsessive love may appear to be the ultimate passion, in reality it has little to do with love or passion. It has to do with neediness and longing. Obsessive lovers never have enough of what they want, whether it is more attention, love, reassurance, or commitment.

Whenever you become obsessive it means there is something more going on than mere attraction. You are desperately trying to fill the void inside yourself by merging with someone else, avoiding being alone, avoiding facing your own internal problems, or replaying some drama from the past.

Obsession is when you love someone for what you need him to be instead of for who he really is. It is when you feel you *must* have someone or you will die. It is when you feel you need the other person so much that life seems unbearable without him.

While real love is easy, gentle, kind, and giving, obsessive love is difficult, possessive, and needy. Dominated by fear and jealousy, it is volatile and sometimes even dangerous.

Tell Yourself the Truth

In chapter 6 I encouraged you to tell the truth about yourself to the men in your life. In order to stop losing yourself in your relationships, it is equally important to tell *yourself* the truth about your relationships and the men you become involved with.

There are several ways women fool or lie to themselves about their relationships. Some imagine a relationship is far more serious that it actually is or that a man is far more interested in them than he really is. They misinterpret innocuous signs of friendliness as deep interest. They read into a man's behavior motives that don't exist. And they assume that if he wants to have sex with them it must mean he is in love.

By the same token, many women assume that their own interest in a man means more than it does. Some women convince themselves an intense attraction is love even though they really don't know the man. Instead of questioning their motives for getting carried away so quickly (e.g., fear of being alone, being "horny," or trying to rewrite the past), they allow themselves to be lulled into a love affair with someone they don't know.

E X E R C I S E : *Question Your Motives*

Part of facing the truth about your relationship is questioning your motives for wanting a relationship at this time. Answering the following questions as honestly as possible may help you uncover some motives you were unaware of:

1. Are you especially needy right now? Are you just getting over a bad love affair in which your self-esteem was damaged or you were made to question your perceptions, your desirability, or your attractiveness?

2. Are you experiencing problems at work, in your career, or in school? Have these problems caused you to doubt your abilities, intelligence, or ability to get along with others?

3. Is your self-esteem at an all-time low because you don't feel good about your body or your lack of accomplishments, or because you've just been dumped by a man?

4. Have you just turned thirty, forty, fifty, or sixty and become overwhelmed with the fear that you'll never have another relationship?

5. Are you tired of being alone?

6. Has an unresolved issue from your childhood suddenly come back to haunt you? Are you desperately trying to avoid dealing with this issue by getting involved in a relationship?

7. Are you really looking for a mother or father substitute?

Tell Yourself the Truth about Who He Is

It is easy to get caught up in the initial rush of excitement a new relationship brings. But sooner or later you will need to come down to earth enough to assess the situation more realistically. If you have taken the time to get to know one another as recommended in chapter 5, you now have a fairly good idea who this man really is and how compatible you are together. The problem is, you may not want to face the truth about the relationship because you don't want it to end.

Even when a woman spots a potential problem in her new lover or in her relationship, she will often fool herself into believing that it isn't that important. She may convince herself that the problem won't affect the relationship that much.

Many women ignore or minimize the importance of certain aspects of a man's personality or a man's life in order to justify their willingness to get involved or to stay involved with him. This was the case with Gloria Steinem in her relationship with Mort Zuckerman, a multimillionaire real estate developer who was strongly disliked by many for his business dealings.

Gloria Steinem: Denying a Lover's Real Nature

According to biographer Carolyn Heilbrun in *The Education of a Woman,* Zuckerman was a man who supported policies that Steinem had worked all her life to change. He advocated trade with governments she had publicly protested against, gave dinner parties at which her closest friends would have felt ill at ease, and yet somehow she was able to ignore these glaring problems to be with him. According to Heilbrun, ". . . she had to ignore aspects of his life that were not and could never be attractive to her."

In *Revolution from Within,* Steinem explained it this way:

> Having for the first time in my life made a lover out of a man who wasn't a friend first—my mistake, not his, since I was the one being untrue to myself—I had a huge stake in justifying what I had done.
>
> When he supported the same policies and hierarchies that I was working to change, I thought: Nobody said we had to have the same views. When I told him about a trip I'd made to raise a few thousand dollars for a battered women's shelter that was about to close down, and he in the next breath celebrated an unexpected six-figure check that, he joked, would buy a good dinner, I said to myself: It's not his fault he can't empathize—and besides, everyone can change.

This brings up an even more typical way that women deceive themselves—by convincing themselves that they can change a man or that he will be different with her. Afterward, of course, this same woman will inevitably ask herself, "How could I have been so stupid to get involved with him? Why didn't I heed the warnings?" This was the case with Crystal:

> I suspected Max was a player when I met him but he told me he'd changed, that he's never felt so much love for a woman before, and I

wanted to believe him. I'd just come out of a six-month relationship with a man who told me he'd never loved me, that he was still in love with his ex-wife. I felt so rejected and undesirable and I desperately needed to believe that a man could love me.

I resisted Max for a while because I didn't want to get hurt again, but eventually I gave in. Now I feel like kicking myself for falling for his line. I mean, how stupid can you get? Max is incapable of loving a woman; he just likes to play the game.

You've no doubt done the same thing that Gloria Steinem and Crystal did—held on to a fantasy about a man rather than face the truth and the pain of ending a relationship. It should take only one time for us to learn our lesson, but unfortunately, many Disappearing Women don't seem to learn from their mistakes. It's as if they develop a sort of amnesia shortly after they recover from the pain of their last disappointment and then start the process all over again without taking with them the lessons from the past.

Don't let this be you. Learn from your past experiences and vow to begin working on letting go of your tendency to pretend, fantasize, or deny the truth.

Rewriting the Past

Another way women step out of the present and reality is by attempting to rewrite the past. For example, most women who lost their father before they were grown either through death or divorce suffer from severe feelings of deprivation and abandonment and are left with an unbearable void and what psychoanalyst Ernest Abelin calls an overwhelming "father thirst." This "father thirst" usually causes a girl to look for father substitutes, either in older brothers, grandfathers, or other male authority figures.

Although these substitutes do not provide the continuity needed to actually replace a father in terms of a girl's development, they can help overcome the absence of the father to some degree.

For a girl to feel free to seek out father substitutes, it is very important that her interest in men be supported and endorsed by her mother. However, some mothers convey the message to their daughters that it is not important or necessary to relate to men, and this will usually discourage the girl from her interest in men at a time when it is crucial to her development. When this occurs, one of two things can happen. The girl may grow into adulthood with either negative or indifferent feelings toward men in general, or, once away from the scrutinizing eyes of her mother, her "father thirst" may take over her life, causing her to become promiscuous and/or to enter intense relationships with men—relationships that are highly charged with her unresolved conflicts and unmet needs. In my case it was the latter.

Looking for a Daddy

I was an only child raised by a single mother. I never knew my father, who died in an airplane crash when I was two. Not only did I grow up fatherless, but I had no other male relatives. Instead, I was raised by women—my mother, her friends, and female baby-sitters. Plus, I had only female teachers all through grammar school. The only men I was around growing up were my girlfriends' fathers, but I was never close to any of them, since they were usually at work. By the time I hit puberty I had mad crushes on several boys at school, but since I was overweight, none of the boys paid any attention to me.

It wasn't until I was out of high school and had lost a lot of weight that men began to notice me. My first real sexual relationship was with a man who was considerably older than I was, and we'd spend every weekend together, most of the time spent having sex. I couldn't seem to get enough affection, and he couldn't get enough sex. When we'd finally get out of bed I'd watch while he shaved and got dressed, fascinated by his maleness, hungry to soak in everything masculine.

For years afterward I had one affair after another, mostly with older men. We'd always have an "instant" kind of attraction, end up having sex the first night, and then be together almost all the time after that. But none of them could tolerate my flirting, nor my insanity. Even though I flirted all the time and usually saw other men behind their back, I was insanely jealous myself, constantly getting angry if they even looked at another woman. I was spoiled and demanding and unreasonable, constantly accusing them of not loving me enough. No matter what they did, I was never satisfied.

People always accused me of looking for a father in these men, especially the older ones, but I always denied it. It seems obvious now that I was desperate to get the fathering I'd missed out on as a child. I wanted all of their attention, just like a spoiled child, but at the same time I constantly tested them to prove their love.

I didn't realize it then, but I was trying to rewrite the past, to provide for myself the father I'd never had. Unfortunately, it doesn't work that way. I would have to discover ways to give to myself what I hadn't received as a child.

You don't want the needy child within you who still hungers for good parenting to be the one who is in charge of choosing your partners. That part of you is so desperate and emotionally hungry that her perceptions are distorted. Moreover, she is unaware of your adult needs. Put very simply, children don't pick very good adult companions. She may pick someone who is very "fatherly" and therefore also very controlling, she may pick a playmate who is probably immature and irresponsible, or she may become attracted to another "wounded soul" like herself who might have even more problems than she has—she won't choose an equal partner who will meet your adult needs.

Try instead to connect with your adult needs and choose a partner who can satisfy them. This is obviously easier said than done, but your continued work on yourself will eventually make this possible.

Unconscious Patterns

Another way by which Disappearing Women attempt to rewrite the past is by unconsciously repeating experiences from their childhood in an attempt to resolve them.

If you have found that you have a pattern of picking a certain kind of man—someone who is always unavailable, someone who is always unfaithful—you may be trying to rewrite the past. Freud called this tendency to reenact the past the "repetition compulsion." Author Judith Viorst writes about this compulsion in her book *Necessary Losses:*

> [W]hom we love and how we love are revivals—unconscious revivals—
> of early experience, even when revival brings us pain. . . . We will act out
> the same old tragedies unless awareness and insight intervene.

E X E R C I S E : *Discover Your Patterns*

To break such patterns you must first recognize them for what they are. The following exercise will help:

1. Draw a line down the middle of a piece of paper. On one half of the page, list the positive personality traits of your most current lover; on the other half, list his most predominant negative personality traits.

2. On two separate sheets, do the same for each of your parents or primary caretakers.

3. Notice if there are similarities between the traits of your most current lover and those of your parents. Pay special attention to whether he shares *negative* traits with one or both of your parents.

4. Now, once again on separate sheets, list the personality traits of your previous three boyfriends (if you have had that many).

5. Notice if they share any personality traits, particularly negative ones.

6. Compare these traits with those of your parents.

7. Circle the negative traits that your partners (both present and past) and your parents have in common.

    Most Disappearing Women notice a close correlation between the traits of their partners and their parents. And with few exceptions, the traits that matched up most closely are the negative traits.

    While it seems logical to look for partners who compensate for, rather than duplicate, our parents' inadequacies, the fact is, we do the opposite—we attempt to re-create the conditions of our upbringing in order to correct them. We attempt to return to the scene of our original frustration or wounding in an effort to resolve our unfinished business. Therefore, if one or both of your parents were over-protective or engulfing, instead of looking for someone who allows you plenty of freedom and space so you can overcome your fear of engulfment, you find yourself repeatedly attracted to men who smother you. If one or both of your parents neglected or abandoned you, either emotionally or physically, instead of looking for someone attentive and reliable so you can overcome your fear of abandonment, you find yourself attracted to men who are unreliable.

More Warning Signs of a Pattern

Any or all of the following warning signs may also help alert you to a pattern:

- You can't really explain why you like him, you just do.
- He's your "type."
- Whenever you're around him it's so intense it feels like there is electricity in the air.
- Something about him feels very familiar.
- You feel so comfortable with him, like you've known each other all your lives.
- You develop extremely intense feelings toward him in a very short time.
- You find yourself doing things you never imagined you'd do with him, things that just aren't like you.
- Ever since you met him you've been obsessive—you can't get him out of your mind.

Once recognized, these patterns can be broken by finishing up your unfinished business from the past. We'll discuss this further in part III.

For now, begin by saying no to an intense attraction to a man who is your "type," and be willing to go out with a man when the intense attraction is not there. This may seem boring at first, but give it a chance.

Confusing the Present with the Past

Another way women step out of reality is to confuse the present with the past. For example, Disappearing Women have a tendency to compare their current boyfriend to someone in the past, whether it be a previous lover, their father, grandfather, or brother.

Just because a current lover broke a date doesn't mean he is always going to disappoint you, as your father did. Sure, the feelings of rejection and disappointment may *feel* the same, and it may bring terrible memories flooding back into your mind, but you must remind yourself that he is *not* your father, this is the first time he has done this, and you need to give him a chance.

To prevent the past from contaminating the present, I suggest you try the following strategies:

- *Take responsibility for your reactions.* Instead of blaming your partner for your reaction or immediately assuming that he is just like someone from your past, first allow yourself to process the feelings that have been stirred up. Then, once you are clearer, see if you can make a connection with the past.

- *Learn from the past, but don't dwell on it.* This is especially true for those who have been hurt in past relationships with men. Take responsibility for releasing your past pain and anger either through therapy or self-help programs, and then work toward learning to trust again. This will take time, and you can do it by taking baby steps, but you can't allow the past to contaminate every new relationship.

- *Become familiar with your buttons.* Each of us has buttons that get pushed—triggers that set us off emotionally. It may be a situation that reminds us of the past, or something someone says that reminds us of what someone from the past said to hurt us. Getting your buttons pushed can send you into a tizzy without warning, causing you to become enraged, deeply hurt, fearful, or depressed. For example, those who were emotionally or verbally abused as children often have strong reactions to verbal comments such as "You're lying," "You're crazy," "You don't know what you're talking about," "You're stupid," "I don't believe you," "I can't trust you," or "You're too fat (skinny, tall, thin, etc.)."

Make a list of your buttons. The next time your partner uses one of these phrases, tell him you do not want him to use it again, that it hurts you deeply and reminds you of your past. If he seems to be sympathetic, you may wish to share your entire list, explaining why each phrase upsets you so much. While you're at it, you might wish to ask him to make his own button list and share it with you.

It obviously requires a great deal of trust on your part to share this kind of information, since knowing your particular buttons can give your partner ammunition with which to deliberately hurt you. If you have not established this kind of trust, by all means do not set yourself up for any more hurt by sharing this information.

Your current partner may be constantly pushing your buttons and reminding you of the past, so it is important that you find ways to bring yourself back into the present.

It is unfair of you to hold your current partner responsible for what others have done to you, and it is unhealthy for you to live in the past in this way. By working on differentiating the past from the present you will begin to feel less insecure or intimidated by your current partner and will be more likely to respond to him as an adult, not as a child. The following suggestions will help you make this distinction:

1. Determine who your partner reminds you of.

2. Make a list of the ways in which your partner is different from this person.

3. Whenever you are reminded of a person from the past, make sure you look at your current partner in the face and bring yourself back to the present. Remind yourself of who you are with now.

This last step is especially important for those who were sexually abused as children. Certain things that partners say and do, particularly when they are making love, can remind survivors of the abuser and cause them to confuse their partner with their abuser, as was the case with my client Lupe:

"Sometimes, when my husband and I are having sex, I will freeze. I don't know if it's the way he's breathing or the smells in the room or what, but suddenly I feel like I'm with my father all over again."

I suggested that at these times Lupe open her eyes and really look at her husband's face and tell herself that she is not with her father but her husband. After several weeks she shared with me the following:

"It's really helping for me to open my eyes like you suggested. In the past we'd have to stop altogether because I was so freaked out, but now we just stop for a little while and I'm okay to continue. Sometimes we both keep our eyes open and it makes our lovemaking much more intense and loving."

As much as your partner may remind you of one of your parents, or of someone who abused or rejected you, he is not that person. Continue to work toward differentiating the past from the present so you can see him for who he really is and your relationship for the way it really is instead of as a replay of past relationships.

Learn to Stay in the Present

Learning to stay in the present takes practice and attention, but it can be very rewarding. The more you do it, the more you will be able to do it. The following suggestions may help.

- *Catch yourself in the act of fantasizing about the future or reliving the past.* Bring your focus into the present by deep breathing.

- *Complete the following exercise each time you drift into the past or the future.*

    1. Take a deep breath.

    2. Whether you are sitting or standing, plant your feet firmly on the ground.

    3. Take another deep breath and clear your eyes by opening them wide and looking around the room.

At first you may be able to be present for only a short time before your eyes glaze over or you go into fantasy, but soon you will be able to do it for longer and longer periods of time and will notice when you have been lost in a dream of the future or a memory of the past.

Staying out of fantasy and in the present may make life more difficult for you at first, since you'll be forced to deal with reality, but ultimately it will save you a great deal of pain. Think of it this way: by enduring the discomfort of facing the present and reality today, you will save yourself the devastation of yet another painful breakup, yet another rude awakening when you are forced to face who he really is or what the relationship has really been about. Besides, by staying in fantasy and in the future or the past, you miss the everyday joys of reality—and of your relationship.

Loving Him

It is very unloving to arbitrarily slip a man into one of your preconceived fantasies as if he were a missing puzzle piece. By doing this you are essentially saying that your fantasy is more important than he is. No one wants to be objectified in this way.

It also isn't very loving of you to punish your present partner for what previous partners have done. There are some very good men out there who appreciate good women if given the chance. Don't blow your chance at finding or keeping one by making assumptions about him. Give him the benefit of the doubt.

9

Commitment 5

Don't Go Changing to
Try to Please Him

We must never allow another person's limited perceptions to define us.
VIRGINIA SATIR

*There's nothing wrong with you. Anyone who says
something is wrong is wrong.*
RENAIS JEANNE HILL

*One is taught by experience to put a premium on those few people who
can appreciate you for who you are.*
GAIL GODWIN

I feel like such a fool. I don't know what got into me. After all, I'm not some
lovesick teenager. I can't believe I was willing to give up my house, leave my
friends, and change my entire life for that man. Thank God my friends took
me aside and warned me that he was just after my money.

GERALDINE, AGE SIXTY-TWO

Women are far more likely than men to try to change themselves to please
their partner. This tendency is one of the primary ways women lose themselves in relationships with men. Women will try to change their behavior,
their values, their looks, even their personalities if they believe it means
pleasing their partner, ensuring his love, his fidelity, or his presence in their

lives. Unfortunately, many women believe that the way to keep a man is to do whatever he wants. Time and time again clients have told me, "I thought if I did everything he asked me to do he wouldn't have a reason to leave me."

Why are women so much more willing to change themselves? There are several reasons:

1. As discussed earlier, women tend to have thinner boundaries than men. This causes women to be less rigid and more easily influenced by their partners' perceptions of them and to be more open to changing themselves to please their partners.

2. Women also have been raised to believe that they must be the more flexible ones in a relationship, and many women take pride in their ability to adapt to situations and "go with the flow" versus what they view as men's tendency to be rigid or uptight.

3. Being sensitive to the needs of others and to creating harmony in relationships, women, to their credit, tend to do whatever they can to change aspects of their behavior they come to believe are hurtful to their partner or disruptive to the relationship. Men, on the other hand, fearful of being smothered by a woman, tend to become defensive and to convince themselves that her complaints have no merit.

4. Women tend to have less self-confidence than men. This is especially true when it comes to women's bodies. In numerous research studies it has been shown that most males are satisfied with the way they look, whereas most females are not. This makes women particularly vulnerable to the comments and suggestions their partners make about how they should improve their appearance.

5. Women are far more likely to become involved with men who have more power, more money, or more achievements than they do. This type of unequal relationship sets the stage for women changing themselves to please their partner, since women in these kinds of relationships tend to feel they must work extra hard to keep a powerful man's interest.

How Women Change to Please Their Partners

The most prevalent type of changes women make to please their partners are to their appearance, especially to the contours of their body. Every year thousands of women go on dangerous diets or undergo needless cosmetic surgery in attempts to please their partner and become more like what men say they want in women.

ALENA: WHEN EVEN PERFECT WASN'T GOOD ENOUGH

This was the case with my client Alena, age twenty-nine, who, during her four-year relationship, underwent three cosmetic surgeries in order to please her partner, Mitchell.

Mitchell made it very clear to me that he preferred women with larger breasts. We couldn't go anywhere without him craning his neck to get a better look at a large-chested woman. I felt so inadequate with my A cups that I couldn't stand it.

After my breast augmentation I felt so happy. Mitchell loved them, and he acted so proud of me it was worth the expense and the pain. He even took me to Bermuda to celebrate. He bought me some new bikinis and told me he loved walking down the beach with me and watching the other guys drool over me.

But shortly after we got back he started talking to me about my thighs being too big. I started working out, but I had those kind of thighs that don't really change that much with exercise. Then one night we saw a television program on liposuction. It showed how they could suck the excess fat right out of my thighs. I really didn't want to do it because it looked so gross, but Mitchell thought I should look into it, so I did. My doctor told me I was a good candidate for it and confirmed my belief that I'd never get my thighs to change any other way, so I finally agreed to do it. The procedure went smoothly, and the results were noticeable.

Mitchell just loved the new look, and I was pretty happy with it, too. He seemed to want to make love to me more, and that made it worth it. But it wasn't long before he was talking about my nose. He told me that I was nearly perfect, that with just a little nose job I'd be gorgeous. I knew my nose was a little too long, but I hadn't known it bothered him so much. When he offered to pay for it this time, I finally agreed.

Now that I was "perfect," I assumed Mitchell would finally be happy with me, and he was for a while. But I noticed he still looked at other women, and before long he started in on my weight. It finally began to sink in that Mitchell was never going to be happy with the way I looked, that he was always going to find something wrong with me. When I told him I was happy with the way I looked and that I felt *he* had a problem, he blew up and accused me of being an ungrateful brat who didn't appreciate all he'd done for me. He told me, "If it hadn't been for me, you'd still be a flat-chested, long-nosed excuse for a woman. I *made you* into the woman you are today, and this is the thanks I get!"

That did it. I suddenly saw the real Mitchell, and I didn't like who I saw. Looking back on it all now, I wish I'd have been strong enough to walk away from him long before I did. I want a man who loves me for who I am inside, not just for how I look.

The second most common change Disappearing Women make to please their partner is their tendency to submerge their need for verbal intimacy with their partner. One of the biggest differences most couples have is their communication styles. Women complain that men don't talk about their feelings enough, that they don't open up and share their personal thoughts and plans, and that they don't take responsibility for the negative or sarcastic statements they make about their female partners. Men complain that women try to force conversation or force them to open up, that they nag too much, that they are always trying to stir up trouble.

While men may complain about their partner's communication style, most will not do much about changing their own. Many women, on the other hand, not only give up trying to draw their male partners into conversation but eventually come to believe that the problem lies within themselves—that they are "too emotional" and "too needy." In the end, both the man and the woman agree that he's not to blame for being unable to meet her needs, and that she was wrong for having such needs in the first place.

Finally, women are far more likely to bend their values and change their beliefs to make themselves more compatible with those of their partner.

Cassandra: The Case of the Missing Values

Cassandra, age thirty-four, told me about her experience:

When I met Otis I strongly believed that couples shouldn't have children together unless they are married. I believed a child needs a mother and a father and that the commitment of marriage makes couples more likely to stay together. I came to these beliefs partly due to my religious upbringing and partly due to the fact that I was raised by a single mother in South-Central Los Angeles. It was very hard on me and my mother, and I was determined that my children wouldn't have to go through what I did.

But Otis didn't think it was necessary for a couple to be married to be committed. He thought a marriage license was just a piece of paper.

After being together for three years I wanted a baby very badly and so did Otis, but he wasn't budging about getting married. He assured me that he was committed to me and that he'd always stay in our baby's life no matter what happened with us.

Eventually my desire for a baby overtook my better judgment, and I got pregnant. Otis was wonderful during my pregnancy, but as soon as she was born, he began to change. He became jealous of the time I was giving to the baby, and he complained constantly that our sexual relationship had changed—that we'd lost the passion.

I'd read enough to know that these are typical problems new parents face, but had we been married I believe we both would have felt more secure knowing we'd work it out eventually. Instead, we became more and more distant. He started spending more time at work, and while I knew he loved our daughter, he didn't spend that much time with her. Before long I began to feel like I was raising her all alone, the very thing I hadn't wanted to do.

Then one day Otis went off to work and just didn't come back. He left a letter for me saying he was sorry but he just wasn't cut out for family life. My worst fear had come true. I was going to have to raise my daughter on my own. If Otis and I had been married, maybe it would have been more difficult for him to just walk away. I wish I'd have been strong enough to hold on to my beliefs and refused to have a child together. It's not that I don't love my daughter, but I really don't like the fact that she doesn't have a father.

In this chapter you'll learn which type of changes are appropriate and healthy to make in a relationship and which are not. You'll also learn strategies that will help you stop the self-defeating behavior of changing yourself for each man you meet.

Distinguishing between Good Changes and Bad

It is particularly important that women don't change themselves to catch or please a man in the beginning of a relationship. By changing your beliefs or your way of behaving, or by pretending to agree with something you are really opposed to as a way of impressing a man or keeping the peace, you give the man the message that you can be easily manipulated, dominated, or controlled.

The only changes you should make in a relationship are those you feel will make you a better person, changes you decide to make on your own, not those that are foisted on you by your partner or those made to please a partner.

Women are masters at the art of compromise and reaching consensus, and we have much to teach men in these areas. But there is a difference between compromising and giving in, a difference between attempting to reach consensus and constantly allowing oneself to be won over by another's reasoning and arguments.

There is no sin in standing firm to defend one's values, beliefs, and preferences, no crime in refusing to allow oneself to be manipulated into becoming the kind of person someone else wants us to be.

GINA: DO YOU THINK I'M TOO RIGID?

My client Gina, age forty-two, recently began seeing a man after quite a long hiatus from dating. She'd stopped dating for several years because she felt she was "addicted" to men—that for years her life had revolved around whatever man she was dating at the time. She wanted to prove to herself she could be alone, to spend some time focusing on herself to work through some issues in her childhood, and to develop a satisfying life separate from men. By the time she'd started dating Ian she had done these things and felt she was now able to maintain her separateness within a relationship.

One day, after several weeks of dating, she came into her session very confused. She said that Ian had told her she should change her hairstyle and the way she dressed. He said her hair and clothes made her look old and drab. Gina didn't know what to do.

"I've been on my own for so long now I'm afraid that maybe I've become rigid. I mean, I want to be open to suggestions."

I asked Gina how she felt about Ian's comments and suggestions.

"Something inside me bristled, and I got very upset. I don't know why exactly. I'm sure he has my best interests in mind, and he told me that other women he's dated have welcomed his suggestions."

I asked her if *she* liked the way she wore her hair.

"Yes, I do. I think it complements my face. And I get lots of positive comments on it. In fact, it's one of my best assets."

"And how about your clothes—are you pleased with them?" I asked.

"I am. I think I have very good taste in clothes. And other people tell me they think I do, too."

"Then why would you even consider listening to a man you've only been dating for such a short time?" I asked.

"I don't know. I don't want a man telling me how I should dress or wear my hair. I guess I just didn't want to give the impression that I was too rigid and set in my ways."

Like most women, Gina felt that unless she was flexible and open to change, she would become rigid. But there is a big difference between rigidity and having healthy boundaries. While a healthy relationship involves some compromise on the part of both partners, compromise should never involve changing important aspects of yourself solely on the basis of a partner's preferences.

Areas That Are Out of Bounds

There are certain areas of a person's life that are out of bounds when it comes to making suggestions for change. No man has the right to find fault or suggest you change any of the following, especially at the beginning of a relationship:

- the way you dress;
- the way you style your hair;
- the way you speak;
- the way you eat or what you eat;
- the way you spend your free time;
- the way you express your emotions, even if he feels you are "too emotional";
- the way your body is shaped, including whether he considers you too fat, or too thin, or whether he feels you should exercise more;
- your choice of friends;
- your job or choice of career;
- your education.

Refusing to change to satisfy the desires of the man you love may seem like an unloving thing to do, but it is not. Men know this, and that is why they are so reluctant to bend to the whims of women. Often accused of being selfish and inconsiderate, men intuitively know that they are defending their identity when they refuse to become what their partner asks them to become. They know that their true self is all they have and that to sacrifice it, even for love, is courting emotional annihilation.

Change needs to come from within, based on your desire to become a better person, not simply in an attempt to please or placate a partner's desires or demands. In this way you don't lose yourself in a relationship but rather become a more fully actualized version of yourself.

DEBORAH: GOING TO EXTREMES TO TRY TO PLEASE

Thirty-one-year-old Deborah told me how she lost herself over the course of a relationship by making changes solely motivated by her desire to please her husband, John. From the time they were first married, John set out on a course to change Deborah. He didn't like the fact that she "wasted" money on a hair-stylist, so he told her she should let her hair grow long and wear it in a braid. Since she knew John preferred her hair longer anyway, she gave in to his demands because of her desire to please him.

Then he started in on Deborah's job. She wasn't making enough money, so he insisted she ask for a raise. When her boss refused, John felt she should quit and find a better-paying job. Even though she loved her job and had many friends within the company, Deborah once again gave in to her husband's suggestions and found a job that paid more.

Several years later, when Deborah told John she wanted to have a child, he refused to even talk to her about it. It wasn't the right time. They needed her salary to have enough money for a down payment on a house.

Deborah once again gave into her husband, but six months later her biological clock was ticking so loudly she couldn't ignore it. She brought up the subject of having a child again, reasoning with John that they already had enough money saved to buy a house and that she would work right up to delivery and miss only a month of work. But John wouldn't hear of it. The fact was, he had decided they shouldn't have children at all. He thought having a child would ruin their marriage. Deborah would become preoccupied with the children and not have any time for him.

This is what brought Deborah into therapy. "I've always tried hard to please John, but having a child is important to me, and he doesn't seem to be flexible at all. I've always told myself that John had my best interests at heart, even if he seemed a little overprotective. But now I'm not so sure. I think it's time I stop trying to please him so much and start pleasing myself."

Make Sure He Wants to Be with You

One of the best ways to prevent yourself from getting into a situation where your partner pressures you to change is to be sure your partner wants to be with *you,* not a fantasy of who he wants you to be, not someone he can mold into someone else. If he wants to make you over like Eliza Doolittle in *My*

Fair Lady, he isn't loving you for who you are. For example, if you are basically an entrepreneur who loves the excitement of being around people and new ideas and he wants a stay-at-home homemaker and mother, you are not what he wants. It would be foolish of you to try to make yourself into someone you aren't just to please him or keep him.

Stay Away from Modern-Day Svengalis

Some men have a Svengali complex and want to "make over" or re-create the women they are involved with. This is especially damaging to a woman's sense of self. If she goes along with this she will eventually lose all sense of who she really is in her attempt to become someone else. Annette, thirty-nine, told me her Svengali story:

> When I met Al I was an insecure kid and he was confident and outgoing and I admired him. From the very beginning he was determined to improve me. I'll never forget the first time we went out to eat in an expensive restaurant. When my appetizer came I started to eat the way I usually did. Al just sat and watched me for a few minutes and then he said, "If you're going to eat with me you'll have to learn the correct way to hold your knife and fork."
>
> At first I welcomed his help. I never knew my own father, and my mother had been too busy to teach me things like correct etiquette. Al taught me not only how to hold my knife and fork but how to hold my own in conversations with people and how to dress like a lady.
>
> But after a while his need to make me over began to feel stifling. He showered me with books and grilled me about what I'd learned. I found I liked to read, but I wasn't always interested in the subjects he wanted me to be interested in. He wanted to make me into an intellectual, and that's just not who I am.
>
> Eventually he began to lose interest in me. I guess I just wasn't per-forming to his expectations. It felt devastating at first not to have his undivided attention, but soon it began to feel like freedom. I began read-ing the kinds of books *I* wanted to read and to discover who I really am. Of course, as soon as this happened, Al didn't want anything to do with me. If he couldn't mold me into the kind of woman he wanted me to be, he didn't want me at all.

As was the situation with both Annette and Al and Deborah and John, the need to change a partner is generally more an issue of control than anything else. If a man doesn't love a woman for who she is, no amount of change by her will create that love. What it will create, however, is a growing lack of respect and even loathing within the man at the realization that you are willing to make such changes in the first place.

In general, the more a woman is willing to change for a man, the less of a sense of self she has. Those with strong identities are seldom willing to give them up just to keep a man. They recognize that their identity is all they have and they cannot risk losing it, not for anyone or anything.

In most cases, the more you give in to a man's expectations that you change, the less he will respect you. Because men value emotional strength and power so much, because they feel they must hold on to their beliefs and values to be respected, many men perceive "giving in" as a sign of weakness and an indication that you are a "loser," which, in their mind, gives them permission to walk all over you.

E X E R C I S E : *How Much Have You Been Willing to Change?*_____

- Make a list of the things about yourself that your current partner would like you to change.
- If you are not currently in a relationship, list those things about yourself that your previous partner wanted you to change.
- Now list the ways in which you did change to please either your current or previous partner.

Whether you are happy with your changes or not, looking at them in this way can bring the point home about how much you tend to lose yourself in relationships and whether you tend to choose partners who are bent on changing you.

Just as the popular Billy Joel song advises, "don't go changing" to try to please your man.

Love shouldn't involve having to change yourself to please a partner. Neither should loving mean you must give up all that makes you who you are. As you've no doubt heard many times, to truly love someone you must first love yourself. If you continually give up yourself to the men you love, you will soon have no self to love.

If you have to give up yourself, the way you truly are inside, to please a man, then you shouldn't be with that man. When someone truly loves you he loves you for who you are—not who he wants you to become or who he thinks you can become. True love involves total acceptance of you as a person, your so-called negative qualities as well as your so-called positive ones.

Loving Him

It goes both ways. You shouldn't expect a man to change for you either. Unfortunately, as we discussed earlier, many Disappearing Women hold to the fantasy that they can change the man they love or that if a man would only make certain changes, they know their relationship would work out. But no matter how much "potential" you think a man has, no matter how much happier you think he'd be if only he'd change certain aspects of his life or his personality, you don't have the right to expect these changes from him.

True love isn't about changing the other person into someone else. It's about *accepting* the person you love the way he is. An important aspect of recognizing that you and your partner are separate individuals is accepting that you have your differences and that there will always be aspects of your partner's personality or way of life that you don't like or don't agree with.

This is not to say that individuals within a relationship can't change or never change. Ideally, within a healthy relationship, both people are transformed by the love of the other and make tremendous changes. But these changes are the kind that come from within and as by-products of the love and acceptance each feels from the other, as opposed to the kinds of changes that one partner may feel the other should make.

10

Commitment 6

CULTIVATE EQUAL RELATIONSHIPS

For some reason I'm always attracted to men I feel are better than I am. They're almost always smarter and more confident, and they usually have more life experience. I guess I want to learn from them. But it always turns ugly somehow. I guess being in that one down position encourages men to become controlling.

JADE, AGE TWENTY-NINE

Another way to ensure that you won't lose yourself in your attempts to please your partner is to make sure you have *equal relationships*. An equal relationship is one in which both parties contribute to the relationship in an equitable way and in which each is seen as an equal in the other's eyes.

Unfortunately, Disappearing Women tend to become involved in relationships in which they have *less* power, money, or accomplishments than their partner, relationships where they have *more* needs, more of a tendency to give, or more willingness to commit. This is especially true of women who become involved with older or more experienced men. This scenario, plus the fact that many women feel "less than" men in the first place, creates relationships that are unequal.

When I was in my twenties I immediately felt diminished whenever I was in the presence of most men, especially men in authority. I felt as if someone had let the air out of me. Whatever feelings of personal power I had seemed to disappear, and I even felt physically smaller (I'm five-eight). Although I was no shrinking violet in any other setting, around these men I became a different person. I was no longer gregarious and outspoken, and a quieter, less confident version of myself took over.

Whenever a boyfriend would take me to a party or to another couple's home I became a silent appendage, quietly listening while others talked. It didn't help that I tended to date older men who were far more established in their careers.

Many young women feel this way around successful men, older men, and men in authority. But hopefully, by the time they mature and gain more self-confidence and experience, they begin to feel more equal to men. They grow to trust that their opinions, their knowledge, and the details of their lives are just as interesting as those of others. When this happens it is a sign that they are becoming a Woman of Substance.

A Woman of Substance is a woman who can hold her own while in the presence of men, even men of power and accomplishment. And because she has gained a sense of her own personal power and her ability to achieve her own goals, she doesn't need to attach herself to those who are substantially older or more accomplished to find completion. She can do it on her own.

Unfortunately, many women don't mature in this way. Instead, they continue to look to men to provide them with the approval they cannot give themselves.

EXERCISE: *Are You in an Equal Relationship?*

When a woman enters a relationship with a man feeling as if she is "less than" he is, she essentially gives away her power to him, and this sets the tone for the entire relationship.

The following questions will help you decide whether the relationship you are now in is an equal one and/or whether your past relationships have been based on equality or an imbalance of power.

1. Who has more personal power in the relationship, you or your partner? By "personal power" I mean who do you feel is the stronger of the two in terms of being able to ask for what you want and being able to take care of yourself emotionally?

2. Which of you has a stronger need to be in control? Who usually gets his or her way in terms of choosing what you will do at any given time?

3. Who has control over the finances?

4. Who is more in control of your sexual relationship?

5. Which of you has more self-confidence? Which one feels better about himself/herself?

6. Which of you is more successful in your career?

7. Who makes more money?

8. Would you say one of you feels superior to the other? If so, who?

9. Who would you say loves the other more?

10. Who is more emotionally dependent on the other? Which of you would have a harder time going on without the other?

If you answered "my partner" to most of questions 1 to 8, and "me" to questions 9 and 10, your partner has more power in the relationship.

When you get involved with someone *you* perceive as being more powerful or "better" than you are in some way—because he seems more intelligent, successful, or attractive—you will tend to give in to him far more than if you feel his equal. You'll tend to keep quiet when you should speak up, to tolerate unacceptable behavior, and to generally allow him to control the relationship.

When you become involved with a man who perceives *himself* as being more powerful or "better" than you are, he will tend to take advantage by pushing limits, taking you for granted, or trying to dominate you.

Therefore it is vital that you aim for equal relationships—ones in which both you and your partner view one another as equals. This doesn't mean you are equal in all respects, but that overall, your qualities balance each other out. For example, perhaps your partner has a better job, makes more money, and has more life experience than you do. This could certainly tip the scales to the point where the relationship is unequal. But let's suppose that you have far more people skills than he has and consequently have more friends. He doesn't do as well relating to others and misses having the kind of social life he'd like to have, so he values what you bring to the relationship. This situation can balance out the relationship to the point where you are equal in each other's eyes.

How Unequal Relationships Can Lead to Abuse

Unequal relationships set women up for abuse. Men who have more power in a relationship tend to expect and demand more from their partner, and women who feel "less than" not only tend to bend over backward to please but also tend to put up with abusive behavior.

As much as men feel threatened by a woman's requests for change and believe they must protect *themselves* from being taken over by a woman, many do not hesitate to make demands of their own. This is especially true of men who tend to be controlling and domineering. Since women genuinely believe in creating harmony and consensus, most women attempt to make the changes their partners request, within reason. The difference between Disappearing Women and those who have a stronger sense of self is that Disappearing Women, under the right amount of pressure, will cave in to almost any request from their partners, whether it is reasonable or not. In many cases this scenario turns into emotional and physical abuse. Often, as in the case of emotional abuse, women are completely unaware that what they are putting up with is actually abuse.

Emotional Abuse

There are many ways of being abused without anyone laying a hand on you. Emotional abuse cuts to the very core of a person, creating scars that may be far deeper and more lasting than physical ones.

Emotional abuse is like brainwashing in that it systematically wears away at your self-confidence, sense of self-worth, even in your trust in your own perceptions. Whether it is done by constant berating and belittling, by intimidation, by manipulation, or under the guise of "guidance" or "teaching," the results are similar. Eventually you lose all sense of self and all remnants of personal value.

In the following sections I will briefly describe several types of emotional abuse that some men are prone to exert, and continue exerting if a woman allows it, along with some case examples to illustrate various forms of emotional abuse.

Domination

Those who have a need to dominate have to have their own way—insisting on making all the decisions, not allowing the other person to have an opinion or to speak her mind. They often get their way by threatening rejection or even physical violence if the other person does not comply. Men who dominate also need to be in charge, and because of this they often try to control their partner's every action.

Unreasonable Expectations

It is difficult enough, even in a healthy relationship, to meet your partner's needs and remain true to yourself. But when your partner's needs and expectations are unreasonable, you can never win. It is unreasonable for a man to expect that you will put everything aside to satisfy his every whim. It is unreasonable for someone to expect you to anticipate his needs unless he communicates them to you. And it is extremely unreasonable for someone to expect that you will put up with selfishness, constant demands, and ingratitude indefinitely. When you are with someone who is never pleased, it is time to stop trying to please him.

BARBARA: THE DUTIFUL WIFE

Barbara, age fifty-one, a woman I interviewed for this book, was abused by the unreasonable expectations of her partner:

> When Abe and I first got married I played the role of the dutiful wife. This is how I'd been raised, and I was happy doing it. I loved him and I loved pleasing him. But as the years went by it was harder and harder to please him. He began complaining about everything I did. I didn't cook the meat just right. I didn't put enough starch in his shirts. I didn't clean the bathroom often enough. This went on for years, all the while with me trying harder to please him.
>
> Then he started in on my personality. I didn't seem cheerful enough when we had guests over for dinner, and I talked too much. When I talked I went off on tangents and never stuck to the subject. I complained too much about what was going on in the world, it was boring.
>
> Each time he criticized me I took it to heart and tried to change. I didn't want to irritate him. I wanted him to be happy. But as much as I tried to change, he always found something else to complain about.

The relationship between Abe and Barbara is an example of how a woman gives up her power and, in essence, invites a man to misuse the power she's given him. Because Barbara had given in to Abe so much in the beginning of their relationship, it set the stage for further demands from him as time went on. The more she gave in to him, the more permission she gave him to continue finding fault in her.

Verbal Abuse

This behavior involves berating, belittling, criticizing, name-calling, screaming, threatening, blaming, and using sarcasm and humiliation. It is extremely damaging to your self-esteem and self-image. Just as assuredly as physical violence assaults the body, verbal abuse assaults the mind and the spirit, causing wounds that are extremely difficult to heal. And when a man verbally assaults a woman he is also often intimidating her with the unspoken threat of physical violence.

Blaming

Blaming can be a form of verbal abuse, but it also constitutes a category of its own. A blamer is a person who automatically assumes that whenever something goes wrong it is someone else's fault. If this kind of person ever does admit to being responsible for something or for doing something wrong, he will always justify or rationalize his behavior by trying to convince you that his behavior is an understandable reaction to some deficiency in you, or that he was provoked into doing it by something you did.

For example, if a blamer has impotence problems he will say, "I wouldn't have this problem is you weren't so fat," or "If you'd be a little more assertive I might not have this problem." If a man who tends to blame has a drinking problem he's likely to blame his girlfriend or his wife for it. And if a blamer has a tendency to be lazy, he will blame the woman in his life because she nags at him so much about his procrastination or blame the fact that he isn't getting ahead in life because she takes up so much of his time.

Disappearing Women are especially susceptible to men who blame because they tend to blame themselves so much. A typical Disappearing Woman will automatically look to herself first as the cause of problems in her relationships. And she will be the first to acknowledge her faults and shortcomings and to admit any mistakes she may have made. This gives a blamer ample ammunition to use against her in the future. The next time there is a disagreement, he will bring up her vulnerabilities as the reasons for his poor behavior.

Constant Criticism

When someone continuously finds fault, can never be pleased, and is unrelentingly critical of you, it is the insidious nature and cumulative effects of the abuse that do the damage. Over time, this type of abuse eats away at your self-confidence and sense of self-worth, undermining any good feelings you have about yourself and your accomplishments or achievements. Eventually you become convinced that nothing you do is worthwhile, and you may feel like giving up.

Emotional Blackmail

Emotional blackmail is one of the most powerful forms of manipulation. It occurs when someone either consciously or unconsciously coerces other people into doing what he wants by playing on their fear, guilt, or compassion.

Women, in particular, are easily exploited because they tend to place others' wishes and feelings ahead of their own. They can easily be made to feel guilty for thinking of their own needs and feelings first.

You are being emotionally blackmailed when a man threatens to end a relationship if you don't give him what he wants, or when he rejects you or distances himself from you until you give in to his demands. If your partner gives you the "cold shoulder" whenever he is displeased with you, threatens to leave you, or uses other fear tactics to get you under his control, he is using the tactic of emotional blackmail.

Threats of emotional blackmail don't have to be overt. In fact, they are often quite subtle. For example, a man may suggest offhandedly that it gets much harder to find a new partner as you get older, or that we often don't know how good we have it until our partner leaves.

The following are warning signs that you are being emotionally black-mailed:

- Your partner asks you to choose between something you want to do and him.

- Your partner asks you to give up something or someone as a way of proving your love for him.

- Your partner threatens to leave you if you don't change.

While we are all sometimes guilty of some of the behaviors I've listed here, there is a vast difference between name-calling or criticizing in the heat of an argument and doing so daily.

Similarly, constant complaining is not necessarily emotionally abusive unless it is destructive and the intent is to make the other person feel bad. For example, a husband who complains that the house isn't clean isn't necessarily being emotionally abusive if the house is in fact not clean. But if he constantly tells his wife that she is bad, lazy, inconsiderate, selfish, and so on because she does not clean the house, then he is being abusive.

True emotional abuse is distinguished by the following:

- It is constant, as opposed to occasional.

- The intent is to devalue and denigrate rather than to simply state a complaint.

- The intent is to dominate and control rather than to provide constructive criticism.

- The person has an *overall* attitude of disrespect toward you, rather than just not liking something specific you are doing.

For a complete listing of the different types of emotional abuse, and more about emotional abusers, please refer to my book *The Emotionally Abused Woman.*

A Woman of Substance chooses to have equal relationships with both men and women. She is no longer searching for a father or mother substitute, since she recognizes the inappropriateness and the danger in doing so (witness the trouble Monica Lewinsky got into by seeking out older men as lovers *and* older women as friends). Instead of attracting and being attracted to "teachers," "nurturers," or "controllers," a Woman of Substance searches out friends and lovers who are her intellectual and emotional peers, those who are capable of more give-and-take in a relationship, those who accept her as she is instead of constantly trying to change her into someone else.

Make sure that the man you love sees you as his equal and that you in turn see yourself as equal to any man. In a healthy relationship both partners complement each other by making up for one another's weaknesses; they don't use their strengths to intimidate or to make their partner feel "less than."

By choosing an equal partner and by creating a relationship based on equality, mutuality, and reciprocity, you create an environment where you feel such acceptance and love that you can become the best you can be, as can your partner.

Loving Him

It is not loving of you to allow your partner to dominate or abuse you, nor is it loving for you to dominate or emotionally abuse your partner.

As unloving as it is for a man to dominate or emotionally abuse a woman, it is equally unloving for a woman to choose a man she feels superior to just so she can be the one who is in control. Don't take the easy way out by choosing a man who feels "less than" you, who will allow you to control or abuse *him*. Hold out for an equal relationship.

Many Disappearing Women, especially those at the extreme end of the continuum, become emotionally abusive in their attempts to maintain their sense of self. As a way of protecting themselves from true intimacy, or in reaction to their fear of engulfment, they criticize, complain to, and demean their partners. Others become abusive by constantly lashing out verbally, releasing on their partners the pent-up anger they should be directing toward their parents or other abusers. If this applies to you, the most loving thing you can do for your partner is to work on releasing your anger in more constructive ways.

11

Commitment 7

SPEAK YOUR MIND

I've tried talking to my husband about the things that bother me, but he just thinks I'm criticizing him and gets defensive. He accuses me of always stirring up trouble when nothing's really wrong, and he doesn't really listen to what I say. So I just clam up for a while. But that doesn't work either because things build up and I end up yelling—which I don't want to do.

SUNNY, AGE FORTY-ONE

Aside from describing how women lose themselves in relationships, another reason I use the term "Disappearing Women" is that many women, particularly those currently in a relationship, complain about not being listened to, heard, or "seen" by their partners. How many of the following statements describe you?

- When you muster up enough strength to voice an opinion or to disagree with your partner, you usually have the experience of being ignored or discounted.

- You seldom if ever feel you are fully acknowledged or appreciated for what you bring to the relationship.

- You often feel as if the help you provide or the favors you give are taken for granted or negated.

- Although you are extremely sensitive to the feelings and the needs of your partner, you often feel that he doesn't reciprocate but instead ignores your feelings and needs.

If even one of these statements describes you and your situation, you are not alone. Many women experience these feelings in their relationships with men, as did my client, Donna.

When Donna first came to see me she was suffering from depression. For several months she had lost interest in all of the things that once excited her—her job, her children's progress at school, even sex with her husband. No matter how much sleep she got, she was tired all the time.

When I asked her how her marriage was going she answered with the proverbial "fine," but after a few sessions it became clear that she had been unhappy for quite some time. Her husband, Cliff, had a very forceful personality, and Donna had long since given up trying to oppose him in any way.

"I learned early on in our marriage that it just wasn't worth it to disagree with him. He wouldn't listen to my point of view anyway and I would just end up feeling upset and confused."

So for years, Donna had just gone along with whatever Cliff wanted, becoming more and more invisible with each passing day. Finally she couldn't do it anymore—her entire system had shut down.

Donna had lost up her voice, and in doing so she had sacrificed a part of herself. While it may have felt hopeless to communicate her feelings to her husband, by giving up trying, she had essentially given up on the relationship. You cannot hope to have a truly intimate, loving relationship if you decide to give up your right to speak out, to voice your opinions, to ask for your needs to be met, and to disagree when necessary.

Giving Up

Donna's story is so typical it is sad. Time after time my clients complain to me that they have given up trying to communicate with their male partners about their needs or about the things that upset them.

"Every time I bring something up my husband sighs, rolls his eyes, and says, 'What is it *this* time?' as if all I ever do is complain. It is so demoralizing. Why should I even keep trying when he has this attitude?"

Eventually these kinds of attitudes and remarks take their toll on a woman, and she may begin to doubt her perceptions and blame herself.

"Maybe my husband is right. Maybe I do look for things to complain about. After all, in most areas my husband treats me very well. Maybe I don't have the right to ask him to change. I'm not perfect either and he doesn't complain about my behavior."

What is sad is that by not treating women with respect and equality, some men set themselves up for their wives and lovers to complain. It is, in fact, the subtle, continuous buildup of slights and condescensions that lead to the "complaining" in the first place. Unfortunately, these men tend to become defensive and retreat behind their walls of condescension and arrogance, blaming a woman for having complaints in the first place and for "starting trouble" instead of focusing on their own behavior.

What is even sadder is that some men actually *need* women to teach them about equality, compromise, and cooperation—attitudes and behaviors that do not come naturally to them. They need the skills that women can teach them about how to relate to others in a more respectful, meaningful way and how to achieve true understanding with others, and yet they push away the lessons and the teachers in their attempt to protect their egos and maintain the status quo.

Much of the arguing that goes on in relationships is an indication that a woman is trying to restructure the relationship to make it more emotionally satisfying to *both* parties. Although women are accused of being "complainers" and "troublemakers," by bringing up the issues and addressing the unspoken concerns they usually are the ones who make it possible for relationships to survive. Not only do women bring up their own problems in the relationship, but also, if their partner seems unhappy, they will try to find out why.

And the saddest thing is that so many women give up and don't try anymore. They either go their own way, try to develop a separate life from their husband or lover, or leave the relationship entirely.

Fortunately, there are several strategies that have proven effective in helping many of the women I've worked with to speak up in their personal relationships. I've listed them in the following steps:

Step 1: Value and voice your opinions, beliefs, and knowledge

Step 2: Speak up for what you need

Step 3: Call your man on his attitudes and behavior

Step 4: State your grievances in a relationship

Step 5: Stand by what you've said

Step 1: Value and Voice Your Opinions, Beliefs, and Knowledge

Let's begin at the beginning—when you first meet a new man. If you can establish emotional equality at the beginning of the relationship, you can avoid the typical problems that most couples encounter once they marry or move in together.

Start off by remembering how delicate the male psyche is. This will help you view the entire situation differently. Realize, from the beginning, that even though you have much to teach the men in your life, they will feel threatened by your attempts.

Then, instead of keeping quiet out of fear of offending a man, continue to be yourself. Take the risk of voicing your opinions, and then follow it up with a reassuring statement such as "I hope we can agree to disagree. I don't always have to be right and I'm sure you don't either," or "I love to debate, don't you? It's so stimulating. In fact, it kind of turns me on."

Only the most controlling of men want a woman who agrees with him all the time, who doesn't have her own opinions and beliefs. As much as men are afraid of being dominated, they don't respect a woman who allows herself to be dominated either. A woman pays the price not only of becoming more and more invisible the less she speaks up, but also of losing the respect of the man she loves. (You will, however, continue to meet men who express horror at women who disagree with them, men who will try to make it very uncomfortable for you to disagree or speak up. While these same men may respect you secretly or in the long run, don't expect them to verbalize this respect.)

In addition, realize that traditionally, thinking has been considered a male province, and women's thought processes have been devalued and downgraded. While women's thinking can be characterized as different from men's, it is not less than men's. Women tend to think in complex, circular patterns rather than in a linear progression.

Because women's minds have been devalued both by society and by dysfunctional families, many women have not explored either how they think or what they think. Therefore, becoming familiar with your thinking—how your mind works, what triggers a thought process, how you solve problems, what prevents you from thinking clearly about an issue—can be informative and empowering.

Step 2: Speak Up for What You Need

Begin to take risks by verbally asking that some of your needs be met by your lover or husband. Don't make the mistake of expecting him to figure out what you need without your telling him. At a very early age girls develop the ability to "intuit" what others are feeling, and in turn, grow up expecting others to be able to figure out what they are feeling without their needing to explain it. But most men don't operate that way. They fully expect you to ask if you want or need something, and many have little inherent ability to figure out what your needs are.

In addition, don't hint at what you want, be vague about what you want, or test him by asking him if he thinks he meets your needs. These tactics make men feel manipulated, and this makes them angry. State your needs clearly and specifically, such as, "I would appreciate it if you'd call me the next time you're going to be late so I don't have to worry."

EXERCISE: *Your Emotional Needs*

In addition to our physical needs for food, shelter, safety, and rest, we have emotional needs that are just as crucial for our survival.

1. Make a list of the things you feel you need for your emotional survival.
2. How many of these needs are you meeting yourself?
3. How many of these needs does your partner meet?

Many Disappearing Women are unaware of their emotional needs. If this is your situation, the following list will give you some ideas. We need to:

- *be heard*—this includes being listened to and understood by those we love;
- *be seen*—this includes not being ignored, not being discounted, and not being falsely perceived;
- *be accepted* for ourselves;
- *be touched*—this includes touching that is nonsexual, that conveys affection and support;
- *be supported* and nurtured—this includes being encouraged when you have an idea or when you wish to explore something new, as well as being complimented for your efforts;
- *be trusted* and trust others;
- *be loved;*
- *be our authentic selves;*
- *know our life* makes a difference and *has a purpose.*

As you can see, not all these needs can be met by your partner (such as your need to be your authentic self and your need for purpose in your life). In part III we will discuss ways for you to begin meeting these needs. But your partner should be able to meet the other needs on this list at least some of the time.

The best way to begin is by letting your partner know what your needs are. A good way to open the discussion is to ask him to list his needs, and then to share your lists with one another. If that goes well you can share with one another which of your needs are being met by one another and which are not. Finally, you can share ideas on how you can begin meeting one another's needs better.

Step 3: Call Your Man on His Attitudes and Behavior

The most effective way for you to call a man on offensive attitudes and behavior is for you to remember that you need to act as a role model to teach him more effective ways of communicating. Instead of taking it personally, realize that many men simply do not know how to communicate their feelings in direct ways. Instead, they couch their feelings in indifference, condescension, humor, or sarcasm. The following is a list of the behaviors and attitudes that most offend and hurt women, along with suggestions on how to call a man on them and how to model more constructive, healthy behaviors and attitudes.

Don't be afraid to exercise your right to call a man on any and all of the following:

• *Criticism.* Many men feel they have a right to criticize a woman they are dating, even at the beginning of a relationship, and they often get away with it under the guise of being "helpful," or as a way of sharing with her their experience or "superior" knowledge. But this is just a way for them to hide their own insecurities and to establish their superiority in the relationship. If you allow this criticism, no matter how subtle, to continue you are essentially agreeing to have an unequal relationship, one in which it will be nearly impossible for you to be treated with respect, mutuality, and reciprocity. Call this behavior what it is—criticism— and state clearly that you do not wish to be criticized by him.

I'm always pleased when I learn tactics from clients. Recently a woman in one of my groups shared with me how she dealt with the constant criticism she was receiving from her husband:

"One day it just hit me and I thought, 'I don't have to accept his criticism.' And so the next time he criticized me I just told him, 'I don't accept your criticism.' He just stared at me for a minute and then walked away. I couldn't believe it! Instead of having to endure minutes and sometimes hours of his haranguing me about something I'd done or not done, it all stopped before it started with just that one statement. After that I said the same thing every time he started in on me, and pretty soon he stopped altogether."

While I can't guarantee you will have the same experience, it has helped several of my other clients. Try it and see what happens with you.

- *Making fun of you.* Many men use humor as a way of subtly putting you down. They do this partly because of habit—it is a common practice among men to tease and make fun of one another—and partly as a way of gaining dominance. But it is also a passive-aggressive way by which some men communicate their hostility. Many men are used to being treated this way by their peers, but this behavior is especially hurtful to women because we can sense the hostility underneath. If one of his "humorous" put-downs hurts your feelings, tell him about it and explain *why* it hurt. If he tries to laugh it off, look him directly in the eyes and say something like, "I'm really serious about this. That comment hurt my feelings. Please don't say that kind of thing to me again."

- *Sarcastic remarks.* This, too, is a way for a man to passively-aggressively let you know how he really feels without taking the risk of coming out and saying it directly. Follow the same suggestions that I made when he makes fun of you.

- *Condescension.* Many men are raised around other male figures who have misogynistic attitudes toward women, and because of this they grow up feeling they are superior to women. Never allow a man to make conde-scending remarks to you, even in the beginning. If you do, you are giving silent permission for him to continue both his behavior and his attitude. Say something like, "Do you realize how condescending that remark was?" or "I'm sure you don't really feel you are superior to me, but that kind of com-ment makes it sound like you do."

- *Not taking you seriously or minimizing and trivializing what you have to say.* The sad truth is that some men simply do not value what women say. They think of women as if they were children to be adored, comforted, and protected, not adults who are equal to them in intelligence, talent, power, and accomplishments.

It is your job to let the men in your life know that you have ideas and opinions and that you expect your ideas and opinions to be listened to and respected. If you find that a man isn't listening to you, or if he changes the subject when you begin to speak, gently call him on it by saying something like, "I really enjoyed listening to you earlier. I think you had a lot of good ideas. Now I'd appreciate it if you'd return the favor and listen to my point of view."

- *Interrupting you.* To many men, a conversation, especially one that has turned into a debate, is like a battle in which the ultimate goal is to defeat your opponent at all costs. This means it is okay to interrupt the other person, to try to outtalk her, to raise his voice and drown her out, or to discredit her in any way possible.

  If he begins to argue with you before you even have a chance to get your ideas across, stop speaking for a minute and say, "I really like to debate with you like this. It's exciting. But it would be so much more fun if you'd stop interrupting me."

  If he continues arguing with you, stop talking again, look him directly in the eyes, and say something like, "I listened without interrupting until you were finished telling me your point of view. Now I expect you to listen to my point of view without interrupting me."

  If he still continues interrupting you to get his point across, stop talking and say something like, "It seems like it's far more important to you to be right, and all I wanted to do was have a lively discussion. Let's talk another time when you're more in the mood to listen."

Don't Fall for These Excuses

Many men are defensive and give excuses for their behavior. Don't fall for any of the following excuses, no matter how good they may sound. They are just ways for him to get out of taking responsibility for his behavior, and some are out-and-out emotionally abusive.

- *You are being "unreasonable."* It is perfectly reasonable for you to state that you don't want to be criticized, made fun of, or condescended to. In fact it is "unreasonable" for him to expect to treat you in any of these ways without repercussions.

- *You are being "hysterical."* This is another typical misogynistic attitude stemming from the very outdated belief that women who are upset are either on their period, premenstrual, menopausal, or crazy. It negates your right to your anger and is very demeaning.

- *You are "trying to start trouble."* Far from trying to start trouble, many women try very hard to avoid it by going along with whatever a man says or does. This comment is condescending and misogynistic and is meant to throw you off track.

Behaviors to Avoid on Your Part

It is also important that you avoid engaging in any of the following behaviors. Many of these behaviors weaken your position or give your partner an excuse for ignoring you, while others merely add to your own frustration.

- *Don't whine or whimper.* The biggest complaint men have about women is that they whine too much. Interestingly, the thing women like the least about men is their arrogance. Your whining makes a man even more arrogant than he might be otherwise because it causes him to perceive you as a victim, a martyr, or a loser—all things that men are programmed from an early age *not* to be and to disrespect in others. That's why so many men say things such as, "Oh, poor little girl" when a woman complains in a whiny fashion.

- *Don't allow things to build up.* By keeping quiet you're sending the message that it's okay for him to act inappropriately. A mistake many women make is to put up with inappropriate behavior for too long in their attempts to keep the peace. Then they get to the point where they can't take it anymore and go into a tirade about all the things he's done wrong. They end up losing control and giving him a good excuse to say they are being "unreasonable" or "hysterical."

  Instead, consistently state your complaints and your needs each time they come up, using "I" statements. This may feel tiresome and it may prompt him to call you a nag, but it will make you feel better for having stood up for yourself.

- *Don't expect him to admit he was wrong or to apologize.* If you demand that he do either of these things he'll likely become just that much more defensive. It's a matter of pride for a man to remain strong, not admit defeat, and continue to believe he is right even when he has been proven wrong. In any case, demanding an apology can give him too much power, since it sends the message that your happiness is in his hands.

- *Don't say you were wrong just to keep the peace.* Never say you were wrong if you don't believe it just so you can appease him or make up with him. Many women, especially Disappearing Women, become afraid that if they don't give in they risk a man's anger or worse yet, risk losing him. Saying you were wrong when you don't believe you were will eventually backfire on you. It will cause you to doubt your own perceptions as you come to believe your own words, and it will cause your partner to lose respect for you and can invite either emotional or physical abuse.

- *Don't start screaming and yelling.* While it is perfectly understandable to lose your cool when a man ignores you, minimizes what you've said, or calls you a liar, if you start screaming at him the discussion will only deteriorate or escalate, both of which are extremely unproductive. In addition, it will only give him a good excuse to accuse you of being crazy, irrational, or hysterical.

  If you've become so frustrated and angry that you need to scream, go into your bedroom, put a pillow over your head, and let loose. Or take a shower and scream your head off.

- *Don't be afraid to get angry.* Anger is a great motivator and provides us with a great sense of power. Far from making you irrational, anger can sometimes cause you to think more clearly, and it usually helps quiet your fears of rejection or abandonment. Just don't let your anger build up to the point where you do become irrational, where you are likely to lose it and begin screaming inappropriately, or where you lash out physically at your partner.

- *Don't allow your partner to verbally, emotionally, or physically abuse you.* Verbal abuse includes calling you derogatory names (bitch, whore), or telling you you are stupid, ugly, fat, or insane. Emotional abuse is trying to make you think you are crazy, threatening to end the relationship if you don't do as he says, or threatening to hit you if you don't be quiet. Physical abuse includes hitting, punching, pushing, tripping, or dragging. It also includes breaking down doors, putting his fist through windows, breaking dishes, or throwing things at you. Tactics of intimidation are forms of abuse, even if he doesn't physically touch you. Don't tolerate these tactics. Call them what they are: abuse.

Step 4: State Your Grievances in a Relationship

Some women have such low self-esteem that they don't feel they have the right to complain. They convince themselves they are making a big thing out of nothing, or they justify their partner's behavior, convincing themselves that he really didn't mean it or that he couldn't help himself.

Others are so dependent on their partner that they are terrified of calling him on his behavior for fear of making him angry. They fear rejection or worse—abandonment—to such an extent that they put up with horrible behavior from their partner. If this is you, you will need to risk making him angry if you are going to have any hope of having a healthy relationship. You will need to find your voice and risk stating your grievances if you are going to become a Woman of Substance.

Still others complain about the same issues over and over to such an extent that their partners simply ignore them. Often frustrated not only by the fact that their requests are being ignored, but also by the fact that harmony has not been established, many women attempt to say the same words differently, hoping that if they can just find the right way of saying it, possibly a more diplomatic way, their partner will be sure to listen. Assuming that he has the same desire to resolve conflicts and differences, they feel continual attempts on their part will be successful. However, many men do not have the same needs for resolution. Their need to protect themselves takes far more precedence, and they shut down even more at each attempt on a woman's part. This is one reason why you so often hear men complaining about women "nagging."

Instead of withholding your anger, whining, nagging, or blowing up, try stating your grievances when they first come up in as honest a manner as possible. Never start out with name-calling and avoid "you," "always," and "never" statements such as "You never ask me how I'm feeling," or "You always assume I'm the one who is wrong." Instead, simply state your grievance using "I" statements such as "I would like it if you'd ask me how I'm feeling sometimes," or "I don't like it when you assume I'm wrong."

State your position and stick to it. Don't back down, and don't apologize for bringing up the issue. There is no need to argue about what you've said. If he defends himself, listen carefully and then say, "I understand you don't agree with me and you have a right to your point of view. But I would appreciate it if you'd think about what I've said."

If you've asked him to do something specific and he insists that he already does it, say something like this: "Maybe you're right. I'll try to pay more attention. On the other hand, maybe you could try a little harder or do it a little more often so that I will notice it next time."

Step 5: Stand By What You've Said

While it is very important to stand up for yourself and state your grievances, if you end up backing down or giving in, the next time he behaves in the same inappropriate way your words of confrontation will mean nothing. Your partner will assume you were just "spouting off" and that he doesn't need to take you seriously.

Therefore, you need to be consistent and state consequences. Don't complain endlessly about his excessive drinking, only to get drunk with him one night. And don't threaten to leave and then not act on it, as my client Gigi did:

"I finally got enough nerve to tell Warren that the relationship was unacceptable. I told him everything I felt and that I couldn't continue. He just stared at me in disbelief. I guess he never thought I'd speak up."

This was a big step for Gigi, since she'd never been able to confront Warren before. But it is not enough to speak up, you must also back up what you say with action, and Gigi couldn't do this.

"But he kept coming over. It was so strange. I didn't know what to do. After several weeks I guess I lost my nerve and we were together again."

Why couldn't she just tell him she didn't want to see him? Where was her voice? The key here was that *she needed him* and was afraid to alienate him completely. He had all the power in the relationship. If she angered him she was afraid he'd go away for good, since she was emotionally dependent on him.

If you aren't willing to stand by your words, if you aren't willing to take the necessary action to create change, then you shouldn't threaten. Threatening to leave if your mate doesn't do as you wish or in a moment of anger without taking any action only weakens your words and your position, and threatening to leave if he doesn't change can be a form of emotional blackmail. If you really don't want the relationship to end but are just trying to get your partner to change, don't threaten to end it or say the relationship is over. Ask for what you need in the relationship, and then if it isn't forthcoming, decide whether you want to stay or leave.

Speaking your mind means never again sitting in silence when a man cuts you off, negates what you are saying, or criticizes you for stating your opinions and your beliefs. Once you have found your voice, you realize that you have as much right to speak as anyone else and as much right to disagree with others.

As you learn to speak your mind, you'll also find out who loves you for being who you really are. Chances are, he'll love you and respect you more in the long run even if there are some bumps in your relationship as you move along the road to self-discovery. Just stick to your path toward authenticity, and the strength of your conviction will sustain you. As a result, healthy relationships will thrive, unhealthy relationships will die. Whatever happens, you've become your own person, and that's the greatest gift you can give yourself.

Loving Him

You can speak your mind and still be loving. While it's important to call a man on inappropriate attitudes or behaviors, you don't need to make him feel like he's an idiot or a monster. Therefore, when you bring something to his attention, practice the following suggestions:

- Remember that most men are not taught to be vulnerable, especially to women.

- Even though men are often unaware of their own emotional state, unable to communicate effectively about their emotions, and sometimes refuse to be vulnerable out of fear of losing their masculinity or their appeal to women, don't try to *pull* emotional responses from your partner.

- Most men automatically go into a defensive stance when women call them on their issues. While we all silently believe that there is something wrong with us and are just waiting for our partner to discover this, the male ego is especially delicate. Therefore, temper your comments with loving care.

- Give your partner a lot of acknowledgment for the positive things he does and for any attempt he makes at changing the way he treats you.

By keeping the seven commitments to yourself you can stop losing yourself in relationships. You will also be far more likely to attract the kind of partner who will respect your need to maintain a separate self instead of merging your life with his.

Interestingly, the very actions I've encouraged you to take to avoid losing yourself in your relationships are the same things men need in order to feel free to be vulnerable and loving. By going slowly and taking the time to get to know a man you inadvertently allow him the space and the time to ease into the relationship more comfortably than he would feel if he were being pressured. By telling the truth about who you are and how you feel, you help a man with his issues of trust and encourage him to be more vulnerable. By maintaining your own separate life you let a man know that you have no intention of entrapping or engulfing him. By staying out of fantasy and in reality you let a man know that you see him and the relationship for what it really is, and this will also help him to build trust. By not allowing a man to change you, you send the message that you are not going to try to change *him* and that you can share a love in which you both accept one another the way you are.

By choosing a man who is your equal you bring out the best in him since he is more likely to treat you with respect. Finally, by speaking your mind you encourage him to do the same.

If women are really going to become equal with men we need to find a way to work with our innate nature, such as our tendency to be nurturers, so we can remain the loving, compassionate people we are while at the same time minimizing and alleviating our tendency to lose ourselves. The work you have done so far has been a beginning.

In the next part of this book we will focus on how to make deeper life changes, such as finding your authentic self, finding your voice, and learning ways to express the creativity that will help you develop a stronger sense of self.

PART III

BECOME A WOMAN
OF SUBSTANCE

Developing a Self and a Life
That Satisfies You

I n this part of the book I offer strategies that will work from the inside out, ways to begin thinking and feeling that change not only the way others see you but the way you see yourself. Some of these strategies can be incorporated into your life fairly easily, while others are life changes that will take more time to create. Some will be fairly painless and may bring almost immediate feelings of autonomy, strength, and independence, while others will be rather painful, and the payoff will be long in coming. Throughout, it is important that you keep your goal in mind—that of becoming a woman who is seen, heard, respected, and honored for who she is, a woman who has such a fulfilling life that she is unwilling to sacrifice it for a relationship, a woman who will be respected by the kind of man she most admires—a man who is dynamic, interesting, loving, and independent.

Because the women who are reading this book are on very different levels in terms of their personal growth—some are just starting out, while others have been focusing in this direction for a long time—some of you will find the information I share with you to be extremely relevant to where you now are, while others will find that some of the information is not new to you. At no time is it my intention to talk down to you but to offer the greatest number of women information that can and will change your lives. On the other hand, you may feel threatened by some of the things I suggest. If this is the case, please don't feel pressured to do anything you are not ready to do.

12

Find Your Authentic Self

You can live a lifetime and, at the end of it, know more about other people than you know of yourself.
BERYL MARKHAM

It all starts with self-reflection. Then you can know and empathize more profoundly with someone else.
SHIRLEY MACLAINE

My life is such a cliché. I worked to put my husband through school and dedicated my life to him and my kids, always trying to be the perfect wife and mother. Then last year my husband left me for a younger woman and my kids are all off to college. Not only am I all alone, but I don't even know who I am.

CONNIE, AGE FIFTY-ONE

The phrase "finding your authentic self" has been overused. But for Disappearing Women there is no better way to describe the process of self-discovery that you must go through in order to stop losing yourself in relationships and become a Woman of Substance.

Many of you have become so lost in your attempts to find completion with or through a man that you will literally need to find your way back to yourself again.

Others have spent so much time taking care of others that you got lost in the process. In *Revolution from Within,* Gloria Steinem called this being "empathy sick," meaning that she had focused so much of her time and attention on helping others and meeting their needs that she had lost touch with herself and her own needs. She had spent so much time relating to others that she knew other people's feelings better than her own.

Ten years ago, I, too, was forced to acknowledge that I had spent so much of my time and energy helping my clients and pouring my soul into one relationship after another that I had lost touch with my own needs. I, too, became burned out physically, emotionally, and spiritually. Both my physical and emotional health were suffering, and I knew I had to do something. I knew I had to get back to myself.

This is a typical scenario—not just for those of us who are committed to social change and the betterment of others, but for all women. We focus so much attention on caring for others, on being empathetic to their needs, that we lose track of our own.

As Carol Gilligan wrote in her book *In a Different Voice:*

> The differences between women and men . . . center on a tendency for women and men to make different relational errors—for men to think that if they know themselves, following Socrates' dictum, they will also know women, and for women to think that if only they know others, they will come to know themselves.

How We've Lost Ourselves

Some women have lost themselves by constantly trying to be what others expected them to be. They haven't given themselves the time and the opportunity to discover what pleases them or to become the person they want to be. Because all their lives, people have told them who they are and what their motivations are for doing the things they do, they haven't focused enough attention on discovering who they really are or on discovering their real motivations.

Still others have become lost through years of trying to "become" someone they aren't. Many women spend their lives trying on the identities of others they admire. It may be a boyfriend, a teacher, a boss at work—any person who seems to embody the qualities they themselves would like to have. This is how Lorraine described it:

"I've come to realize that I don't know who I really am underneath all my playacting. I've finally reached a point in my life where I want to find out."

And some of you had such neglectful or abusive childhoods that you never developed a fully autonomous self in the first place and will need to literally develop your true self.

This was the case with Drew Barrymore, the actress who became drug- and alcohol-addicted by the time she was fourteen. In her autobiography *Little Girl Lost*, she wrote:

> Someone once explained to me what the word *veneer* meant. Gloss. A shiny surface that's supposed to protect an inferior material underneath. That's me exactly. Whenever I'd look in the mirror, I'd think, "You're lost. Totally lost. How can anyone like you? You don't even like yourself." Those moments when I realized how estranged I'd become from myself, not to mention the rest of the world, sent me spiraling into a depression.

How We Find Ourselves

No matter what your situation, finding yourself will involve time, a great deal of focus, and a willingness to put aside all your preconceived ideas about who you should be, how you should act, and how you should feel. Instead, the focus will be on discovering who you really are, how you really behave, and how you really feel.

Beyond all your fantasies of who you want to be and the expectations of who you should be lies the real you. Underneath your public self and your false self, underneath your masks and facades, there is a core—your authentic self. Each of us travels through the journey of life with only one constant companion, and that is ourself. How sad if your closest companion is someone you don't even know.

You've been hiding from yourself by getting lost in one relationship after another. Now you need to take some time to put your life in perspective, to heal from your past relationships, and to do some deep inner reflection.

Now is the time. There is absolutely nothing as important as taking time out for self-discovery.

We cannot be intimate with another person until we are able to be intimate with ourselves, which includes establishing our own identity and discovering what we feel, prefer, and desire. As you no doubt experienced while reading chapter 6, if you don't know these things about yourself, you cannot share them with another person.

There are a number of ways by which you can begin your journey toward self-discovery. In this chapter I will suggest some of the most effective ways—paths that women, including myself, have found to be most effective and most rewarding.

Find Yourself through Solitude

What is necessary, after all, is only this: solitude, vast inner solitude.
To walk inside yourself and meet no one for hours . . .
RAINER MARIA RILKE

She would not exchange her solitude for anything. Never again
to be forced to move to the rhythms of others.
TILLIE OLSEN

I am happy to be alone—time to think, time to be. This kind of
open-ended time is the only luxury that really counts and
I feel stupendously rich to have it.
MAY SARTON, JOURNAL OF A SOLITUDE

A good marriage is one in which each partner appoints the other
to be the guardian of his solitude. . . .
RAINER MARIA RILKE

One of the most effective ways of discovering your true self is to face and embrace solitude. As frightening as the prospect of this may seem, you need time alone to discover who you really are, to learn to rely on yourself, to learn to like your own company, and to break your tendency to merge completely with others.

Spending time alone with yourself will help you develop your own personality, retrieve or establish a stronger sense of self, and find your own individual lifestyle instead of automatically conforming to society's pressures.

The time you take alone now may be the only time you have ever stood alone, not depending on anyone else to help hold you up. Your fear of being alone has likely propelled you into continually seeking relationships or staying in unsatisfying or even destructive ones. You need to know that you can be alone and find completeness within yourself. In that way you will never be in a relationship again out of fear of being alone.

For those of you who have a history of unfulfilling relationships, taking time to be alone will help you gather the courage to avoid unfulfilling, unequal, or abusive relationships in the future and to face issues that you've avoided by focusing on others. From this position you will be less desperate to immediately attach yourself to someone in an attempt to avoid yourself.

Most important, instead of looking to others to validate you, keep you company, entertain you, or fill up the emptiness inside, solitude will help you discover that you can do these things for yourself. This will, in turn, make you a stronger, more complete woman who will be far more interesting to the kind of man who will truly appreciate you.

More Than Being Alone

Solitude is much more than just being alone with yourself. It is a time for self-reflection, soul-searching, and self-discovery. It is a time for reaching inside yourself for answers, for solace, for inspiration, for healing. It is a time to discover your inner voice and your inner wisdom.

Practicing solitude needs to be an important aspect of each major stage of our development as individuals. It is the development of the capacity for isolating oneself from the environment that helps adolescents begin to individuate in a more clear and evident way.

When Cameron was an adolescent she sought solitude by disappearing into the attic, where she would sit in an old rocking chair by the window. There she would write in her diary, read, and stare out the window. This was the only place where she felt like she could have her own thoughts, dream her own dreams, experience her own feelings. When she was not in the attic, her mother, a very domineering, possessive woman, watched her like a hawk, constantly monitoring her behavior. If she felt pensive her mother would say, "What have you got to feel sad about? You've got it made." If she felt angry her mother would yell, "Wipe that scowl off your face or I'll wipe it off for you!"

According to Joanne Wieland-Burston in her book *Contemporary Solitude*, what Cameron was unconsciously practicing was the custom of incubation, which is practiced by so-called primitive peoples in many parts of the world. This is a meaningful ritual for adolescents as well as for people in other difficult life phases. During incubation, a bird sits on eggs to hatch them through the warmth of the body. This kind of withdrawal is needed for concentrating one's energies on an important stage of development.

Of the many tribal rites for puberty in "primitive" cultures, all involve some kind of seclusion. Young boys are subjected to intense experiences, first being taken out of the family, away from their mothers, to go through masculinity rites with a new social group—their masculine peers. They emerge as adult members of the community, but only after having gone through a trial of sorts in which a ritual death or dismemberment has been acted out. They must die in their old roles in order to emerge prepared for their new ones. Girls' puberty rites offer even more impressive images of seclusion, for the girls are often placed alone in huts, where their feet are not even allowed to touch the ground. These rites institutionalize the need to be alone, which Donald W. Winnicott, a renowned pediatrician turned psychoanalyst, speaks of as being all-important in puberty.

By practicing solitude, adolescents turn inward, concentrating all their life energies on the inner developmental processes. As a Disappearing Woman, you need to do the same thing, particularly if you were unable to do so when you were an adolescent or if you are going through midlife.

If you sensed too much disapproval or even the threat of rejection or abandonment from your parents when you attempted to isolate and/or separate yourself as a child or an adolescent, you likely gave up on your efforts and instead remained overly connected to your parents. The fear of losing your parents' love or the security of your environment became a definite impediment to your development, since it also prevented you from daring to risk becoming yourself and to speak, dress, and act differently from what was expected of you.

EXERCISE: *Start with Fifteen Minutes a Day* ———————

To experience solitude you do not need to seclude yourself in a remote area or lock yourself up in your home for days or weeks at a time. You can begin by spending just fifteen minutes a day alone, without the distractions of the telephone, the Internet, television, or the radio, and by following these simple suggestions:

- Unplug the phone and go into a quiet part of the house where you won't be interrupted. If there are others in the house, ask them not to disturb you, or put a "Do not disturb" sign on your door.

- Sit quietly or lie down and take some deep breaths.

- Let your mind wander but try not to spend your time obsessing about other people. Instead, concentrate only on yourself—your feelings, your awarenesses, your thoughts, and your body.

In her book *Journal of a Solitude,* the poet May Sarton wrote about how difficult it is to put the needs of others aside:

It may be outwardly silent here but in the back of my mind is a clamor of human voices, too many needs, hopes, fears. I hardly ever sit still without being haunted by the "undone" and the "unsent." I often feel exhausted, but it is not my work that tires (work is a rest); it is the effort of pushing away the lives and needs of others before I can come to the work with any freshness and zest.

What to Expect

It can be extremely difficult to focus this much attention on yourself and your feelings. Most people have a very hard time spending even a few minutes focusing in this way. You may become nervous and agitated, and you may find all kinds of ways to distract yourself from yourself.

May Sarton writes about the fear that emerged as she once again embarked on her solitary journey:

> The ambience here is order and beauty. This is what frightens me when I am first alone again. I feel inadequate. I have made an open place, a place for meditation. What if I cannot find myself inside it?
>
> Now I hope to break through into the rough, rocky depths, to the matrix itself. There is violence there and anger never resolved. . . . My need to be alone is balanced against my fear of what will happen when suddenly I enter the huge empty silence if I cannot find support there.

Of course, one of the major benefits of solitude—that there is nothing to cushion you against attacks from within—can also be one of the greatest drawbacks. As May Sarton explained it:

> . . . [T]he storm, painful as it is, might have had some truth in it. So sometimes one has simply to endure a period of depression for what it may hold of illumination if one can live through it, attentive to what it exposes or demands.

Your time of solitude may at first bring you only anxiety, fear, and sadness. Some women find that as soon as they spend even a few minutes alone they are overwhelmed with a great sadness and that they spend their time of solitude in tears. If this happens to you, don't be afraid, and don't let this discourage you. Although it can be painful to cry all the tears you've been storing up for years, it can be liberating and healing as well. This is particularly true for those of you who had traumatic or painful childhoods and who now need to mourn your losses, disappointments, and woundings.

Others become so anxious, they can't keep still. Instead they spend their time alone pacing up and down the floor, trying to calm themselves long enough to connect with what they are actually feeling. This is usually caused by the realization that one is thrown back onto oneself, with no one else to rely on—the moment when one is faced with one's aloneness in the world.

Be prepared for anything—tears, intense anxiety, fear, rage. Don't be surprised if your mind races a mile a minute and you are unable to get in touch with anything at first. Just be patient with yourself and keep trying. Soon your efforts will be rewarded.

Only by facing your fear of aloneness once and for all, only by confronting your inner pain can you achieve contemplation instead of boredom, wisdom instead of despair, serenity instead of conflict.

A Little Solitude Can Go a Long Way

Don't be critical of yourself if you can't spend much time alone at first. If you stick with it and continue for just a few minutes at a time, you'll gradually be able to work your way up to an hour or more.

I began by consolidating my workweek to four days, giving me three days off instead of two. This enabled me to spend one entire day with myself, since my partner at the time worked five days a week.

I was so burned out that at first I just lay on the couch and read or watched television during the day. But I also did something else. I cried. I cried over sad movies. I cried over the news. I even cried over commercials.

I was so disconnected from myself that I didn't even know what I was crying about. On the surface I had a good life. A good relationship with someone who was my equal. A successful practice doing work I was passionate about, work that felt satisfying and fulfilling.

Not knowing what my tears were about was frustrating and confusing. I clearly didn't know myself as well as I thought I did.

Then I decided I needed even more time alone. I drove up the coast of California and rented a little house to stay in for the weekend. I went to the store and bought all the groceries I'd need, unpacked, and set out on a walk. I was not going to let anything get in my way of facing myself and discovering what was going on with me.

A Place of Mysteries and Answers

During the previous year I had begun to take long walks. I had originally done it for exercise, but I discovered that walking became a moving meditation for me, a time to clear my head and connect with my emotions and my spirit.

As anticipated, my walk along the cliffs of the ocean began to calm me down. As I took in the fresh sea air and felt the ocean spray against my face, my mind began to clear of all the superfluous chatter and minutiae of my daily life. Soon all I was aware of were the intense deep colors of the ocean, the sea-gulls flying overhead, and the pounding of my own heartbeat. In those moments, my fear of what I was to face subsided, and I knew I had the courage to confront whatever came up.

I went back to my little house and began to write in the journal I had bought for my trip. I wrote for hours without stopping and without con-sciously thinking. My hand seemed to have a mind of its own as it glided across the paper. When I finally stopped writing I was exhausted, but at the same time exhilarated. I knew I'd connected with myself in a way that I hadn't done for years, perhaps ever. I had written down my deepest, darkest feelings. I had written without censoring myself, without fear of what my words would mean or what the confessions of my soul would sound like to others.

Through my writing I discovered the truths I'd suppressed and denied by staying busy, by seldom being alone, by focusing my attention on the needs of others. I discovered truths about myself that I needed to face if I was going to continue growing. Truths about how much like my emotionally abusive mother I had become. Truths about how much more work I still needed to do to clear up issues from my childhood. And equally painful, I discovered that after years of therapy I was still making the same mistakes in my relation-ships. Even though I was in the most equal relationship I'd ever had, I had still lost myself in it. I was still putting my own needs aside to please my partner. I was still pretending that I was much more easygoing than I really was. And I was still putting up with unacceptable behavior to keep my relationship intact.

The next morning, even though I was exhausted from the hours and hours of writing, and the hours and hours of crying that came afterward, I forced myself to get up and go for another walk. I walked slower this time, since my body ached from the effects of my emotional outpouring. Instead of going down to the ocean, I walked deeper into the woods. It was quieter and darker there, a place that seemed to hold both mysteries and answers.

There, among the dark shadows of the pine trees, I heard a voice inside my head, a voice I hadn't heard for a long time. It was my inner voice telling me what I needed to do next, what path I needed to take.

That weekend of solitude set the course for my life for the next several years. My inner voice told me I needed to end my relationship. It told me I needed to move away from Los Angeles and surround myself with the healing power of nature. And it told me that I needed a break from helping others in order to devote much more time to my own healing.

By giving myself the gift of solitude I have been rewarded with a treasure chest of self-knowledge. By following my inner voice I changed my entire life—for the better. Today I am doing the things I truly want to do, not only the things I think I *should* be doing. I have learned who I truly am and have grown to love myself for who I am instead of constantly trying to be someone I'm not.

For several years I lived in the woods, surrounded by those beautiful pines, immersed in the shadows. I dug deep into the rich soil and found great treasures buried there. Like many others, I found that being alone with nature was the most healing, enlightening, and productive time I had ever spent.

Away from the distractions of their household, away from other people, many women are free to connect with themselves and with nature in a profound way. Being alone with nature can help you discover your own true nature, achieve a different perspective on your problems, and come away with a deeper appreciation for the things that are truly important.

My time of solitude helped prepare me for an intimate relationship based on a desire for true sharing. I no longer felt I would lose myself in a relationship with a man and was ready for an intimate relationship based not on need but on desire.

The Power of Journaling

As an aid to self-discovery I suggest that you, too, start a journal if you haven't already done so. Your journal can act as a silent companion that listens without judgment and reflects back to you aspects of yourself you are unaware of. This is vital for those Disappearing Women who when growing up had a parental figure constantly judging, criticizing, or demanding something from them.

As you begin to put your thoughts and feelings down on paper you will find that you feel less alone in your solitude, that you are becoming your own loving companion.

Writing in your journal will help you stay focused and provide you with an outlet for self-expression. In it you can record your feelings and your innermost thoughts and dreams, discovering more about yourself than you ever imagined possible. You will discover thoughts and feelings long buried, solutions and alternatives to problem situations, new ways of looking at lifelong issues, and most important—new ways of looking at yourself.

Alice Koller spent three months alone in the middle of winter on the island of Nantucket in order to find herself and to face all that she had fled from throughout her thirty-seven years. This is how she described the purpose and method of her inner journey in her book *An Unknown Woman: A Journey of Self-Discovery:*

> I'm here to understand myself, deliberately to turn myself open to my own view. I know, as I sit here, what I must have known for many years, that I can recognize what's true about myself when I see it. It's whatever I find myself refusing to admit, whatever I say no to very fast. That blanket admission right at the start may save me a lot of time. May save me, period. I'm using that "no" to protect myself from something. What? I'll find out. I'll write down everything I can remember, so that I can see the full extent of it, pick out some patterns in what I've been denying for so long.
>
> So, that's first: to get it all written, no matter how ugly.

You may want to structure your journal writing in a similar way. Writing down the story of your life, especially if you allow yourself to reexperience your emotions all along the way, can be very rewarding and enlightening. It can help you recognize the origins of your problems and the patterns in your life. Your memories, when examined in the light of your current awareness, can reveal a pattern discernible only when your life is considered as a whole.

EXERCISE: *Your Life in Review*

The following exercise is an invaluable tool to get you started examining your life. The information you gather can help you discover important patterns and can be used for further exploration of the self, such as giving you ideas for journal and autobiographical writings, poems, short stories, drawings, and paintings.

Set up a space for yourself where you will not be disturbed. I recommend lying down in a darkened room, but you may also choose to sit up. Put paper and a pen where you can easily reach them. Please read the following instructions through completely before beginning. Once you have them clear in your mind, you can begin the exercise.

1. Take some deep breaths and clear your mind of all thoughts. Think of your life as if it were a movie. Imagine that you have a magic button you can push that will "rewind" your life, much like you can do with

a video player. Keep going back until you have reached your very first memory. Try to recall, as vividly as possible, the feelings associated with this memory.

Now go forward and remember another significant scene from your life. Continue playing your movie (your life) in your mind, picking out the most significant scenes and recalling the emotions you felt at the time.

2. Open your eyes, go back over your memories, and choose moments in time when you experienced an intense emotion or those moments where time stood still, those moments that stand out from all the rest. Write these memories down.

   Don't just write about major events in your life. When you choose a scene, there should be a significant emotional charge to it. Don't take too much time thinking; just write as events come to your mind, letting your life flash before you. Breathe deeply. You might be surprised by the events you have chosen and the ones you have skipped over.

3. Now go over your writing and put a star beside those memories that really stand out, those that still hold an emotional charge (i.e., those that make your stomach flip-flop, that still bring back intense feelings).

4. Working with just the starred items, write about these incidents and why they were so significant, powerful, and meaningful to you. Take note of any patterns, themes, cycles, or lessons revealed there and write about them in your journal.

5. Using what you have written, see if you can condense or characterize each of these significant experiences down to only a few words. Examples: loneliness, fear, hope, friendship.

If you look carefully and deeply enough you will find in childhood the seeds of the life you have lived. You can begin to recognize that your life was made inevitable by your childhood, and in so doing, can begin to forgive yourself for your adult behavior.

By the same token, *your childhood does not have to be your destiny.* While you can't undo what was or wasn't done to you in childhood, you can find ways to purge yourself of much of the pain, guilt, and anger created by your negative experiences. Journal writing is one such way. You need not do anything so formal or structured as writing your life story. Simply writing down your feelings at the moment can be very revealing.

Keeping a journal will help you to discover and stay in touch with your emotions. By using different techniques such as writing with your nondominant hand (the hand you don't usually use) or stream-of-consciousness writing (writing whatever occurs to you without editing or stopping), you can bypass your internal censors and discover feelings that are buried below the surface.

Your journal can also be the place where you allow yourself to be completely who you are—no facades, no pretense, no saying what you think others want you to say, just the truth. Being totally honest with yourself can be extremely difficult, but without complete honesty it is not possible for you to develop a true sense of who you are.

I suggest you make a commitment to yourself to write only the truth in your journal, or that you start a "truth book" in which you write only the truth.

EXERCISE: *Sentence Completion*

The following are some topics to help get you started. If you find them either boring or overwhelming, feel free to adapt them in any way you like.

Complete each sentence in the list below in as many ways as you can. Try to push past the obvious and the superficial and attempt to move into deeper, more meaningful answers. Allow yourself to connect with your emotions and your memories as you write. Each sentence can become an entire journal entry if you allow yourself to really get into it.

When I am alone I feel _____

I feel afraid when _____

I feel insecure when _____

I feel sad when _____

I feel angry when _____

I feel embarrassed when _____

I feel guilty when _____

I feel safe when _____

I feel comforted when _____

I feel at peace when _____

The thing I am most angry about in my life is _____

The thing I am most ashamed of in my life is _____

The thing I am saddest about in my life is _____

The thing I am proudest of in my life is _____

Completing these sentences can help you connect more deeply with your emotions, remind you of important events in your life, and help you further discover the unfinished business you will need to complete in order to become a Woman of Substance.

Choosing Your Equipment

Make a commitment to begin your journal by buying the supplies you will need. Because writing is a physical act, it is affected by the equipment you use. The following guidelines will help you with your decisions.

• Start by choosing the type of pen you wish to use. Most people prefer a fast-writing pen, since our thoughts are always much faster than our hands. The new roller pens are fast; ballpoints and felt tips are slow. Go to a stationery store and try out different kinds until you find one that feels good to you.

• Next, pick out your journal or notebook. Some women choose hardcover journals with artistic covers that mean something special to them or that inspire them—reminders of nature, pictures of famous women writers or artists, or reproductions of artwork. Others feel that these are too bulky, and because they are expensive, they feel restricted, as if they can only write something that is profound or especially good in them. For this reason these women choose inexpensive spiral notebooks, the kind schoolchildren use, because they then feel permission to write anything and everything their heart desires.

  Experiment with different formats—hardcovers, softcovers, large, small, blank, wide-lined, thin-lined until you find what works best for you. Some women even like to write on large drawing pads using felt pens.

• Some women choose to use their computers as their journal because their hands can keep up with their minds better than when they write by hand. Others feel that handwriting helps them stay more heart-centered when they are writing something emotional.

- Still others choose to speak into a tape recorder. They like how it feels to directly record their own voice as they speak their thoughts. This is also convenient when you need your hands free to be doing something else, such as driving, cooking, or painting.

How to Create a Refuge

The self-knowledge you gain by opening inward can be profoundly gratifying. But *finding yourself doesn't require you to go off to the woods for weeks or months at a time.* It does require you to take some time alone to focus on yourself, listen to your inner voice, discover your most hidden secrets and your deepest desires.

Most of us think of a refuge as a place that is away from our home, but to create a refuge of solitude all you really need is a place where you can experience silence and experience yourself. The following suggestions will help you create such a place:

- Begin by unplugging the phone, removing distracting reminders of work such as computers and fax machines, and telling others in the house not to disturb you for a given period of time.

- Because you want to connect with yourself, get rid of clutter and any distracting reminders of previous or present relationships, and replace them with pictures of yourself or pictures of places and things you love.

- Some women set up a table or altar on which they place photographs of themselves and special mementos. Many include a photograph of themselves as a child to help them reconnect with or stay connected to their "inner child."

- Because you want your refuge to be a place where you can find solace, strength, and comfort, make it as visually appealing as possible. For example, fill the room with candles, plants, or other items that are comforting and meaningful to you, and decorate it in colors you like.

- Even if you don't have enough space to designate an entire room as your refuge, you can set up a corner in a room. One woman who lives in a crowded New York apartment had only enough room for a lap desk that she brought out when her husband wasn't home, and yet her desk symbolized solitude to her.

- Some women create a ceremony to designate their refuge as a special, sacred space by performing such rituals as lighting a candle, burning incense, meditating, praying, playing or singing a special song, or reading a poem.

The only way some women are able to be alone without feeling abandoned is by creating a space that feels comforting, safe, and nurturing. The following exercise will help you reconnect with memories of comforting and soothing from your childhood that you can incorporate into your refuge of solitude.

EXERCISE: *Comforting and Soothing*

- Write about any childhood memories you have of being comforted and soothed. Who was the person who comforted you the most?

- How did you comfort yourself as a child? Did you have a favorite blanket, pillow, or toy that you used to comfort yourself?

- When you think of self-nurturing, what comes to mind?

- Do you still use the same methods of self-nurturing and comforting you did as a child, or have you developed other ways?

- Do you feel good about the way you nurture and comfort yourself today, or do you wish you had healthier ways?

Many Disappearing Women do not come into adulthood with a reservoir of pleasurable, soothing experiences—memories they can call on in times of stress to comfort them. If this is your situation, you will need to create a soothing, comforting environment based on your current needs. In Briana's case, she needed to design a space where she could integrate maternal comfort and at the same time feel rooted in herself.

To begin, she spent hours cutting out pictures from magazines of loving mothers and phrases of support such as "Be all that you can be" and "You are loved." She then made several collages using the pictures and put them on her bedroom wall. Then she cut out pictures that represented various aspects of herself or the self she wanted to become. Once again she made collages and put them on her wall.

Then she scattered several large, colorful pillows as well as some stuffed animals on her bed. Lying on her bed, surrounded by her stuffed animals, her pillows, and her collages, she felt far more able to spend time alone with herself.

If you, like Briana, can create a space of your own in which you feel comfortable, you can begin to feel at home with yourself. Creating your refuge of solitude will serve as a physical reminder of your commitment to discover yourself. For those of you who are in a relationship, it can also offer a place where you can go to get some space and come back to yourself.

Virginia Woolf wrote about a woman's need for a "room of one's own" in order for her to be able to write, a space in which a woman can be on her own without continuous interruptions. While it is true that solitude and a room of one's own are necessary for creativity, they are also necessary for individuation.

Cultivate Your Attitudes and Intentions

While it is important to create a refuge that is inviting and comforting, it is the attitude with which you approach your time of solitude that influences the experience far more than the actual place.

It is important that you begin each time of solitude with a clear intention. For example, your intention might be to connect with yourself or your spirit, to solve a particular problem, or simply to relax. Many people think of their time of solitude as a way to go beyond day-to-day reality, a time and a place where they can connect with greater truths.

Begin your time of solitude by taking a deep breath and stating your intention to yourself, either out loud or silently.

Many women use rituals to enhance their time of solitude. These rituals can be especially effective if you use your refuge for other purposes throughout the day.

By spending only a half hour a day for honest self-discovery, you will slowly begin to know yourself in a way you may never have thought possible. You can spend your time in silence, in meditation, writing in your journal, or just allowing yourself to feel.

Find Your Authentic Self through Your Emotions

Focusing on how you feel is another important way to discover yourself. Only by knowing yourself through your emotions can you grow to trust yourself, your perceptions, your thoughts, and your actions. Knowing what you are feeling at any given time is one of the best ways of connecting with your authentic self, as well as grounding or centering yourself.

One of the most significant ways women lose themselves is by becoming disconnected from their emotions. If you don't know what you are feeling at any given time you can't expect yourself to act in your best interest. You will do things that are unhealthy without even realizing it, and you will be more inclined to let others make your decisions for you. In addition, if you aren't in touch with how you feel, you are much more susceptible to being controlled by those who will tell you what you are feeling and who you are.

To discover what you are feeling at any given time you must first be able to distinguish between feelings, thoughts, and behavior. This is a typical conversation I have with clients:

Me: "How are you *feeling* about what John did?"

Client: "I just don't understand why he does it."

Me: "So how do you feel about it?"

Client: "I wish he would stop."

Me: "And how do you feel about the fact that he isn't stopping?"

Client: "I get upset."

Me: "Upset in what way?"

Client: "I get frustrated."

As you can see, I was having a difficult time getting the client to connect with and express her feelings. She started off telling me what she *thought* (she couldn't understand it), and what she *wished for,* but she didn't tell me how she *felt.* The closest she could come was to explain that she felt upset, and then only after being pressed still further, to say she was frustrated, which are rather vague descriptions of feelings. It was very difficult for her to realize, much less admit that she was angry.

While the words "upset" and "frustrated" may describe a vague reaction to a situation, these are usually merely euphemisms for what are considered more primal emotions, such as anger, hurt, and fear. For example, saying you are "upset" is often a more socially acceptable way of saying you are hurt or angry, and saying you are "frustrated" is a more acceptable way of saying you are angry. Saying you are "anxious" is less revealing than saying you are afraid, and saying you are "confused" is often a way of not having to own up to your emotions at all. While it can be an honest articulation of your state of mind, it doesn't really describe your emotions.

It may not have been acceptable to express the so-called negative emotions of anger, fear, or sadness in your family. Or one or both of your parents may have been cut off from their feelings and were therefore poor role models. As a child, you may have been told that you were "too sensitive" or that you "felt too strongly about things." You may have been told that you overreacted to situations. Ironically, you were probably reacting normally, but your parents may have felt threatened by your emotional expression because they tended to avoid their own feelings.

We also become disconnected from our emotions by dissociating from ourselves. Many of you have experienced the sensation of "leaving your body" in which your mind seems to rise up, leaving your body, but not your awareness, to deal with a situation. Those who were sexually or physically abused as children frequently dissociate in this way to survive unbearable pain and anguish. Others, such as those raised in chaotic and/or alcoholic households, have experienced the sensation of "spacing out" (all your senses become dulled and your mind seems to take a vacation), or the sensation of your body becoming numb or paralyzed when you are faced with something you feel incapable of coping with.

All these are natural coping mechanisms meant to protect us. Unfortunately, they can become habitual and cause us to disconnect from our emotions to such an extent that we literally do not know what we are feeling at any given time.

If you have grown numb to your feelings for whatever reason, the following exercise will help you begin to reconnect with your emotions.

E X E R C I S E : *Journaling about Your Feelings*

- Carry your journal or a notebook around with you, and whenever you have a spare moment ask yourself, "What am I feeling?" and write the answer down.

- If you don't think you're feeling anything, or if you are not aware of what you are feeling, write that down.

By continuing this process for several weeks you will eventually sensitize yourself to your emotions, becoming more and more aware of what you are feeling at any given time.

The Price We Pay for Repressing and Suppressing Our Emotions

The more you repress and suppress your emotions, the more you will lose contact with who you are and what you really want. When we become alienated from our own emotions we tend to "figure out" in our heads what to feel rather than simply and spontaneously feeling from our hearts.

Also, the more we repress or suppress our "negative emotions" such as anger, fear, and sadness, the more we also restrict our ability to feel the "positive emotions" such as love, joy, and passion. This is because we can't repress or suppress one emotion without affecting our ability to feel and express *all* our emotions.

Each emotion has a purpose, and that emotion will remain with you, buried in your body, locked in your psyche, until that purpose is recognized and understood. For example, anger arises within us to tell us that what is occurring is undesirable or unhealthy. Fear arises to warn us that there is potential loss, pain, failure, or danger. Sadness or hurt arises to tell us we have lost something or will soon lose something, or that we are missing something we want or need. Finally, guilt arises to remind us that we have done something that goes against our own moral code or that we are in some way responsible for causing an undesirable circumstance, such as hurting another person.

Suppressing your emotions—consciously trying to bury them—does not eliminate them. In addition to causing you to become more and more numb to your feelings, including your positive feelings, your suppressed emotions will no doubt also cause physical symptoms such as muscle tension, stomach distress, back problems, headaches, constipation, diarrhea, or maybe even hypertension.

Moreover, your suppressed emotions will likely cause you to overreact to people and situations in inappropriate ways. Unexpressed emotions can cause you to be irritable, irrational, and prone to emotional outbursts and episodes of depression. Something someone says or does may trigger memories of past incidents, causing you to react far more intensely than the present situation warrants. It may send you into a deep depression without your ever knowing why.

If you carry around a lot of suppressed or repressed *anger* (anger you have unconsciously buried), you may lash out at people, blaming them or punishing them for something someone else did long ago. Because you were unable or unwilling to express how you felt at the time, you may overreact in the present, damaging your present relationships.

If you carry around a lot of suppressed or repressed *guilt,* you may live in fear of receiving punishment from authority figures such as bosses or the police, you may set yourself up for punishment by acting out, or you may punish yourself by being self-destructive.

If you carry around a lot of suppressed or repressed *fear,* you may unconsciously avoid meeting people, or you may tell yourself you don't like or need others.

Now is the time to uncover the layers of self-doubt and fear that have prevented you from discovering your true self. You do this by uncovering the emotions that lie hidden deep inside you.

Tear Down the Wall Brick by Brick

A large part of our identity lies in whatever emotions we are feeling at any given time. Denying our feelings is denying a part of our very self, pushing it down and smothering it. Allowing yourself to express your feelings—whether it be anger, pain, or fear—is an assertion of your right to feel and to be your true self.

Earlier in this book I explained how many of us develop what is commonly referred to as a "false self," a facade we present to the world portraying us as stronger, more together, more sure of ourselves than we truly are. This false self protects our more vulnerable, true self that we keep hidden from others and often from ourselves.

Creating a false self is like building a brick wall to protect the true self. Unfortunately, this same brick wall that enables us to appear to be far more self-confident than we truly are also keeps us from making contact with our true selves.

To connect with your authentic self and discover your true feelings you will first need to recognize the wall that blocks access to them and then begin to tear down the wall brick by brick. This will obviously take time and focus, but the alternative is to remain disconnected from your emotions and yourself, something you undoubtedly don't want to do.

Don't Let Your Fear of Your Emotions Stop You

One of the best ways to avoid your emotions is to make sure you are never alone long enough for your feelings to emerge. Once you spend some time alone, you will find that your suppressed and repressed feelings will bubble up and cry out for expression. This experience is often frightening and can drive you back out into the world, where your feelings can get drowned out by the noises around you.

We often become frightened when we feel anything intensely, whether it is anger, fear, pain, or even love and joy. We are afraid that our feelings will overpower us or that we will go crazy from them. We imagine our emotions spilling out all over the place, creating havoc in our lives.

In reality, it is what we *don't* express that can get us into trouble. The more we repress our feelings, the more likely it is that they will burst out when we least expect it. Rest assured, you will not go crazy if you allow yourself to feel and express your strong emotions. If you consistently allow yourself to express your feelings when they occur instead of holding them in, you will find you will actually feel more in control of your emotions, not less.

It takes a great deal of vital energy to push down feelings of anger and sadness. When these emotions are released, on the other hand, most people feel energized and far more free to create the kind of life they want to live.

It is never too late to reclaim those disowned emotions, to open yourself up gradually and allow your feelings to peek out. Test the waters if you must, choose safe people to expose your tender feelings to, but vow to wake up from your emotional slumber and join the living.

It is impossible in one book to explore all the avenues of self-discovery. Instead, in the back of this book I suggest books for you to read that will help you explore other options that have worked for other women, such as meditation and connecting with your spirit. For many women, cultivating their inner life through a spiritual connection to nature and creative expression can be especially rewarding.

No matter which path you take, the important thing is that you dedicate yourself to discovering your authentic self instead of focusing all your time and energy on meeting a man, pleasing a man, or figuring out a man. Until you do, you will be unable to experience true intimacy with a man.

13

Find Your Voice

*Only when you are fully able to say no will you become able
to say yes! from your whole being.*

WILLIAM ASHOKA ROSS

*So often I have listened to everyone else's truth and tried to make it
mine. Now, I am listening deep inside for my own voice and I am
softly, yet firmly, speaking my truth.*

LIANE CORDES

I can't believe I'm forty years old and just learning to stand up for myself.
All my life I've done what others wanted me to do, first my parents and then
my husband. But I'm tired of it and tired of being unhappy. I want a life. I
want to be someone who has opinions and demands, someone who isn't
afraid to voice them. I want other people to listen to me while I tell them
what I think and how I feel for a change.

JOANIE, AGE FORTY

Finding your voice means many things to many people. For some it means
finding a better way to communicate their needs and desires; for others it
means being able to speak up when they disagree instead of remaining passive. For some, finding their voice means finding a way to say NO!—when
they don't want to do something, when they strongly disapprove of another's

actions, when they've finally had enough. For others, finding their voice means learning to say YES!—to stand up for what they believe in, to assert their right to do as they please, to find the courage to live an independent life with or without a relationship.

For some Disappearing Women, finding your voice will involve speaking the words of anger, pain, fear, guilt, and shame that you've repressed or suppressed for years. It will mean finally being able to speak out loud about the abuse and neglect you experienced as a child. For others it will mean being able to finally speak about the domestic violence or rape you experienced as an adult.

Finding your voice can also mean discovering a way to communicate your beliefs, your deepest feelings, or your ideas about how to improve your environment, the world, or the way women are treated in the world. Some women find their voice through politics, social action, or protest, while others find their voice through creative endeavors.

In this chapter I'll explain how women in general have come to lose their voices and provide strategies to help you begin finding your individual voice. These strategies vary in difficulty from relatively simple to very difficult. Do not judge yourself if your attempts don't bring you immediate success, but remember that each attempt on your part will bring you that much closer to finding your voice and your inner strength. Even seemingly unsuccessful attempts will cause you to feel better about yourself if you just give yourself credit for trying.

Women of Substance

Women of Substance aren't afraid to voice their opinion or to say what is on their mind. They know they have a right to their feelings and their point of view, and they aren't afraid of others disagreeing with them. They don't see life as a popularity contest, and they don't take it personally if someone disagrees with them.

Women of Substance know they can't please everyone, and they don't try. They know their limits and know when to say no.

Women of Substance know that if they don't speak up for themselves, no one else will. They know that by keeping silent when others treat them inappropriately, without respect or abusively, they are giving silent permission to this very treatment.

Women of Substance know that if they don't make their needs known, they can't very well expect others to meet them. They don't expect others to read their minds or to know intuitively what they want or need but take responsibility for asking for what they want in a clear, unashamed way.

Why Women Have Lost Their Voices

The Harvard Project on Women's Psychology and the Development of Girls investigated women's lives, moving backward developmentally from adulthood to adolescence and from adolescence to childhood.

They came to realize that girls' initiation or passage into adulthood "in a world psychologically rooted and historically anchored in the experiences of powerful men" forced the girls toward relinquishing what they knew and to silence their own voices:

> . . . the coming not to know what one knows, the difficulty hearing or listening to one's voice, the disconnection between mind and body, thoughts and feelings, and the use of one's voice to cover rather than to convey one's inner world, so that relationships no longer provide channels for exploring the connections between one's inner life and the world of others.

Far more than male children, girls are taught to obey adults, even at the cost of their own comfort or safety. The following example illustrates this point.

When Kendra was a little girl, her mother taught her that it was unladylike for girls to complain or make a fuss. During the summer of her eleventh year she began feeling pain on her right side. When she politely told her mother, she was told to stop complaining—that she probably just ate too much for lunch. Because Kendra did tend to overeat, she thought her mother was probably right. Even though the pain continued, Kendra never complained again. Two weeks later she passed out at a family picnic and was rushed to the hospital with acute appendicitis. The doctors were shocked when they saw her appendix, which was close to becoming gangrenous.

Talk to any voice coach and he or she will talk about "freeing the natural voice," which is the process of freeing the voice from blocks created by inhibitions and fears. Those who were told to be quiet, to keep their thoughts and feelings to themselves, and those who have been traumatized will often have more difficulty connecting with their natural voice than those who are encouraged to express themselves and those who have not been traumatized. Whenever I see an adult female client who has a high-pitched, childlike voice, I usually suspect that there was some trauma in her background that prevented her from fully developing her voice.

Mallory: The Big Woman with the Little-Girl Voice

This was the case with a client I saw several years ago whom I will call Mallory. The first thing I noticed about her was that although she had a rather large frame and was quite tall, her voice was that of a child's—almost "squeaky" in nature. At thirty-four, her voice didn't match her body or her age, and it was almost comical, making it quite disconcerting to listen to her. I immediately suspected that either some trauma had occurred in her childhood or there was something about the way she had been raised that accounted for this arrest in her development. Although she denied any such experience, as time went by it became evident that she had been so strongly dominated by her father that her voice had become constricted with fear. Her father, a very large and angry man, had forbidden his wife or daughter from "talking back" to him, which meant he would not tolerate any dissenting voice. In addition, because he treated his wife as if she were a child, making fun of her requests and constantly talking down to her, Mallory remained childlike in other ways in addition to her voice. She was extremely passive in her relationships and had a series of bad experiences with men who were domineering, like her father.

With encouragement, Mallory began talking about how she felt about her father's domination. At first all she could do was whisper to me some of the horrible things he had said to her and how it made her feel. As she discovered that nothing bad happened to her because she was talking against her father, she began to talk in her normal voice, which was still choked with fear. Suspecting that in addition to fear there was also a great deal of anger trapped in her chest, just waiting to come up and out through her voice, I encouraged her to begin speaking louder and to add more power to her voice. Eventually, with time, encouragement, and support, Mallory was able to yell out the words of anger that had been buried for years. By the time she completed therapy, her voice was deeper, more powerful, and far more adult. Mallory had found her voice.

Not Being Taken Seriously

While not all women have high-pitched, squeaky voices like Mallory's, it is common for women to speak so softly they can barely be heard or to speak even strong words in such a way that they aren't taken seriously. If a girl consistently has the experience of not being heard by those she cares about, she may deduce that it isn't worth it to speak up. If what she says is constantly ridiculed, or if her words are continually countered with opposing arguments, she may opt for silence rather than risk being hurt or humiliated. And if her words don't seem to be understood by others or echoed by others, she will assume her words and her opinions are incorrect. This was Lee's experience:

> My parents were rather simple, old-fashioned people. They were loving toward me, but neither one of them took me seriously, especially my father. When I started school and began to have my own ideas about things, my father would say things like, "That's a crazy idea" or "What in the world made you think of that?" After a while I stopped sharing my thoughts with my parents because I knew they wouldn't understand. Unfortunately, it took me years to discover that there were other people who thought like I did, and that it had been my parents' problem, not mine.

By the time many girls have become women, they have already lost their voice. They have learned it is better to keep the peace than to speak out and risk rejection, humiliation, or retaliation. They have learned that many men assume that what a woman has to say has no merit in the first place and that their words are to be tolerated but not taken seriously. And many have been taught that when they do speak up in a relationship they are considered "nags" or "whiners."

When it comes to voicing their opinions, beliefs, and knowledge around a man they are attracted to, even the most confident and successful women can become intimidated. This is often because they are afraid of turning off or appearing too dominant to a man. Women sense, and rightly so, that many men are afraid of being controlled and dominated by a woman. This fear often goes back to adolescence, when boys are acutely afraid of being rejected and dominated by girls. No matter how attracted to her he is, a boy will likely reject a girl he thinks is too controlling or possessive. Many grown men never get past this stage.

Women also become intimidated because men take on dominance patterns in conversation, through louder voices, physical contact, or by cutting off conversation. In fact, male conversation relies heavily on one-upping and dominance patterns, a fact that Deborah Tannen, in *You Just Don't Understand,* has made so brilliantly clear.

Because of their conditioning, men tend to generate a more intense, attention-getting energy than do women. To see the phenomenon occur, one only need notice what happens when one man joins a group of women. The energy in the room changes, and unless the man is totally inadequate socially and doesn't say anything, he will end up doing most of the talking and the women most of the listening.

Sneak Past Your Censor

Many women find they must sneak past their inner censor to find their true voice. Our inner censor is that insistent, critical voice inside that tells us we can't do something or that tries to convince us that what we are doing isn't good enough. Nowhere is this truer than in the practice of writing. In her fine book *Writing Down the Bones,* Natalie Goldberg recommends the timed exercise as a way to bypass your inner censor when you begin to write. You may wish to start small (ten minutes) and after a week increase your time. Goldberg suggests the following rules:

1. *Keep your hand moving*—don't pause to reread what you have written.

2. *Don't cross out*—that's editing as you write. Separate the creator from the editor or internal censor so the creator has free space to explore and express herself.

3. *Don't worry about spelling, punctuation, or grammar.*

4. *Lose control.*

5. *Don't think. Don't get logical.*

6. *Go for the jugular*—if something comes up that's frightening or what Goldberg calls "naked"—dive in!

These rules will help you to burn through to what Goldberg calls "first thoughts"—to "the place where energy is unobstructed by social politeness or the internal censor, to the place where you are writing what your mind actually sees and feels, not what it *thinks* it should see or feel."

As Goldberg explained, our internal censor usually squelches our first thoughts, "so we live in the realm of second and third thoughts, thoughts on thoughts, twice or three times removed from the direct connection of the first fresh flash." But if we can persist in giving our first thoughts free rein and getting them down on paper uncensored, we will find that they are unencumbered by our ego (that mechanism in us that tries to be in control), and we will be able to express the truth of the way things are.

The more your true, first thoughts have a chance to pour out of you, the more you will learn to trust your deep self and not give in to your inner censor as often. When you learn to trust your own voice through spontaneous writing, you can then transfer this experience to other areas of your life.

EXERCISE: *Voice Your Anger and Pain*

In the previous chapter I explained how repressed emotions from the past can interfere with your life today. For many of you it will be necessary to find a way to express these emotions from the past to find your voice and be able to live more assertively in the present.

There are many ways of voicing your anger and pain from the past:

- Write a letter to the person who hurt or angered you, expressing exactly how you feel. Do not ask *questions* such as "How could you . . . ?" or "Why did you . . . ?" Such questions keep you in the role of victim. Instead, make *statements* using "I" messages, such as "I'm angry with you for . . ." or "I don't like what you did. . . ." Be assertive. Whether you choose to mail the letter or simply use it as an exercise, it still has the same basic effect of helping you rid yourself of pent-up emotions.

  For many, writing doesn't do the trick. They need to vocalize their anger and pain—let out the screams and the sobs that are buried deep inside. They need to say the words that repeat in their heads over and over but never get spoken. They need to stop the self-critical words that play like a never-ending tape in their heads, by giving them back to those who have criticized them. If this is true for you, try any or all of the following:

- Have an imaginary conversation with the person you are angry with. Tell that person exactly how you feel; don't hold back anything.

- Pretend the person you are angry with is sitting in a chair across from you. It may help to put a picture of the person on the chair. Talk to the empty chair or the picture and tell off that person.

- Express your feelings of anger into a tape recorder.

To find your voice and become a Woman of Substance you must give yourself permission to express your sorrow and rage, especially if you experienced trauma in your childhood or adulthood. Otherwise you will continue to turn it inward on yourself, damaging your self-esteem, causing depression and even bodily symptoms, and generally paralyzing your life.

Overcome Your Fear of Anger

Even though you may understand that releasing your anger will help you recover from your childhood and help you find your voice today, you may still fear actually doing it. If you were punished whenever you spoke up as a child, you may be afraid of retaliation. This is especially true of those who were physically abused as children and those who were threatened with physical punishment whenever they became angry.

Although those who neglected or abused you may have little or no power over you today and even though you don't plan to confront them directly, this fear of retaliation may be overwhelming. It is actually your "inner child," that part of you who holds the memories of your childhood, who is afraid. Therefore you will need to assure that child part of you that the "adult" you will protect her. This may seem foolish to you, but over the years I have worked with countless women who have been helped by visualizing their inner child and then talking to her and reassuring her that she is safe now, that no one can hurt her. Just as you would promise to protect an actual child, your promise will be heard by that child part of you who is still so frightened, and this will enable you to begin letting your anger out a little bit at a time until you are assured it is indeed safe to do so.

As mentioned earlier, some women are afraid that once they begin releasing their anger they will lose control, "go crazy," or hurt someone. Unless you have a history of losing control and acting in these ways, there is probably little danger of you doing so now, but the following visualization exercise may help you get more comfortable with your anger and learn that you have far more control than you realize.

EXERCISE: *Anger Visualization*

1. Lie down or sit in a comfortable chair, relax, and close your eyes. Begin to breathe deeply and evenly.
2. Visualize what you imagine you might do if you became extremely angry and totally "lost control." Really "see" what might happen.

This visualization will give you valuable information about how you might react if you actually did begin to express your anger. Having in a sense already experienced the situation in your mind can put you more in control. You now have a choice whether you feel safe enough to actually begin releasing your anger or whether you should seek professional help before attempting it.

If you found yourself merely screaming or throwing things, you will probably feel relieved to realize that this is the extent of your "loss of control."

If, on the other hand, you imagined yourself destroying someone with your rage and chopping that person into little pieces, going "berserk," or curling up in a corner completely catatonic and having to be hospitalized, you may have reason to be afraid. This does not mean that you would actually do any of these things, but it does show you just how angry you are and that you must begin to release your anger slowly and carefully.

EXERCISE: *Gradual Anger Release*

This exercise will help you visualize a way to begin releasing your anger a little at a time:

1. Get into a comfortable position again. Close your eyes and begin to breathe deeply.

2. Visualize your anger as steam that has built up in some pipes. Imagine that the steam (anger) had filled the pipes almost to the bursting point (losing control).

3. Slowly let some of the steam out of the pipes by carefully and gradually opening a valve. Allow only a small amount of steam out at a time. Eventually all the steam will be released and no pipes will burst.

Your anger is the steam building up inside you. If you release your anger a little at a time, you will not lose control.

EXERCISE: *"Sneak Past" Your Resistance and Fear*

You can "sneak past" your resistance and fear by finding ways to begin releasing your anger as part of your daily schedule. For example:

- When taking out the garbage and recycling, stomp on egg cartons, aluminum cans, or any other packaging that makes a loud or crisp sound, and imagine you are stomping on those who hurt you.

- As you garden, release your anger as you hoe the soil, cut limbs, or tear out weeds.

- As you take your daily walk, imagine that each time you take a step you are stomping on the person you are angry with.

- Tear an old phone book or newspapers into pieces.

- Yell and scream in the shower

- Go to a batting cage, driving range, or tennis court and practice hitting balls, focusing on releasing your anger instead of on performance.

- Throw balls or darts at a target.

Whichever anger-release technique you use, be prepared for more resistance on your part. Resistance will take many different forms: worrying about what other people will think; feeling too tired right after you've started; worrying about hurting your back, blistering your hands, feeling silly, and so on.

You can find lots of excuses for not releasing your anger. There will always seem to be a better time. But don't fool yourself. There is no better time than now!

Releasing Anger Is Not for Everyone

If you are the type of person who has a difficult time expressing your anger, who puts up with inappropriate behavior from others rather than risking retaliation or rejection, and who has not been able to express your rage concerning the neglect or abuse you experienced as a child, you need to find ways to vent your anger—to express it in safe, constructive ways.

On the other hand, if you are the type of person who frequently loses your temper, who has emotional outbursts that seem to come out of nowhere, or who seems to have more trouble controlling your anger than expressing it, you will need to find ways to *contain* your anger.

Sometimes a woman's wounds are so deep and her rage is so explosive that it is destructive. Such rage is often rooted in feelings of abandonment, betrayal, and rejection from childhood and often comes up over and over again in her current relationships. Many women destroy their relationships this way through continual outbursts or suicidal threats and attempts. If this describes you, your work will be in focusing on what is behind the rage—usually pain and fear—and getting access to those emotions as well as your rage. Equally important will be for you to distinguish which part of your rage is the unresolved anger from childhood and what belongs to the present situation.

Transform Your Rage

Your rage, while unfocused and perhaps even explosive, carries powerful energy that, if utilized constructively, can release your true potential as a woman.

Kali, the Hindu goddess of creation and destruction, symbolizes the power many women need to develop in themselves—the power to assert themselves, to set limits, and to say no when necessary. While Kali's rage can destroy, it also can create, and so it can provide the fire for transformation.

In *The Wounded Woman: Healing the Father-Daughter Relationship,*

Linda Schierse Leonard compared how one releases one's rage to the way one deals with a forest fire—by essentially "fighting fire with fire"—setting smaller fires around the larger, more dangerous fire in order to limit it:

> In the same way, letting the rage out into the open with a burst of feeling can actually limit the rage by releasing it. For rage can be an act of assertion that sets limits and establishes identity by saying, "I won't take any more of this!"

Ultimately, this expression of rage needs to be not only forceful but also formed and focused. Once women become conscious of their rage they must take responsibility for giving it form and shape.

There are two stages to transforming rage. First we must get the rage out, and then we must transform the power of our anger into creative energy.

Containing the energy means not dissipating it in formless rage but asserting it creatively. This might be in a work of art, through a political act, by raising an emotionally healthy child, or in the quality of one's own life.

Throughout history women have transformed their anger into powerful acts of transformation: women such as Rosa Parks, the American civil rights activist who sparked the successful 1955-1956 Montgomery, Alabama, city bus boycott when she refused a driver's order to give her seat to a white man simply because she was black, as mandated by city ordinance; Dian Fossey, the American primatologist who engaged in an economic and political battle to preserve the mountain gorilla in Rwanda and who has become a hero to wildlife preservationists and environmentalists throughout the world; and Rachel Carson, the American biologist and writer whose scientific accuracy and thoroughness made *Silent Spring* a powerful warning of the growing danger of unrestricted use of chemical pesticides and herbicides.

Experiment with different ways of expressing yourself (through art, writing, music, political action) until you find a way to transform your rage and find your true voice.

Finding your voice can be as important as finding yourself, because if you can't speak up for yourself and your rights, you are in constant danger of losing yourself all over again. Those who can't ask for what they want will end up taking what they can get and hating themselves for it. Those who can't say no to unreasonable demands will end up doing things that lower their self-esteem and cause them to lose respect for themselves. And those who can't speak their minds will soon become confused about what they actually believe.

Finding your voice also means that you have finally been able to express the anger, pain, and fear that you have held in from the past out of fear of retaliation, humiliation, or losing control.

You have a right to your anger. By expressing it instead of holding it in, you can become empowered by it instead of diminished.

14

Find Your Shadow

*If you bring forth what is within you, what you bring forth
will save you. If you do not bring forth what is within you,
what you do bring forth will destroy you.*

JESUS

*The web of our life is of a mingled yarn, good and ill together:
our virtues would be proud, if our faults whipped them not; and our
crimes would despair, if they were not cherished by our virtues.*

WILLIAM SHAKESPEARE

When my mother was still alive she often told me this story: One day, as she dropped me off at the baby-sitter and gave me her usual admonishment—"Now you be good for Mrs. Jones today"—I turned to her and said, "I have to be good for Mrs. Jones, I have to be good for you, I have to be good at school, I have to be good when I go to church. When can I be bad?"

My mother always laughed when she told this story, since in many ways she loved my precociousness. But I doubt that she truly appreciated what I was trying to tell her—that I felt too much pressure to be good and needed a time and a place where I could be "bad."

As human beings, we contain within ourselves a spectrum of urges and potential behaviors, but our parents, society, and religion reinforce some and discourage others. While it is important for children to learn certain social behaviors in the process of growing up, the very act of encouraging some while discouraging others creates within us all a shadow personality. These rejected qualities do not cease to exist simply because they've been denied expression. Instead, they live on within us and form the secondary personality that psychology calls the Shadow.

Therefore there is a part of ourselves we hide away not only from others but also from ourselves. This dark side is made up of forbidden thoughts and feelings such as rage, jealousy, shame, resentment, lust, greed; undesirable and therefore rejected personality traits, and all the violent and sexual tendencies we consider evil, dangerous, or forbidden.

Sometimes we are aware of our dark side, and out of fear of being propelled into acting in ways that we will regret, we consciously work at pushing down and controlling our more prurient or unacceptable urges. More often, though, we are entirely unaware of it.

Only by owning our Shadow can we gain control over it. We've all heard the old saying that it's what we don't know that can hurt us. Once we are aware of our dark side, we can exercise real control over it: not by suppressing it, but by respecting it, finding constructive outlets for it, and setting limits.

How do we meet the Shadow? By conceding that there are parts of ourselves that we abhor, despise, or deny; by acknowledging those parts, no matter how horrific they are; and by seeing that we are still ourselves. These acts in themselves become peace offerings that encourage the Shadow to emerge.

When we are immunized against disease, our bodies know instinctively how to make good use of the poison or disease-producing substance that in larger or altered amounts would harm us. The ability to admit the Shadow, to allow it into consciousness in manageable doses, similarly allows us to immunize the psyche.

It is a paradox of consciousness that allowing and admitting the Shadow reduces its power, producing the opposite of what we feared. By making ourselves vulnerable to it, we achieve an immunity to its deadliness. Instead of being overwhelmed by our darker urges, we learn to coexist with them, nodding knowingly when they appear, gratefully taking the lessons they give us, and turning them into healthy emotional or creative expressions. I've seen time and again in my practice that recognizing the dark side produces a powerful and beneficial change in consciousness.

In this chapter we will discuss four ways in which you can begin to discover and own your Shadow:

- Take back your projections.
- Own your own talents, intelligence, and beauty.
- Own your envy and your hidden treasures.
- Accept that you and others are both good and bad.

Take Back Your Projections

Projection is the act of attributing to others those feelings and reactions that we ourselves are having but do not want to acknowledge, or in some cases, feelings that we fear we may have or have had in the past. Just as a movie camera *projects* an image onto a screen, we project onto others all those aspects of ourselves we are fearful of or ashamed of.

Why do we project? Projection is an unconscious defense mechanism. Therefore, we are not necessarily aware of our behavior. In fact, more often than not we are unaware of it. Projection happens whenever a trait or characteristic of our personality that has no relationship to consciousness becomes activated. As a result of the unconscious projection, we observe and react to this unrecognized personal trait in other people. We see in them something that is a part of ourselves but that we fail to see in ourselves.

Usually the feelings, traits, and qualities that we project onto others are ones we consider negative. Sometimes, though, we deny positive qualities and feelings as well. The former often take the form of the Shadow, while the latter take the form of envy, which we will discuss later in this chapter.

To become a Woman of Substance you need to take back your projections—all the disowned qualities within yourself that you attribute instead to others. For example, instead of owning their own anger, Disappearing Women will often be especially sensitive to or critical of the anger of others. Instead of owning their own neediness, they become critical of others who are needy. And instead of owning their own dishonesty, they focus on the dishonesty of the men in their lives.

EXERCISE: *Shadow Work*

For you to begin taking back your Shadow projections, you must first identify them. The following exercise will help you do so.

1. List all the qualities you do not like in other people—for instance, conceit, short temper, selfishness, bad manners, and greed.

2. When your list is complete, extract those characteristics that you not only dislike in others but hate, loathe, and despise.

This shorter list is a fairly accurate picture of your personal Shadow.

Of course, not all our criticisms of others are projections of our own undesirable qualities, but any time our response to another person involves excessive emotion or overreaction, we can be certain that something unconscious within us is being prodded. For example, if your partner is sometimes arrogant, it is reasonable for you to find his behavior offensive. But in true Shadow projection your condemnation of him will far exceed his demonstration of the fault, in which case it would be wise of you to examine your own behavior for arrogance.

Conflict situations, which usually bring up strong emotions and highlight important issues, provide an excellent opportunity for you to discover your Shadow projections. The next time you are in an argument with your partner and find yourself expressing intense feelings about one of his characteristics, look within yourself to see if you can find that very same attribute tucked away in some corner inside yourself.

We all have parts of ourselves that we have denied or disowned, but Women of Substance have the integrity to take back their projections. Don't continue to avoid dealing with your own negative qualities by *projecting* them onto others or by getting involved with others who act them out for you.

Own Your Own Talents, Intelligence, and Beauty

If you tend to get involved with men who have the qualities you admire but lack, it is time for you to begin to either develop these qualities in yourself or take a closer look at yourself to find the positive qualities you do have. For example, if you have a pattern of getting involved with men who are extremely attractive and then proceed to lose yourself in the relationship by constantly fearing that the man will leave you for someone else, perhaps you need to focus instead on improving your own body image and owning your own beauty (inner and outer).

If you constantly get involved with wealthy, successful, or talented men and then proceed to get lost in the relationship because of the imbalance of power between you and your partner, perhaps it is time for you to begin creating the life you aspire to instead of trying to get it vicariously from someone else.

After some self-reflection, Gloria Steinem began to realize that there was, in fact, a reason why she had become involved with Mort Zuckerman:

> Slowly, I began to realize there might be a reason why I was attracted to someone so obviously wrong for me. If I had been drawn to a man totally focused on his own agenda, *maybe I needed to have an agenda of my own.* Finally, I began to make time to write. If I had felt comforted by the elaborate organization of his life, *maybe I needed some comfort and organization in my own.* Therefore, I enlisted the help of friends to

take the stacks of cardboard boxes out of my apartment and started the long process of making it into a pleasant place to live. I even began to save money for the first time in my life. . . . And perhaps most of all, if I had fallen in love with a powerful man, I had to realize that I was in mourning for the power women need and rarely have, myself included.

If you are like many Disappearing Women, you have spent your life envying the lives and accomplishments of others. You have felt like a child out in the cold, pressing your nose up against the windows of those who seem to have what you most desire. Some of you may have patterned your life after those you admire, emulating their behavior as a guideline for how to act and how to feel.

Now is the time to begin to dig up your own treasures instead of envying those of others, to begin focusing your attention on your own talents and pursuing your own dreams instead of idolizing the talents and lives of others.

Own Your Envy and Your Hidden Treasures

Our Shadow includes not only our forbidden thoughts and feelings, undesirable and rejected personality traits, but *any* aspect of ourselves that we have denied, including our talents, ambitions, and dreams. Just as we project our anger, greed, lust, and rage onto others as a way of denying these qualities within ourselves, so we also project our talents, ambitions, and dreams. This is at the core of our need to idealize others and put them on pedestals. It is also at the core of the emotion of envy.

Envy is one of our most destructive emotions. The person who envies wants to possess what the admired person holds most dear—their possessions, their good qualities, their lifestyle, their loved ones. Ultimately (albeit unconsciously), they want to destroy the person and take over his or her life.

Envy is at the core of our exaggerated respect of other people and the celebration of their achievements. At the same time it is a rejection of the good things within ourselves, for when we envy we unconsciously project our own positive attributes onto others. The tragedy is that our envy blinds us to the good that is within ourselves.

Although it can be extremely upsetting to be faced with the realization that our Shadow includes the demons of envy and covetousness, particularly when we have endeavored to always look up to others and applaud their achievements, such acceptance allows these Shadow attitudes to provide us with the positive dimension of motivation—motivation to achieve goals, to develop ourselves, and to enrich our own lives.

When we envy others for what they have been able to achieve, our own unique gifts and talents are lost to us. Instead, we see our own neglected talents in others and feel that somehow those who possess them have taken these talents from us.

E X E R C I S E : *Mining for the Gold of Your Shadow*—————————————

Jung said that our Shadow is a gold mine of depth, mystery, richness, substance, knowledge, creativity, insight, and power—the very qualities we all seem to be striving for, the very qualities we admire and envy in others.

The Shadow can be positive, particularly when an individual is not living up to his or her potential. Jung said that the personal Shadow contains psychic features of the individual that are unlived or scarcely lived. In repressed people, the Shadow is often the most alive part of the personality. Therefore, only if the Shadow is recognized and integrated will a woman be able to actualize her full potential.

The following exercises will help you come closer to reaching your Shadow and your full potential:

1. On a piece of paper or in your journal, list those qualities you most admire in other people (e.g., ambition, beauty, talent).

   Although you may be convinced that you could never possess such attributes, they are undoubtedly part of what William A. Miller refers to as your Golden Shadow. Begin looking for these qualities in yourself. No matter how deeply they are buried or how undeveloped they are, they are hidden somewhere inside you, and you can find them if you just keep digging.

2. List those qualities you most admire in your current partner. If you are not in a relationship, list those qualities you most admired in your previous relationship or in the men you are currently attracted to.

   These characteristics are likely to be the very attributes within yourself that you have denied. Caught up in their desire for the other person, many Disappearing Women project their own unconscious positive attributes onto the men they become romantically involved with. While the trait projected may in fact be there to some degree, usually it is there nowhere to the degree that they perceive it to be. In all likelihood the admired trait lies more within the Disappearing Woman than in the admired.

3. Give yourself credit for your positive attributes. Women tend to be far

more self-effacing and modest than men are. In most families it is considered inappropriate for girls to point out their accomplishments or acknowledge their looks, whereas boys are encouraged to boast and build themselves up. The following exercise will help you to counter this conditioning and to recognize your positive attributes:

- On a piece of paper or in your journal, list five of your most positive characteristics, those attributes that you feel best about and are proudest of.

- If you cannot think of five things, continue thinking about it and observing yourself until you can. If, after a week, you still cannot think of five positive attributes, ask a close friend to tell you what she values and admires most in you. Then see if you agree with any of the qualities she has named, and if you do, add them to your list. If you still cannot think of five items, work with what you have for now. Hopefully, as you continue working on owning your positive attributes, you will be able to list five attributes and possibly more.

- Write your five positive attributes on an index card and place it in a conspicuous place where you will have to look at it often. Some women have placed their card on their bathroom mirror, others on their nightstand, and still others on the dashboard or taped across their ashtray in their car.

- Stop to read your attributes list at least twice a day. Begin by taking a deep breath. Now read each item out loud, taking a deep breath after each item. As you take in your breath, take in the knowledge that you possess this attribute. By reading your list in this way you will gradually come to the realization that you possess these positive characteristics. Don't expect it to happen overnight, but over time this knowledge will gradually seep into your consciousness, especially if you are no longer surrounding yourself with those who counter these positive messages with criticism.

4. Last but certainly not least, stop comparing yourself with others.

    When we compare ourselves with others we always end up feeling either "less than" or "better than."

    Generally speaking, comparing yourself to others only serves to increase feelings of inferiority and envy. Disappearing Women in particular tend to imagine that others have it better than they do and that others are more talented, beautiful, or lovable than they are. In reality we are all blessed with talent, we are all beautiful in our own way, and we are definitely all lovable.

Instead of wasting time comparing yourself to others, focus your time and attention on tapping your own resources. Instead of coveting the beauty, success, or talents of others, begin to cultivate your own. Instead of living vicariously through the men in your life, begin to develop your own talents and abilities.

Accept That You and Others Are Both Good and Bad

As a Disappearing Woman you probably tend to perceive others as either all good or all bad. You idealize others and put them on a pedestal. Then, when they behave like normal, fallible human beings, you cast them out of your life. When people hurt you, disappoint you, or do something that seems unfair to you, you immediately see them as all bad, lacking in any redeeming qualities. But in reality, we are all both good and bad. No one is perfect, we all make mistakes, we've all disappointed and hurt others.

Many Disappearing Women maintain this all-or-nothing, black-or-white-thinking because they did not pass through a normal developmental process in childhood. They stayed stuck in a child's way of perceiving reality.

An infant sees no distinction between herself and her mother—they are one. Eventually the child realizes that she is separate from her mother, but her mother must remain "all good" for the child to feel safe and secure. Therefore, even if a mother is a not-so-good mother, even if she leaves her baby unattended for hours or doesn't feed her baby when she is hungry, the child cannot perceive of the mother as "bad" because she is all the child has. Nor can the child perceive the mother as "sometimes bad" (when not taking care of her needs) and "sometimes good" (when she is there to comfort and feed her baby) because the child still perceives the world in all-or-nothing terms. The child deduces, therefore, that it is she who is the bad one, not the mother, or that there is a "bad" mother and a "good" mother—two separate mothers.

In the normal course of development, most children move past this "all or nothing" view of life and begin to recognize that the "bad" mother who doesn't come when her child cries is the same "good" mother who does come. Unfortunately, if a child is neglected or abused, she may never reach this stage of development and therefore will continue seeing others, as well as herself, as either "all good" (when she doesn't do anything wrong) or "all bad" (when she does).

This way of thinking is not only naive and childlike but dangerous. No one is all good or all bad. We are all made up of both so-called good and bad qualities. We all have greed, lust, fear, envy, rage, and jealousy in our hearts. And we are all capable of acting on these emotions.

As a way of denying these qualities within ourselves, we do two things. First, we put others on pedestals, attributing to them those qualities we admire and divesting them of those qualities we do not admire. So we have celebrities, gurus, and evangelists—and idealized romantic love. Second, we project all our so-called bad qualities onto those we deem "monsters"—those who get caught for doing what we have done or what we've longed to do.

Our culture teaches us from early infancy to split and polarize dark and light. But not all cultures believe this way. For example, the ancient Chinese culture emphasizes the yin-yang symbol, which shows us the white part of the personality and the black part of the personality united and overlapping inside a circle.

Shadow work—owning those aspects of ourselves we have denied—forces us again and again to take another point of view, to respond to life with our undeveloped traits and our instinctual sides, and to live what Jung called the tension of the opposites—holding both good and evil, right and wrong, light and dark, in our own hearts.

In every dark and undesirable attribute in our personality, there is an opposite *desirable* characteristic in our Shadow that we can bring into consciousness and employ for a richer experience of life.

And perhaps most importantly, a decision to fight the dark side of oneself can cause "the conscious" and "the unconscious" to take up adversary positions, causing us to have a split within ourselves. By embracing our Shadow we heal the split and become whole; by forming a partnership with the Shadow we gain its riches.

Becoming a Whole Person

When my client Caroline began to explore her dark side in therapy, she found that she had tried so hard to be the opposite of her mother, a very selfish woman, that her normal, healthy need to have time away from her family had become transformed into Shadow material. Her need to be *all good* had caused her to be only half a person. Once she was able to acknowledge the fact that she didn't always have to be giving to her family and that they even got on her nerves sometimes, she stopped taking herself so seriously and regained her sense of humor. She suddenly began to have far more energy and was able to bring a new vitality to all aspects of her life—including her sex life with her husband.

Like Caroline, many people go through life bent on being good. Detached from their dark side, they are also detached from the wonderful things the dark side offers us—passion, depth, creativity, sensuous pleasures, and a sense of humor.

When we disown our dark side, we are indeed less alive, less spirited. A rich vitality lies bottled up beneath our "acceptable" personality. Only by finding and redeeming those wishes and traits that we chronically deny in ourselves can we move toward wholeness and healing.

For example, those who are in touch with their personal Shadow are far more likely to be empathetic and compassionate toward others. Because they have owned their not-so-perfect personality traits and their forbidden thoughts and feelings, they are less likely to feel they have a right to sit in judgment of others.

Whereas judging others makes us pompous, self-righteous, and hardhearted, empathy softens us, gives us wisdom and depth and makes us fuller, more interesting people. While judging blinds us to others, empathy helps us see others more clearly—both their positive and their negative qualities. It is like a magic telescope helping us to see inside others, to view their heart and soul.

As Carl Jung said, the dark side is 90 percent gold. But unless we can mine those riches, we are presenting to the world and to ourselves only half a person. Exploring and owning our dark sides make us whole, transforming us not into monsters but into more empathetic, less judgmental *human* beings.

Integrating your Shadow cannot be accomplished by a simple method. It is a complex, ongoing struggle that calls for commitment, dedication, and the loving support of others. In the back of the book I will recommend several books you can read on the Shadow, and in appendix I, I will discuss the option of forming an Empowerment Circle of like-minded women who will offer you the support you need for Shadow work.

15

Find Your Substance

The woman's place of power . . . is dark, it is ancient, and it is deep.
AUDRE LORDE

If we imagine . . . the individual as a larger or smaller room,
it is obvious that most people come to know only one corner of their
room, one spot near the window, one narrow strip on which they keep
walking back and forth. In this way they have a certain security.
RAINER MARIA RILKE

The territory of the self is a vast, unexplored, and prohibited geography . . .
our experiences, feelings, insights, understandings are often off-limits. As
often as we are imprisoned inside ourselves, so often are we actually living
in exile outside ourselves. One can say that one of the basic conditions of
contemporary life is the unfulfilled longing of the self for itself.
DEENA METZGER, WRITING FOR YOUR LIFE

Disappearing Women are often difficult to see, hear, and take seriously because they tend to be amorphous and transparent and may sometimes even appear to be shallow. They don't have a firm foundation; they have shaky boundaries and constantly changing value systems. In other words, they don't have enough substance.

Heather: The Emptiness Inside

Although Heather is forty-four years old, she looks and acts like a woman in her late twenties. There is a breezy quality about her, augmented by the fact that she is extremely thin and walks and moves about rapidly. Although she is very intelligent, she is often perplexed and overwhelmed by life and is constantly trying to figure out where to focus her attention. At any given time she is obsessing about finding either a life partner, a more meaningful career, or the right place to live.

Her life is marked by uncertainty: Should I continue to date a man even though I wouldn't want to marry him? Should I continue working at my job because it pays well, or should I risk making less money but gain more fulfillment doing something else? Should I continue a friendship even though the person has certain beliefs I am strongly opposed to? Should I continue trying to resolve my problems with my mother or just keep my distance from her?

But mostly her life is focused on one unresolved relationship after another. She is constantly in conflict concerning a relationship with either a friend, her ex-husband, one of her siblings, her mother, or a man she is seeing. She spends a great deal of her time in conversations with her friends, usually trying to elicit advice from them about how she can resolve a conflict or whether she should continue a relationship.

In addition, she continually becomes swept up into one cause after another, one fad after another. If a friend becomes involved in a new cause, Heather gets caught up in it, too. She starts going to meetings, volunteers her time, and makes the issue the focus of her attention for a time. But nothing ever sticks. She inevitably becomes disillusioned with the cause, and because she has gone to such an extreme with it, she soon tires of it.

She does the same with people. She'll get a new friend, and for a time all her old friends will hear about how wonderful this person is, how much they have in common, how much fun they had at a particular event. For a time, usually a few months, her old friends won't see her as much because she is so busy with her new friend. But soon she'll make contact again and they'll hear her complaining about her new friend or questioning her new friend's ethics, beliefs, or actions. Before long, Heather is coming around as much as before, maybe even more, telling her old friends how grateful she is for their friendship, how she can't believe she could have gotten so swept up with someone who is so selfish, controlling, or messed up.

I don't mean to imply that Heather is uncaring or selfish, because she isn't. She cares for those close to her and she can be very generous. She is just so distracted by her internal conflicts that she can't connect deeply, either with others or with an activity or cause.

Because of this she has been unable to sustain a romantic relationship for any extended period of time. Although she was married once, she was miserably unhappy during most of the marriage, and she divorced him after two years because, as she explained it to me, "I was no longer living the kind of life that meant anything to me."

Her ex-husband, the vice president of a bank, focused most of his attention on achieving status and accumulating wealth and material possessions. "I got caught up in it for a while. Buying and decorating our house, entertaining his business associates, traveling. But then I got bored. It all seemed so empty."

But Heather did not escape the feeling of boredom when she left her husband. The sad truth is that the emptiness is inside of Heather. No matter who or what she becomes involved with, she will become bored because she is looking outside of herself for meaning and purpose.

This is a kind of "Catch-22." She frantically looks outside herself for something or someone who can fill up her emptiness, which then prevents her from focusing on herself enough to *develop* a stronger sense of self, which will, in turn, help her fill up the emptiness inside.

Become Full of Yourself

In contrast to Disappearing Women such as Heather, Women of Substance stand with their feet firmly planted on the ground. They are full of themselves, not in the derogatory sense, but full of their own emotions, ideas, beliefs, and values. Unlike the will of the wisp who can be blown over or carried away by any strong wind, a Woman of Substance is more like the sturdy oak whose roots are so firmly grounded that she can weather any storm.

Women of Substance are not likely to drop everything they are doing to be with a man, because their lives are meaningful and full. They envision a man adding to their already satisfying life instead of galloping in on a white horse to take them away to a fantasyland. Neither do they try to gain recognition, fame, or wealth by hitching their horse to someone else's wagon. They know what they want, believe they can get it on their own, and fight for it until they get it.

A Woman of Substance doesn't need validation from a man to feel good about herself and is therefore not desperate for a man. Although she wants to have an intimate, loving, *equal* relationship with a man, she doesn't devote her life to obtaining it.

Becoming a Woman of Substance may seem like a tall order and, indeed, it is. We normally develop our sense of self or our identity when we are children, and many believe that those who missed this opportunity are always plagued with symptoms of a weak identity such as dependency, anger toward authority figures, inappropriate boundaries, and/or idealization and over-identification with adored figures. But there are some very specific steps women can take to help them develop a stronger self. In this chapter I will identify and elaborate on the steps you will need to focus on and keep focusing on until you have mastered them.

In the previous three chapters we focused on strategies to help you find your authentic self, your voice, and your Shadow. To become a Woman of Substance you will need to continue focusing on these areas:

- Continue to face and embrace solitude.

- Develop a strong inner life (introspection, dreams, journal).

- Recognize your needs and honor your feelings.

- Remain connected to your emotions and your body.

- Continue to communicate your needs and opinions to others.

- Take back your projections.

In this chapter we will focus on helping you complete the individuation process—a big task, and one that is best accomplished by dividing it up into steps. Unfortunately, there is not enough room in this book to fully elaborate on each step. Instead, I offer you a basic introduction and include a list of recommended books for further exploration.

By practicing the following steps you will not only get over your tendency to lose yourself with a man but also become a Woman of Substance. While these steps are listed in the recommended order, you do not have to complete one step before moving on to the next. In fact, many of the steps work together to help you achieve a more difficult task.

1. Complete your unfinished business from the past.

2. Become involved in some form of creative expression.

3. Stop looking to romance or to a man for completion.

4. Risk making your own decisions.

5. Stop giving yourself away.

6. Create balance in your life.

7. Continue to work on the individuation process.

Step I: Complete Your Unfinished Business from the Past

The life which is not examined is not worth living.
SOCRATES

Freedom is what you do with what's been done to you.
JEAN-PAUL SARTRE

No matter what your childhood history is, even if it was marked by abuse and neglect, you can overcome it, get past it, and become a Woman of Substance. The key is in consciously and diligently working on completing your unfinished business from the past. Unfinished business can include any or all of the following: emotions you haven't expressed, things you have left unsaid, false hopes you are still holding on to, and conflicts left unresolved.

Since the need to repeat the past in an attempt to master it is a compelling, albeit unconscious drive, unless you complete your unfinished business you are destined to continue repeating the same kind of patterns, becoming involved time after time with the same type of person, repeating the same type of relationship.

EXERCISE: *How Much Unfinished Business Do You Have?*_____

Aside from continually being involved with the same type of unavailable, abusive, or otherwise inappropriate partners, another sign that you have unfinished business with your parents or others from your past is the amount of time you spend thinking about the past. Answer the following questions as honestly as possible to help determine whether you have unfinished business:

- Do you think about your childhood a great deal, wishing things had been different?

- Do you continually go over in your mind all the ways that your parent or parents neglected or abused you?

- Do you constantly try to figure out why they treated you as they did?

- Do you ruminate about what you would like to say to those who hurt you or what you would like to do to them?

- Are you continually thinking vengeful thoughts about people in your past, planning ways of getting back at them, or hurting them?

- Or do you do the opposite, completely avoid thinking about your childhood and your parents—trying to block out the pain, anger, fear, guilt, and shame?

If you answered yes to any of these questions, you have unfinished business that is interfering with your current life, preventing you from being all you can be—unfinished business that likely prevents you from loving and being loved in a healthy way.

Express Emotions from Your Past

Most Disappearing Women carry with them a tremendous amount of built-up anger and pain left over from childhood. Most were not allowed to express these emotions as children, and many still fear that if they allow their feelings to come to the surface, horrible things will happen—they will hurt the feelings of those they love, alienate those they love, or lose control.

It is vitally important to work past these fears and begin to express your pent-up emotions. Then and only then can you begin living your life in the present and stop projecting your anger and hurt onto every man you become involved with. Then and only then can you begin to genuinely trust a man.

EXERCISE: *Your Anger List*

- Begin by making a list of all the people you are angry with (e.g., your parents, your siblings for calling you an airhead, the teacher who sexually harassed you, your first boyfriend for having sex with you and then dumping you).

- Rank your list, giving the person you have the most anger toward a #1 and so forth.

- Make a commitment to yourself to do something toward resolving your anger toward each person on your list.

    If you have a great deal of fear about releasing your anger, begin at the bottom of your list and work your way up. Each attempt will give you the encouragement to move up farther on your list until you've reached those you are most afraid to deal with.

    If you feel pumped up and ready to go, tackle the most difficult people first and make your way down the list until you have completed all your unfinished business.

- Decide which method you wish to use to confront each person (e.g., face-to-face, on the telephone, in a letter you do not send, in a letter that you do send). Refer to chapter 13 for suggestions on how to release your anger and pain, including how to do so if the person is not available or if it is too risky to encounter the person directly. For those of you who were sexually abused, please refer to my book *The Right to Innocence: Healing the Trauma of Childhood Sexual Abuse* for suggestions about how to confront a perpetrator as well as members of your family whom you felt did not protect you.

Let Go of False Hope

In addition to releasing emotions from the past, you also need to let go of false hope. For example, a major part of resolving your relationship with your parents may be letting go of any false hope that you will ever get from them what you didn't get as a child. If you were severely neglected or abused as a child, instead of staying lost in fantasies of false hope, you need to mourn the loss of your childhood, and some of you may also have to acknowledge that your parents will never be the loving, supportive parents you always wanted them to be.

In addition, you will need to acknowledge that no one is going to come along and bestow on you what you so longed to get from your parents. It is now up to you to begin to nurture yourself.

In her book *Necessary Losses,* Judith Viorst writes about this:

> For we cannot climb into a time machine, become that long-gone child and get what we want when we oh so desperately wanted it. The days for that getting are over, finished, done. We have needs we can meet in different ways, in better ways, in ways that create new experiences. But until we can mourn the past, until we can mourn and let go of the past, we are doomed to repeat it.

Become Your Own Good Parent

Even though you cannot expect anyone else to give to you what you were deprived of as a child, you can begin to provide these things for yourself. Becoming your own good parent, giving yourself the nurturing and caring that you are still so much in need of, is an important part of completing your unfinished business. Once you have done so you will feel less resentful of those in your childhood who deprived or abused you, and you will be less needy and dependent in your relationships.

EXERCISE: *Your Childhood Wish List*

The following exercise will help you determine which of your needs and desires were not met as a child.

- List all the things you wish you had received in childhood but did not. This list tells you the things that you now need to do for yourself.

- Begin today to meet some of these needs. When you have successfully met one, cross it off your list, and focus on the next item. Don't get overwhelmed and feel you have to do everything on the list at once. Take your time and relish the little steps—whether you're able to cross one item off the list a week or one item a month, you're starting to take care of your needs, and that's what matters most.

Resolve Your Relationship with Your Parents

Resolving your relationship with your parents is one of the most important things you can do both in terms of the individuation process and in becoming a Woman of Substance. Some of you reading this book need to work toward separating from your parents—that is, not allowing your parents to influence and control your lives as much as they currently do. Others need to reconcile with your parents after years of distance or estrangement.

Some Disappearing Women cling to their mother, father, or both out of fear that they cannot survive without their guidance and support. Because they either weren't given the necessary foundation required to become a mature, capable adult or because they were overly controlled or emotionally smothered, they lack the confidence to strike out on their own. At the same time, most of these women harbor a tremendous amount of anger toward their parents, either because they feel so controlled by them or because they didn't get what they needed from them to complete the individuation process as adolescents. Some of you may have been raging at your parents for years, either in direct confrontations or by constantly complaining about them to friends and lovers, while others may be totally unaware of the amount of seething anger you have stored up.

This need, coupled with anger, creates a powerful and debilitating conflict that must be resolved in order for you to leave your childhood behind, become an emancipated adult, and form a healthy, adult relationship with a man.

In contrast, some of you may have cut off all ties to your parents or may be so distant from them that you might as well have. While you may not have the daily pain and may not experience the intense conflicts you once experienced with them, you probably feel the loss of them in your life in a profound way.

Whether you are too dependent or too distant, to complete your unfinished business you will need to resolve your relationship with your parents in one way or another.

How to Resolve Your Relationship with Your Parents

1. Those of you who are too dependent on your parents will need to begin making your own decisions (there will be more on this later on in this chapter) and rely less on your parents for guidance and feedback. This may also entail severing any financial ties that keep you in a dependent relationship with your parents and from gaining the confidence of knowing you can take care of yourself.

2. Those who have parents who continue to be overly controlling or smothering will need to let your parents know, in a nonblaming way, if possible, that you are no longer comfortable with the old pattern of relating. Once you have done this you will need to maintain your position and your boundaries despite any threats or manipulation from your parents.

3. Those who have parents who continue to be abusive, either emotionally, physically, or sexually, may need to confront your parents about their unacceptable behavior or temporarily separate from your parents to gain enough strength to confront them.

4. Finally, those of you who have been estranged from your parents may need to gradually reestablish the relationship on your own terms.

Let Go of Blame

After you have released your anger about what was done or left undone to you as a child, you will need to begin to move beyond your blame and resentment. One way to do this is to realize that underneath your anger lies sadness, and that to get past the anger you must allow yourself to feel and express this sadness.

Anger is empowering, freeing, and motivating. Blame, on the other hand, depletes our energy and keeps us caught up in the problem. Healthy, constructive anger can be your way out of your past, but blame keeps you stuck in it.

Many people have a difficult time moving away from their blame and toward forgiveness. They insist they must receive an apology or at the very least an acknowledgment of the fact that they were hurt or damaged before they can forgive. Although apologies can be tremendously healing, an apology or an acknowledgment of responsibility is not always forthcoming. Holding on to anger and blame does you more harm than it does the person responsible for hurting you. It not only keeps you stuck in the past but also colors all your present and future relationships, imbuing them with hostility and distrust. When you harbor bitterness against someone, that bitterness eats away at you. The only way to get the poison out of your system is to forgive.

For many, forgiveness is a natural by-product of the recovery process, and it takes time. The first step is allowing yourself to acknowledge and release your anger in constructive ways. The next step is determining that you wish to move on and not allow the past to continue to limit your future.

Some people have gained the ability to forgive by developing empathy for the person who hurt them. For example, by learning more about your parents' background you may come to understand why they treated you as they did. Many of us know very little about the forces that shaped our parents' lives, and this lack of information can keep us stuck in blame, as it did in my case.

GAINING EMPATHY FOR MY MOTHER

My mother was a very proud woman who believed, as so many of her generation did, in keeping her business to herself. It wasn't until just before she died that I was able to persuade her to share with me some important information about her own mother. Up to this point she had always insisted that her mother was a warm, caring woman, and I could never understand why my own mother was so distant and unaffectionate.

Even though she finally came to understand how her behavior toward me had negatively affected me, she continued to insist that her behavior had nothing to do with the way she had been raised. Finally, in response to my continual encouragement, she admitted that her mother could be very rigid in her expectations of her children and that she was, in fact, an alcoholic.

Others, including myself, have gained empathy for those who harmed them by recognizing that they, too, have hurt people in similar ways. In my case, it was only after I came to realize that I had become emotionally abusive in my relationships that I was open to forgiving my mother for her emotionally abusive behavior toward me.

Don't let anyone try to force you to forgive, but allow the process to evolve naturally. Forgiving without the acknowledgment of and the release of anger is seldom a true forgiveness but more an intellectual act, but when forgiveness does come it can be a powerful and healing experience that can transform your life and the lives of those around you. *Letting go of blame can free you to love and be loved.*

The Power of Apology

Finally, completing unfinished business often involves apologizing to those you have hurt, often for negative behavior and attitudes you took on as a result of your upbringing.

Whether we act on it or not, we all secretly long to admit our mistakes and ask for forgiveness. But why is it so difficult for us to do it? Why doesn't such a natural drive come more naturally to us? The answer is that there is an equally powerful opposing drive—that of protecting our ego, our pride, and our carefully constructed and defended public self. We don't apologize because to do so is to admit we are flawed and fallible. To apologize is to set aside our pride long enough to admit our imperfections, and for some, this feels too dangerous and makes us feel too vulnerable. This is especially true for men, who often have a difficult time apologizing, but some women do as well. If this is true for you, you will find that by working toward setting aside your pride and being willing to expose your vulnerability you will discover that you are not diminished or destroyed in the process but will become more of a person because of it.

The healing power of apology is phenomenal, both for the person who is being apologized to and the person doing the apologizing. The person who apologizes can finally remove the heavy cloak of shame they have been carrying around and unburden themselves of their guilt and self-hatred. By admitting you were wrong, by taking responsibility for your actions, you will slowly discover that you truly are better than your worst deeds. You will discover that you have another chance to do better, another chance at life.

For further reading:

- *The Dance of Anger* by Harriet Lerner. Written for women, this wonderful book helps you to change your patterns of anger.
- *Necessary Losses* by Judith Viorst. Helps you let go of the illusions, dependencies, and impossible expectations that keep you stuck.
- *Forgive and Forget* by Lewis B. Smedes. Tells the truth about what forgiveness is and what it isn't and presents the four stages of forgiveness.
- *Families in Recovery: Working Together to Heal the Damage of Childhood Sexual Abuse* by Beverly Engel. Discusses how to release your anger and how to confront your parents in constructive ways, as well as suggestions for reconciliation.

Step 2: Become Involved in Some Form of Creative Expression

For each of us as women, there is a deep place within, where hidden and growing our true spirit rises . . . an incredible reserve of creativity and power.

AUDRE LORDE

The creative, when it is pursued freely, is generally therapeutic, is in the interest of the self, even if it disturbs us and arouses fear or despair . . . there is an intrinsic relationship between creativity and self-knowledge. Ultimately, one informs the other. Soon creativity and self-knowledge will seem like twin sisters, similar but distinct comrades who have a common origin.

DEENA METZGER

To complete the individuation process we must take the risk of stepping out and declaring ourselves separate from others. There is no better way to do this than through the act of creativity. When we create something, whether it be a poem or a painting, we are taking one of the greatest risks anyone can take in terms of saying "This is who I am." Involving yourself in creative projects is one of the most powerful ways of developing a stronger sense of self and one of the most exciting.

By engaging in the act of creativity we step into the unknown. We declare our willingness to see and hear things that others haven't seen or heard, our willingness to step away from ideas and beliefs of others and discover a new reality through the unique possibilities of our own vision.

The act of creating ourselves is also a step into the unknown within ourselves. It is a willingness to see and hear things about *ourselves* that no one else has seen or heard. It is a willingness to step away from the ideas and beliefs others have about us and risk creating our own.

Creativity can teach us things about ourselves we never knew, plummeting us to depths within ourselves we would never venture to in any other way. It can help us find strength, resolve, commitment, wisdom, and passion we never knew we possessed.

The act of creating offers a way to express our personal voice and to clear up confusion by allowing us to focus our energies.

Creativity is also another way of merging with something, and yet it doesn't tend to diminish us the way merging dysfunctionally with another person does. Instead, it can connect us with deeper aspects of ourselves, provide catharsis for repressed and suppressed emotions and memories, and fill empty spaces inside us so we don't feel as compelled to become totally absorbed by others.

Creativity is also a wonderful companion. Many Disappearing Women have shared with me through the years how they can get lost in their writing or painting, in their sculpting or in playing a musical instrument, and that hours can go by without their realizing it. Instead of feeling empty and alone, they feel filled up with the excitement of creation. They are soothed and comforted by their own artistry.

Create Your Self

Ultimately, creating art and creating ourselves is the same act.

Writing is an especially fruitful way of learning about oneself and creating oneself, of making a serious commitment to discover who one is and how one sees the world.

As frightening as it can be to step out and declare oneself, ironically, creativity is one of the safest forms of self-expression. Through creativity you can take the risk of asserting yourself, of expressing your deepest emotions, of exploring issues and themes you would normally be afraid to uncover. For example, many survivors of childhood abuse, particularly survivors of sexual abuse, have found that art and writing offer safe avenues of expression that have helped them deal with their pain, fear, guilt, shame, and rage. By getting their feelings down on paper they release them from their hiding places and become stronger, more grounded, and more liberated from the past.

Those of you who were severely criticized whenever you attempted to express yourself as a child may carry forward fears of being ridiculed or chastised for your artistic pursuits. But the wonderful thing about creativity is that most artistic expressions can be done away from the eyes and judgments of others. Alone in your home you can express yourself any way you choose. No one ever has to see your work unless you feel willing to show it to them.

In fact, there are dangers in showing your work to others prematurely. By asking for feedback from others you may be giving them too much power. You may be asking that they approve of your work and therefore your *self.* Or you may be unconsciously asking to be censored. Our creative works, like our innermost selves, require patience and the protection of seclusion.

Another danger in exposing your work prematurely is that you may be distracted from going farther, deeper. You may begin to think that the work (the creative work and your work on yourself) is complete when, in fact, it has only begun.

Still another danger is in using your creative work as an entrée to intimacy with friends or lovers. While you may feel a need to be understood by others and the sharing of your work may ease your feelings of alienation momentarily, if you feel overexposed by the sharing you may cover yourself with an even thicker skin.

By keeping your work private until it is actually finished you may find that you have achieved intimacy with yourself, which is more important, and which is necessary to have intimacy with others.

How to Begin to Create

The most difficult part is knowing how to begin. The act of beginning—whether it is writing your first word on a blank piece of paper or making your first brush stroke on a blank canvas—is itself an act of individuation and can therefore be very frightening, especially for women. As women we haven't been encouraged to create or to individuate. We have been encouraged to conform, to follow the rules, to follow the tried and true, to stay safe. Men, on the other hand, have always been encouraged to explore, to investigate new territory, to forge new paths, to step out. No wonder beginnings are so frightening for us. By taking on the challenge of creating something, you are, perhaps for the first time, stepping out and forging new territory instead of following in someone else's footsteps.

In her book *Writing for Your Life*, Deena Metzger writes about the subject of facing the fear and welcoming the creative:

> Beginning is difficult. We are afraid of failing. We are afraid we will have nothing to say. We are afraid that what we will say will be banal or boring. We are afraid it may endanger us. We are afraid it may be a lie. We are afraid that what we say may be the truth. We are afraid of succeeding. We are afraid no one will notice. We are afraid someone will learn what we've said—and it may be ourselves. We are afraid there will be consequences. We are afraid we will pay attention. We are afraid we will have to change our lives. We are afraid we won't be able to change. We are most afraid that we will.
>
> It is right that we are afraid. If we are fortunate, we *will* say something, it *will* be the truth, it *will* be eloquent, it *will* have power to it, we *will* listen, and we *will* change our lives.

Allow yourself to begin.

For further reading:

- *Writing for Your Life* by Deena Metzger. A beautifully written book that will help you experience the wonder of self-knowledge and the joy of creation.

- *The Creative Journal* by Lucia Capacchione. A classic in the field of art therapy and creativity, it contains exercises for getting in touch with one's feelings, dreams, and creative self as well as techniques for removing blocks to creativity.

- *The Artist's Way* by Julia Cameron. This book can help you manifest any work of art, idea, vision, project, or part of yourself. Encourages readers to write what she calls "morning pages," which help you to get in the habit of writing every day.

- *Writing Down the Bones: Freeing the Writer Within* by Natalie Goldberg.

- *Bird by Bird: Some Instructions on Writing and Life* by Anne Lamott.

Step 3: Stop Looking to Romance or to a Man for Completion

I may not reach [my aspirations], but I can look up and see their beauty, believe in them, and try to follow where they lead.

LOUISA MAY ALCOTT

Women of Substance have rejected the erroneous belief that a woman is "nothing without a man" or "needs a man to complete her." They realize it is useless to look for completion outside themselves. They know that they are the only ones who can make themselves feel worthy and whole. While we can look to people and activities outside ourselves for some *validation* of our lives and worth, ultimately it must come from within.

No one can think for you, feel for you, or give your life meaning for you. As frightening as this may be to face, it is absolutely necessary that you face it head-on in order to break your dependence on others, especially men.

You are no longer a child who must follow blindly the beliefs of others; you are no longer an adolescent who disowns her own feelings and beliefs to "belong." And hopefully, after reading this book you are no longer playing the role of the helpless woman who will "die" if she can't have the love of a certain man or who spends her life trying to manipulate men into giving her love.

You are an adult who can and must take an independent stand. While it no doubt will be painful at times, there is nothing more liberating and empowering than to realize you can rely on your own resources to pull you through even the most difficult dilemmas.

This doesn't mean you don't reach out to others for *connection*. We are all dependent on one another to some degree. No woman or man can do it all alone, and even the most successful of "self-made" women and men have achieved their success through the help of others. But there is a vast difference between looking to others for connection and assistance and depending on them for approval and completion.

Instead of looking to a man to complete you or fill you up, ask yourself, "What is the emptiness inside of me, and how can I fill it up?" If your emptiness is caused by not getting your needs met in childhood, begin meeting those needs yourself. Instead of looking for a new "daddy" (or "mommy") to adopt you, become your own good parent, nurturing the needy child inside you and comforting the scared one.

If your emptiness is caused by the fact that you are disconnected from your feelings, continue to work past your fears and slowly allow yourself to feel and express your emotions. Each time you experience an emotion fully you fill up the emptiness inside a little more until eventually you will find you are no longer empty inside. Instead, you will be filled up with your emotions, filled up with your self.

If the emptiness comes from not having a sense of purpose or meaning in your life, begin focusing your energies on discovering where your "bliss" or fulfillment lies. Another reason why men don't tend to lose themselves in relationships as much as women is that many men have found their passion or purpose in life. As they are growing up, boys have more encouragement and more time to explore their interests and discover their passions. They are more often introduced to and taught skills such as mechanics, woodworking, electronics, and computer programming, and various forms of science-related hobbies such as astronomy, both in school and by their relatives. In contrast, it is usually only girls from privileged environments who are given the opportunity to take such courses as dancing and music lessons, and few are introduced to hobbies that pique their interest enough to become lifelong vocations or avocations.

If your emptiness comes from not having meaningful connections with others, begin to reach out to others of like mind and heart who can nurture your ideas, desires, and individuality.

Most important, if your emptiness comes from not connecting with your true, authentic self, from not discovering who you really are, then continue to follow the suggestions throughout this chapter and throughout this book.

For further reading:

- *Women and Self-Esteem* by Linda Tschirhart Sanford and Mary Ellen Donovan. Examines how women's harmful attitudes about themselves are shaped, including the idea that they need romance or a man to complete them; also offers concrete help to assist you in building your self-esteem.

- *Follow Your Bliss* by Hal Zina Bennett and Susan L. Sparrows. A comprehensive guide to help you discover what excites you and gives your life meaning.

- *How to Find Your Mission in Life* by Richard Bolles. A practical and supportive guide.

- *Creating Community Anywhere* by Carolyn R. Shaffer and Kristina Anundsen. Offers step-by-step plans for finding and creating community.

- *Visioning: Ten Steps to Designing the Life of Your Dreams* by Lucia Capacchione. Using collage to help you clarify your goals.

Step 4: Risk Making Your Own Decisions

Life shrinks or expands in proportion to one's courage.
ANAÏS NIN

Taking a new step, uttering a new word is what people fear most.
FYODOR DOSTOYEVSKY

Take a risk a day—one small or bold stroke that will make you feel great once you have done it.
SUSAN JEFFERS

Ask yourself, and yourself alone, one question: Does this path have a heart? . . . If it does, the path is good; if it doesn't, it is of no use.
CARLOS CASTANEDA

A Woman of Substance makes her own decisions. She doesn't allow others to make them for her, and she doesn't rely on others to tell her what she should do. She trusts her judgment and her ability to choose what is right for her. She knows how to research a situation so she can discover the facts before making her decision, but she doesn't rely on the advice of others. She has grown to trust her instincts and her intuition.

Disappearing Women, on the other hand, encourage others to make their decisions for them because they are afraid of standing on their own or of making a mistake. They cannot make a decision without asking their partner or their friends what they think, which, unfortunately, only tends to confuse them more.

Many Disappearing Women overload their friendships by constantly asking their friends for advice and by continually using their friends as sounding boards for all their complaints about life. Moreover, some tend to identify so strongly with other women that they turn to them for the kind of mothering they did not get in childhood. Not surprisingly, their friends can't meet all their expectations and often grow to resent their demands, resulting in withdrawal and often abandonment.

In addition to constantly asking their friends for advice, many Disappearing Women allow their lover to make their decisions for them. Over time this causes them to become more and more dependent on him and eventually causes them to feel controlled by him. By abdicating their responsibility for themselves in this way they send the message to their partner that their perceptions, knowledge, opinions, and wisdom cannot be trusted.

To make the transition from Disappearing Woman to Woman of Substance you will need to go cold turkey for a while and stop asking your friends, your partner, and others for advice. You will need to stand alone and begin making your own decisions.

Making decisions on your own based on your feelings, logic, and intuition is an especially valuable tool in the individuation process. The more you practice making your own decisions, the more you will realize that you know a lot more than you think, and the more you will realize that you are quite capable of deciding things for yourself. And the more decisions you make, the more you will learn to trust your own judgment, as my client Carly experienced:

"I used to always ask Don what I should wear or whether I should say something to someone or not, and a million other questions throughout the day. Now I find that I'm more sure of myself and that I don't need to constantly get his advice, and it feels good. I'm sure he likes it, too, since I probably used to bug him with my incessant questions."

Making your own decisions, whether they are small or large, without relying on input from others can be one of the most courageous actions you take and the most empowering. You will undoubtedly make some mistakes, but at least you'll be standing on your own and living your own life. Besides, as you've no doubt heard before, we learn and grow from our mistakes. They strengthen us and teach us important lessons. Don't get me wrong: it's fine to get information and advice from others when you make important decisions about your career, your finances, or your health. But in the final analysis you need to trust yourself.

Understandably, those with low self-esteem try to avoid making mistakes because to do so tends to make them feel even worse about themselves. But if you begin to view mistakes, as many successful people have done in the past, as a learning experience, opening up the doors of creativity as you search for more successful ways of accomplishing something, you won't ever experience mistakes in the same way again.

Step 5: Stop Giving Yourself Away

I have another duty equally sacred . . . my duty to myself.
NONA IN A DOLL'S HOUSE BY HENRIK IBSEN

As women we are raised to be caregivers instead of care receivers, as most men are. From an early age most of us learn to derive a great deal of our sense of self and our self-esteem from giving to others. We tend to give pieces of ourselves away until we have little or nothing left.

As a child I learned to cover up my insecurity by being extremely polite and helpful. I gave away everything in my attempt to buy love—my possessions, my body, and my self. Nothing epitomizes this more than what happened when I was nine years old.

Several years earlier, I had found a large, pink quartz crystal in a riverbed. I had always loved pretty rocks, so when I found this beautiful crystal I thought it was the most wonderful thing I had ever seen. I felt so lucky to have found it that I treasured it for years, taking it out to look at it often, being comforted by its cool, smooth texture.

When I was nine we moved to a new neighborhood. As a way of trying to gain acceptance from the other kids on the block, I brought out my crystal to show off. As all the kids admired my rock, I finally began to feel like part of the group. Then one of the kids suggested we drop the crystal and break it into pieces so that everyone could have a piece of it.

In my desperate attempt to be accepted, I dropped my beloved crystal on the hard asphalt street and gave away pieces of it to the other children. When it was over, all I had left was one little piece.

This incident was a perfect metaphor for my life for a long time. I continued to give away different parts of myself until I had very little left for myself. I took care of others' needs and was generous to a fault—but I didn't take care of my own needs.

If you can relate to this story, you need to start saving some of yourself for yourself, giving to yourself in the same way you so generously give to others. Begin listening to yourself, comforting yourself, and providing for yourself instead of giving all your energy and time to others.

EXERCISE: *Give Yourself Gifts of Pleasure*

Unfortunately, many women have spent so much time focusing on the needs of others and taking care of others that they literally do not know what gives them pleasure. The following exercise will help you discover what gifts of pleasure you need to begin giving to yourself:

- Write down—in detail—five of your most positive memories, preferably your most recent. Include how the experience made you feel and which of your five senses was stimulated (e.g., "I can still remember the smell of the night-blooming jasmine and the cool breeze as it brushed against my face. I felt at peace within myself. For that time at least, I ceased worrying about what I had to do next and who I had to please. It was just me and the moon and the night," or "I could hardly catch my breath as I reached the top of the hill but I felt good, strong, and proud of myself for persevering. I was further rewarded by a magnificent sunset—mauve and purple and gray streaks against the sky," or "I felt so loved being surrounded by the women and men I've grown to love and trust. Looking out over their smiling faces my heart warmed, realizing this was the greatest gift they could give me").

- As you read over and reexperience your memories, think about what they say about you. What brings you the most pleasure in your life? Is it connecting with nature and your inner spirit? Is it being physically active and/or testing your physical strength? Is it being in the company of those you love and who love you? These favorite memories will give you hints about what pleases you most, what makes you feel the most at peace, the most joyful, and the most alive, and in so doing they will help you connect with who you are.

- Now make a list of five things you can do to give yourself pleasure, things that will nurture you and make you feel good about yourself.

- Starting at either the top or the bottom of your list, make a commitment to give yourself each of these gifts within the next month.

Notice as time goes by how much resistance you have to giving yourself these gifts and how many excuses you will likely come up with—you don't have the time or the money, you'll do it after you meet your current deadline at work, you're not feeling well enough. Don't allow yourself to buy into any of your excuses but see them for what they are—ways to avoid giving yourself the pleasure and the joy you deserve.

Healthy Interdependency versus Unhealthy Dependency

An important by-product of beginning to take care of your own needs—instead of always focusing on those of the men in your life—is that you won't be as needy in your relationships. As my client Lacy told me, "I realize that I always looked for a man to take care of me so I wouldn't have to take care of myself."

Unhealthy dependency is believing that it is your partner's responsibility to make you happy. Healthy *interdependency* is appreciating the ways you and your partner complement each other while at the same time maintaining your separate identities. And it is recognizing that each of you is ultimately responsible for his or her own well-being.

While it is important to be able to ask your partner to meet some of your needs, if he can't or won't, you need to be able to meet those needs yourself. For example, most women understand that our bodies need proper nutrition, adequate sleep, and exercise. But we have other physical needs that must be met in addition to these basic needs, such as the need for touch.

Often Disappearing Women were deprived of physical touch when they were children, and they enter adulthood hungry for touch and affection. Unfortunately, they often confuse their need for touch with their need for sexual connection. This confusion is often the reason why Disappearing Women become so needy in their relationships and why so many women engage in sexual activities even when they are not feeling sexual. If this is your situation, begin to meet your physical need for touch by getting a weekly massage, or by giving yourself a sensual massage.

Taking care of yourself involves taking care of your physical needs (touch, exercise, buying, preparing and eating nutritious food, proper hygiene, and getting plenty of rest); your emotional needs (allowing yourself the time and the solitude needed to process both your daily life and your past, allowing yourself to express pent-up emotions, experiencing intimate connections with others); your mental needs (stimulating your intellect by reading, learning, and having lively conversations); and your spiritual needs (meditation, prayer, connecting with nature, meaningful experiences with music or art). As you can see, it takes a lot of time and energy to take care of yourself properly so you won't have as much time on your hands. And because you'll feel less needy, you'll be less desperate to find a man to take care of you. If you are currently in a relationship, you'll feel more independent and less likely to expect your partner to take care of all your needs.

Once you've learned you can meet your own needs, you won't be dependent on men to meet them. You also won't become as hurt, depressed, or angry when the man in your life isn't able or willing to meet them.

EXERCISE: *Discover the Reasons for Your Guilt*

If you are currently in a relationship and feel guilty or conflicted about taking time for yourself, try the following writing exercise to help you get in touch with childhood messages that may be influencing you. This may help you work through your guilt and conflicts about taking care of yourself.

Complete the following sentences with as many responses as you can think of.

When I was a child I learned that giving to yourself was _____.

When I take time for myself I feel _____.

When I spend money on myself I feel _____.

I deserve more time for myself because _____.

Ironically, once your partner realizes you can take care of yourself, he may feel much freer to take care of you at times, since he will realize you are not a bottomless pit of need. He will respect you more for your independence and your ability to meet your own needs and will feel less pressure to give to you on demand, freeing him to give to you out of desire, as opposed to expectation.

For further reading:

- *The Woman's Comfort Book* by Jennifer Louden. Shares body-and-soul sustenance skills to help you connect with and nurture yourself.

Step 6: Create Balance in Your Life

Like Heather, the woman I described at the beginning of this chapter, many Disappearing Women tend to go to extremes. They fall in love too fast, and when they do, they tend to neglect everything else in their lives, including their own needs.

They either like someone intensely, or they intensely dislike them. They become impressed with people and put them on a pedestal, only to knock them off it when they inevitably become disappointed. They come on strong but burn out fast, becoming enamored with a cause, a pastime, or a subject, and immersing themselves in it to the exclusion of everything else, only to tire of it or become disillusioned with it.

To become a Woman of Substance you will need to work toward giving up your extremes and finding some balance in your life. Otherwise you'll never feel like you are on solid ground. You'll always feel like you're being tossed about in the wind with no roots to secure you.

The most significant way of creating balance is what we have been discussing throughout this book—not allowing yourself to lose yourself in a relationship by making certain that you go slowly, that you don't give up your friends and interests, and that you give yourself time and space away from the relationship to maintain your sense of self. But there are many other ways of creating balance as well.

One way is to recognize that we all have physical, emotional, mental, and spiritual needs, and if all these needs are not met, our life becomes out of balance. Earlier we discussed the importance of recognizing and meeting your own needs instead of expecting others to meet them. But many women are out of touch with what their needs actually are. Sure, they recognize their physical needs, even though they might not always meet them, but they may not have a clue when it comes to what their emotional, mental, and spiritual needs are. Earlier I gave you some examples of how to meet each of these needs, but it is far more important that you discover ways of meeting them yourself. The following exercise will help.

EXERCISE: *Determine and Meet All Your Needs*

- Make four separate lists, one for each type of need (physical, emotional, mental, spiritual). Under each heading list the people, things, places, and activities in your life that not only meet each need but help to *develop* this aspect of your self.

- Now take a hard look at your lists. Do you find you have many examples under physical and mental but very few under emotional and even fewer under spiritual? Or is it the opposite? Do you have several examples under emotional and spiritual and hardly any under physical and mental?

• Begin to bring balance into your life by making a commitment to do something, no matter how small, to nurture and develop each of these aspects of yourself every day. As a reminder, write a plan of what you intend to do for the next few days. For example:

Monday
  Physical: Take a walk to the park.
  Emotional: Write in my journal about an emotional experience.
  Mental: Read for half an hour before bed.
  Spiritual: Visit a park and focus on nature.

Tuesday
  Physical: Exercise for half an hour at home.
  Emotional: Meet with my best friend for lunch.
  Mental: Watch a program on PBS.
  Spiritual: Meditate.

Wednesday
  Physical: Ride a bike.
  Emotional: Go to a support group.
  Mental: Go to a museum at lunchtime.
  Spiritual: Write down everything I am grateful for.

While it may seem overly ambitious to make an effort to satisfy all four major needs each day, it is the general idea that is important. And as you can see, you can often meet several needs with the same activity, such as walking to a park (exercising meets your physical need, enjoying nature fulfills your spiritual need).

If you find that you are having a problem coming up with a variety of ways of meeting a particular need, this is an indication that you are out of touch with this aspect of yourself. Continue to focus on this area of your self until you can create extra opportunities for expression and development of it.

Each of the four major types of needs represents a different aspect of yourself. By becoming more aware of and expressing the four aspects of your self, you will create more balance in your life since each part of you will be getting positive attention. And by focusing on all four aspects of your self you will continue to develop your whole self.

Step 7: Continue to Work on the Individuation Process

Continue to work toward individuation by practicing the strategies in this book. The following information will help you notice signs of progress as they develop.

Signs That You Are Successfully Individuating

1. As you complete the individuation process, your perception of your parents will change.

Many experience their parent or parents as suddenly seeming less powerful or all-knowing. The following quotes from some of my clients show how much they have achieved individuation.

Norma, age thirty-four:

"I used to think my mother was so together, that she had all the answers. But now I realize she's as confused as I am, maybe more."

Consuela, forty-seven, had seen her father from the same child's perspective. She told me of a recent argument she'd had with him:

"For the first time in my life I felt like there was an adult talking to my father instead of a child. I could stand back and be more objective. In the past I was always a child defending myself and being devastated.

"This time it didn't hurt so much. I reminded myself that I was an adult and that I don't have to listen to his insults—that I can walk away."

2. You are less afraid to be alone.

Many Disappearing Women discover that as they begin to discover themselves, express themselves, and take care of themselves, they feel less afraid of being alone. Those who were once desperate to have a relationship to assuage their feelings of loneliness and emptiness find that they now feel comfortable being alone, or at least until they find the right partner. And those in relationships who once felt horribly abandoned when their partner had to be away find that they actually enjoy their time alone, as was the case with my client Phoebe:

I was surprised to find that when Kyle went out of town this time I didn't freak out. In fact, I had a good time with myself. I wrote poetry and played my harmonica and rented lots of "girl'" movies that I never see when he's here. When he called in the middle of the week to see how I was doing, instead of hearing me whine and cry about how much I missed him and how lonely I was, I told him about the fun I was having.

I'm sure he felt relieved to not have to worry about me or feel guilty because he'd left me alone.

3. You are more willing and able to confront abusive parents or abusive partners.

4. You are less willing to put up with abusive or controlling behavior from your partner (or anyone).

5. You are more able to recognize your positive attributes.

6. You are more able to express yourself.

7. You are more able to express your creativity.

8. You are less afraid to take risks—going back to school, changing jobs, leaving bad relationships.

9. You are better able to hear your own inner voice instead of the internalized voice of your parent.

10. You are better able to trust your own perceptions.

Many people believe that life is about learning how to give and receive love, and this is certainly true. Ultimately we all want to meet our soul mate and experience the kind of transformation that can come from opening our hearts fully. But there are other important lessons in life as well. Many have found that their life purpose is to become the best person they can be. They want to be able to overcome their pettiness, their selfishness, their tendency to judge others, their envy of others. They want to learn the important lessons of forgiveness and compassion.

Women of Substance are too busy working on themselves to focus all their time and attention on finding a man. They are dedicated to becoming healthier, more productive, more creative individuals, so they continue working on those aspects of themselves they feel are incomplete, unfinished, or lacking. For example, if you have unfinished business from the past, continue to face the past and release your pent-up emotions. If you have a great deal of anger toward your domineering mother and find that because of this you misinterpret every suggestion or word of advice from others as an attempt to control you, continue working on releasing this anger in safe, constructive ways, and continue working on differentiating the present from the past.

If you feel overwhelmed with envy at other people's talents, work toward discovering and honing your own. If you feel insecure and invisible because of your weight, it is important that you work toward understanding why you overeat and that you learn alternative ways of comforting yourself. And if you feel insecure about your intellect and uncertain about your opinions, set out on a course to become better educated. Go back to school or obtain a reading list from your local librarian of books relevant to your area of interest.

Women of Substance know that until they work through their own unresolved issues they will only attract men who reflect their problems. They know that needy people attract other needy people. And they know they must be happy with themselves before they will ever be happy with another person.

By working on yourself in these ways you will be ready, willing, and able when and if the right man comes along to have a healthy, intimate, meaningful relationship. And if you're in a relationship now, you'll be able to improve the quality of your relationship.

Becoming the Best You Can Be for You and for Him

While most women definitely want an intimate romantic relationship, no woman should put her life on hold waiting until the right man happens to come along in order to live a "real life." You need to be a full human being, on your own terms. Divorce, death, separation—these are the facts of life that are not always within our control. We owe it to ourselves to face the challenges and changes of life, with or without the presence of a romantic partner.

The most loving thing you can do for a man is to continue striving to be the best person you can be. By becoming a Woman of Substance, a woman who has discovered herself, her voice, her Shadow, and her substance, you will also become more loving, more compassionate, more empathetic, and more giving. You will become the kind of woman your man will admire and respect, a woman who will bring out the best in him, including a desire to be more compassionate, empathetic, and giving to you.

Please refer to the appendixes at the back of this book for more information on where to go from here—how to start a women's Empowerment Circle, a Disappearing Women's support group, or, for those of you who need professional help, how to find the right kind of therapy and the right kind of therapist.

Conclusion

Blending and Balancing

*[It is] . . . the paradoxical truths of human existence—that we know
ourselves as separate only insofar as we live in connection with others, and
that we experience relationship only insofar as we differentiate other from self.*
Carol Gilligan

As you've seen throughout this book, being yourself and being in a relationship are not mutually exclusive. You can be loving to the man in your life and
still be loving to yourself. You can be giving to him without giving yourself
away. And you can be compassionate and cooperative and still stand up for
yourself.

*Loving a man should never make you love yourself less. It should make
you love yourself more.* When you are truly loved you are accepted for who
you are, for your so-called negative traits as well as for your so-called positive ones. When you are truly loved you and your partner bring out the best
in each other. You become not a false self, not a public self, but your authentic self.

Loving a man without losing yourself means many things. It means not
allowing your "feminine" qualities—a need for connectedness, cooperation,
and compassion—to control your life so much that you aren't able to find
meaning and purpose in "masculine" traits such as autonomy, achievement,
and action.

It means learning and practicing the strategies that will empower you in
relationships—including slowing down, telling the truth about who you are

and how you feel, maintaining a separate life, staying out of fantasy and in the present, not allowing a man to change you, and having equal relationships.

It means creating a balance between self and others, including focusing on yourself to complete the work you must do before you are free to truly love.

Loving him without losing yourself means finding and honoring yourself and your voice so you will never again allow your fear of aloneness to propel you into or keep you in unequal, unfulfilling, or unhealthy relationships.

It means not being afraid to feel and express your feelings no matter how negative or unacceptable they are to others, and at the same time learning to contain those very emotions instead of dumping them on whoever is around.

It means having the courage to take back your projections, including your envy and your Shadow, and to begin to take responsibility for completing yourself instead of continuously searching for someone else to do it for you.

It means knowing when to focus on completing the past and when it is time to let it go, when to express your anger, and when to work toward forgiveness.

It means allowing your creative urges to flourish, taking the kinds of risks that will set you free, and giving to yourself the love, guidance, and support you so freely give to others.

What Men Can Learn from Women

Throughout much of this book I have encouraged you to get in touch with and nurture what are often considered masculine traits, such as autonomous thinking, clear decision-making, and responsible action. But I would be remiss if I left you with the idea that there is more value in so-called male qualities and values or that you should be ashamed of or reject your feminine qualities and values such as compassion, empathy, vulnerability, and the need for connection and consensus. Although women definitely need to balance their tendency to take care of others with healthy doses of self-care, a woman's tendency to focus outward and her seemingly inexhaustible fascination with and concern for others and their needs are what make women such good mothers, mates, and friends.

A woman's sense of self tends to come from her relatedness to the people around her, whereas a man's sense of self tends to come from pitting himself against others in a process of individuation. While this self-focus enables a man to act more decisively and with more self-confidence in the world, it presents a tremendous obstacle to his ability to form and maintain intimate relationships.

As much as women's tendency to lose ourselves in relationships is our weakness, in many ways it is our strength that we place such importance on relationships. We know how important relationships are in terms of healing individual wounds and universal wounds. We know that connection is as important as autonomy.

To create a healthy, meaningful relationship with someone else, there must be connection. True connection requires the capacity to empathize with the other person. It requires the ability to truly listen to the other person in order to learn his or her language and understand his or her point of view. This is what men can learn from women.

Just as women need to learn to be more independent and to stop losing themselves in their relationships with men, men need to learn to be more vulnerable and to stop defending themselves so much in their relationships with women. By being positive role models to men concerning the importance of connection, as they have been to us concerning the importance of individuation, we can help create the kind of balance we are all striving for.

Men need women to teach them how to communicate in a way that nurtures and encourages intimacy and trust in relationships. They need us to encourage them to let their walls down and connect with the more vulnerable, loving feelings that lie dormant within. And they need us to teach them what we know about empathy, compassion, and the benefits of consensus.

To encourage the men in your life to become more of these things, practice the following:

1. Remember that men tend to need more distance in their relationships than women and that men have a tendency to feel smothered or engulfed with too much intimacy. Don't expect your male partner or partners to act like your women friends who desire and need intimacy as much as you do.

2. Learn to recognize the *general* symptoms that men exhibit when they are feeling engulfed—such as acting distant, tense, tight, angry, and making comments such as "Lighten up" or "Get off my back."

3. Learn to recognize the *specific* symptoms that your partner exhibits when he is feeling engulfed.

4. Notice how men's engulfment feelings and actions provoke your fear of abandonment. Instead of blaming him for your reaction, take responsibility for it. Instead of taking it personally, recognize it as a normal male reaction and find ways to comfort yourself or attain intimacy outside the relationship.

Be careful that you don't fall into the trap of trying to change men or teach them. This is what codependency is all about. The best we can do is show men, by example, how to be more vulnerable, trusting, and empathetic.

If you are in love with a man who has trouble dealing with strong emotions, try the following:

- Don't overwhelm your partner by pouring out your emotions all at once or by trying to talk to him when you are very upset. Calm down first, take your time, and be clear about what you want to say instead of rambling on and on with no direction.

- Don't expect him to respond immediately. Men need time to access their emotions. Therefore, give him time to digest what you've said. Often when a man is silent he's not ignoring you but processing the information you gave him and trying to get in touch with his feelings. If you push him for a response right away, he'll likely shut down altogether.

- As a way to help him get out of his head and into his feelings, try touching him gently as you speak—hold his hand or rest your hand on his arm, leg, or shoulder. Men are very identified with their bodies, and this can help shift the conversation from an intellectual discussion or battle to a more emotional, even loving exchange.

Blending and Balancing

The truth is, we all need a balance between so-called masculine and feminine qualities, both within our individual personalities and in our culture. Carl Jung believed that to be fully realized human beings, to be whole, both men and women need to integrate the male and the female within.

Good relationships are about *blending* and *balancing*. Women must learn to blend their qualities with those of men, not try to make them into women, and men should not try to make women into men. A balance needs to be created between male and female traits, since both men and women can benefit from what the other has to offer.

We all have issues that we bring into our relationships for healing. Many men have a fear of entrapment or betrayal, being caught in a smothering relationship or humiliated by rejection and deceit. Women fear isolation—we fear that by standing out or being set apart by success, we will be left alone.

Honor yourself and your fear of separation. Allow your partner to honor himself and his fear of abandonment. Allow yourself to have the space to be yourself, and allow your partner to do the same. Only by doing this can you find the loving space to blend your lives. Only then will it be safe to come together.

In a truly healthy, loving relationship both partners are able to connect on an intimate level without completely giving over their individuality to the relationship or to their partner.

In an equal, loving relationship each partner learns from the other. Through the love and security a lasting relationship can bring, women can learn to be less dependent and more secure, and men can learn to be more trusting and vulnerable.

While it is often difficult to create a balance between loving a man and loving yourself, by continuing to follow the suggestions and strategies outlined in this book, you can be one of the exceptional women who are able to do it.

WHERE DO YOU GO FROM HERE?

Appendixes I, II, and III

I n my opinion, it is wrong for a self-help book to promise a cure for all that ails you. First, no book can do this, and second, it gives you the impression that the book itself holds all the answers and that you don't have to do any work yourself. This is not the impression I want to give. As I said earlier, some of you, especially those on the extreme end of the continuum, will need additional help in the form of long-term psychotherapy. In addition, for all of you reading this book, no matter where you lie on the continuum, you will need to devote yourself to the work that is necessary to facilitate the changes you desire. This work can be made a lot easier with the support of other women, either in a support group or an Empowerment Circle.

Embracing Your Femininity

ESPECIALLY FOR THOSE ON THE MILD END OF THE CONTINUUM

Much of what women want in their relationships with men is a deep emotional sharing and a sense of connectedness. Instead of waiting for a man to come along who can offer this kind of sharing or trying to force the man you are involved with into becoming what he is not, try looking to your female friendships for this deep sharing.

Unfortunately, many women continue to have superficial relationships with their female friends, partly because their focus is on the men in their life and partly because of competition and envy. If you can begin to work past your tendency to view every other woman as a potential rival, you will begin to see that deeper friendships with women can offer the support and caring that few other relationships can offer, including relationships with the opposite sex. Begin to honor and respect your female friends and recognize what they bring to your life instead of taking them for granted or using them as substitute connections only when there is no man around.

In addition, although this book has done much to counter the cultural conditioning that caused you to have the tendency to lose yourself in relationships, you will need to continue countering the cultural messages that bombard you daily. The most effective way to do this is to actively embrace feminine qualities and values.

While regular self-help groups offer valuable assistance and support, in the past few years women have begun to meet together in a new way—in circles.

What is a circle? How is it different from a support group? Circles are similar to support groups in that they offer much-needed support to those who are struggling with various issues. But the circle offers a unique format that provides even more.

A circle is not just a gathering of people who sit in a circle on the floor or a meeting where the chairs are arranged in a circle. As Christina Baldwin wrote in her groundbreaking book *Calling the Circle: The First and Future Culture,* it is a way of thinking and doing things that is radically different from the way we normally think and act, and at the same time it is a return to our original form of community, a return to an ancient process of communion.

In circles, advice-giving is discouraged, as is cross talk. Instead, circle members pass a talking piece or talking stick around the circle. When someone is holding the talking piece, this signals to others that it is their turn to speak and that everyone's focus needs to be on the speaker. When it is someone else's turn to talk, others are encouraged to focus all their attention on what this person is saying, as opposed to thinking about how they wish to respond. And everyone is encouraged to open their hearts and minds and to listen nonjudgmentally and lovingly to what the speaker has to say.

If we women want to be positive role models for the importance of connection, we need to continue practicing the ethic of care ourselves. And if you want to find a man who has the qualities of compassion, empathy, and vulnerability, you need to continue developing these qualities in yourself. Meeting with other women in circle can help you connect further with your capacity for compassion and empathy as well as help you develop your intuition and inner wisdom.

Meeting in circle can also help satisfy our hunger for spirituality and for the sacred. It can help us to reconnect with what is genuine and true about ourselves, others, and the world in general. It can help fill us up with meaning, depth, and purpose and assist us in defining values that are meaningful, that we can believe in and live by.

Once we have learned the lessons of the circle we can then pass the information along to others. Our men need us to show them a different way of communicating and connecting with one another and a different way of conducting business. Our children need us to act as role models, showing them a new way of relating to one another. This will, in turn, create a whole new generation of people who are truly open to seeing one another, hearing one another, and connecting with one another on a more empathetic level.

How to Structure a Circle

Sitting in a circle provides part of the structure needed to contain the energy generated in the circle. This is part of the reason why it is very important that your group literally form a circle with your bodies. You can choose to sit on the floor or in chairs, but make sure you form a complete circle.

When we rearrange our seating it causes us to rearrange our expectations as well. By each person sitting on what Christina Baldwin calls the "rim" or the edge of the circle, we are also symbolically removing ourselves and our self-interests from the middle of the group. As she explains it, this moving of our bodies from rows to circles and our self-interests from the center to the edge enable us to reclaim our innate knowledge of circle.

Most people find it useful to mark the physical center of their circle with a cloth placed on the floor or a low table, on which they place objects that remind them that they are gathered in a sacred place for a sacred purpose. Often objects are placed on the altar that are sacred to group members or that signify something meaningful to them. The center also can be formed by each member placing something on the altar that is personally meaningful to that person.

You can form a circle of women just by inviting at least four like-minded women together and by observing the following requirements of circle:

- Intention
- Heart-consciousness
- Gratitude
- Equality
- Sacredness
- Commitment

How to Start Your Own Empowerment Circle

There are many types of circles—sacred circles and council circles, to name only two. Some of you reading this book may wish to create an Empowerment Circle as an alternative to a regular support group. I created Empowerment Circles as an offshoot of my years of working with victims of childhood abuse and my dedication to helping those women who tend to continually give their power to others, and to the literally thousands of women who have been suffering alone with their problem of losing themselves in relationships. I wanted these women to discover, through circle, that they are not alone and to feel the empowerment that can come from connecting with and being supported by other women.

Empowerment Circles help women in many other ways as well:

- By being able to talk openly about their issues, women will begin to feel they are really being heard, seen, and respected, perhaps for the first time in their lives.

- By learning to ask for the kind of feedback and support they want, women will become not only more assertive, but also clearer about what their real needs are.

- By receiving feedback from other women about what they have said in the past and what they have said they wanted, they will begin to know themselves better and take more responsibility for their words and actions.

- By learning to give feedback without judgment they will learn to remain more objective (thus more separate), learn to respect the right and need of others to be separate, and begin to judge themselves less harshly.

The core belief of Empowerment Circles is:

Our deepest fear is not our fear of being inadequate, but the fear of our power. It is much easier to let others control our lives than to take charge ourselves. It is much easier to pretend to be meek than to take responsibility for our power. It is much easier to allow others to abuse us than it is to own our own tendency to abuse ourselves.

Empowerment Circles keep women honest—about their power, feelings, and intentions. If a woman states an intention or makes a proclamation about what is really important to her in front of a circle of women she deeply respects, it is far more difficult to take actions outside the circle that go against her stated intention or beliefs.

Empowerment Circle Guidelines

- We share leadership of the group and meet in a circle to remind us that we are all equal. Since we are all still learning about ourselves, no one can afford to take on the role of leader as a way of distracting herself from her own work.

- We use the talking stick (a Native American tradition) to remind us that each person has something important to say, that we each deserve a turn at speaking, and that only one person speaks at a time.

- We will endeavor to focus our entire attention on the person who is speaking, not allowing our minds to wander or our hearts to close. We know how painful it is to go unheard, unseen, and misunderstood, so we give our attention and our understanding as gifts whenever possible.

- We refrain from giving advice to one another because we believe that deep inside, each woman knows what is best for her, and we want to encourage each woman to come to her own decisions.

- We refrain from criticism and judgment of one another because we understand how it robs us all of our self-confidence, our trust in ourselves, and our ability to be strong and independent.

- We offer our own experiences, not to take the focus off of someone else, not to show that we know best, but to let others know they are not alone, to help us feel connected with others, and to remind ourselves of our own issues.

- We expect each woman in the group to be responsible for asking for what she needs from the group.

- We hold each woman accountable for what she has stated she wants from the group and for her life. Therefore, if a woman is doing something counter to her stated objectives, we will point this out. While we all have a right to change our minds, we need to be aware that we are doing so.

- Even though we have, in fact, been victimized by our families and by the way women are treated in our culture, we do not see ourselves as victims today, nor do we wish to continue to behave like victims. This means that whenever possible, we take responsibility for our actions, particularly when it comes to our relationship with men.

For more information about Empowerment Circles you can contact me in one of two ways:

- Visit me at my web site at www.BeverlyEngel.com.
- Write me at:

  P.O. Box 6412

  Los Osos, CA 93412-6412

There is no one way to form a circle. Generally speaking, one learns to create and participate in circles by being a part of them. You will undoubtedly learn new ways of circling as you go along, but for some general guidelines for starting a circle, please refer to the following books:

- *Calling the Circle* by Christina Baldwin
- *Wisdom Circles* by Charles Garfield, Cindy Spring, and Sedonia Cahill
- *Sacred Circles* by Robin Deen Carnes and Sally Craig
- *The Ceremonial Circle* by Sedonia Cahill and Joshua Halpern
- *Women Circling the Earth: Fostering Community, Healing, and Empowerment through Women's Circles* by Beverly Engel

APPENDIX II

Women of Substance Support Groups

ESPECIALLY FOR THOSE NEAR THE MIDDLE OF THE CONTINUUM

Those of you who fall near the middle of the continuum, especially those who were emotionally, physically, or sexually abused as a child, will need to seek specialized treatment for this abuse before or in addition to working on your problem of losing yourself with men. Group therapy is especially beneficial for the treatment of such issues as sexual abuse as are twelve-step groups.

Today we have twelve-step and other support groups for most addictive behaviors, including alcoholism, compulsive overeating, and sexual addiction, as well as for survivors of child sexual abuse, adult children of alcoholics, and the family and partners of alcoholics. For those of you who come from alcoholic or otherwise dysfunctional families, I strongly recommend that you look into these valuable resources.

As part of your recovery process many of you may already be a member of one of these groups. If this is the case, I strongly encourage you to continue with these important groups.

Women have always looked to one another for support whenever they begin to deal with their problems. Back in the 1980s, books on codependency such as *Women Who Love Too Much* inspired a network of support groups throughout the United States, Canada, and even abroad. While there are still groups for codependency (CODA) and a smattering of Women Who Love Too Much groups, these groups don't address many of the issues we have focused on in this book, nor on the individuation process that is necessary to recover from the Disappearing Woman syndrome.

For this reason, I strongly recommend you start or join a Woman of Substance support group. At the time of the first printing of this book there are already a few such groups, and as the years go by, there will be many others. Before starting a group of your own, make sure there isn't already a group in your area. You can do this by either:

- logging on to my web site at: www.BeverlyEngel.com *or*
- writing me at:

  Beverly Engel
  P.O. Box 6412
  Los Osos, CA 93412-6412

Starting Your Own Women of Substance Support Group

There are several ways for you to get the word out that you are starting a Women of Substance support group. Begin by going to your local bookstore and asking if they are willing to donate space for your first meeting. Many bookstores are more than willing to hold such meetings because it brings women into their store. They will no doubt advertise the group in their store windows, their monthly flyer if they have one, and they may place announcements in local newspapers. (You can also ask the bookstore owner to call the publisher to set up a book signing to help get your group off the ground. If I am available I will come to your area, give a workshop, and help you get started.)

Unfortunately, most bookstores don't have a space that is private enough for ongoing meetings. Therefore, you'll need to find a permanent space. Some of you may decide to meet in your homes. In addition, many churches and banks have rooms they rent out for very little money, and some banks offer meeting rooms free of charge to the public.

It helps to place an ad in your local newspaper announcing the formation of your new group. Many local papers are willing to run such ads for little or no cost. Your ad might read something like this:

Women, are you tired of losing yourself in your relationships with men? Tired of sacrificing your integrity, your values, your very soul to the men in your life? A free self-help group is now being formed based on the book *Loving Him without Losing You.* If you are interested, please call [give your first name and phone number] for more information and the location of the meeting.

By running this ad only a few times you should be able to fill your group. The ideal number of members is seven to ten, but you can start with fewer women if necessary.

You may also wish to put a notice on local bulletin boards and on the Internet.

Your First Meeting

The following suggestions will help you organize and conduct your first meeting:

1. *Start on time and end on time.* An hour and a half is usually sufficient time, but you may wish to allot two hours if you have a larger group. Whatever time period you decide on, don't allow your meetings to go overtime. Many Disappearing Women have thin boundaries and therefore need structure and clear limits. Also, discovering how to stop losing yourself in relationships takes time, so allowing your meetings to drag on won't help anyone and may cause some members to burn out emotionally.

2. Introduce yourself and state why you have started such a group and that you'd like the group to be an ongoing source of support for yourself and others.

3. Emphasize that *everything said at the meeting will be confidential.* That means that members will never discuss what other people say in the meetings, nor share who was at the meeting. Suggest that everyone use only their first names when introducing themselves.

4. Decide what the guidelines and rules of your group will be. To create a truly democratic group, each member should have a say in establishing its structure and guidelines. Begin by asking what each woman needs to feel safe. Each suggestion needs to be heard, honored, examined, and discussed. This process will begin the bonding experience.

    Your guidelines or rules empower each member to take full responsibility for how she interacts, behaves, and contributes to the group. It is especially helpful to have them written down and available to all members at the next meeting and to give to new members as they come in. Bring agreements up for review from time to time.

    The following are some basic guidelines that have proven to be effective for self-help support groups:

    • *Commitment.* Most groups function best if each person makes a commitment, which includes making the group a priority, making every attempt to attend every meeting, and notifying someone if they cannot attend.

- *Rotate leadership.* To form a group, someone has to be responsible for initiating it, and since this person has such a commitment to the group, it is often assumed she will be the leader. Also, if the group meets at the home or office of the convener, more responsibility will naturally fall on that person, and this, too, can be interpreted as leadership. But experience has shown that rotating leadership works much better for these types of groups.

  Leadership should be rotated weekly or monthly. The leader is often the person who is hosting the meeting. It is the leader's responsibility to start and end the meeting on time, to welcome any new members, and to make sure another leader is chosen for the next meeting. It is also the leader's job to pick a topic if that is the group's format.

- *No advice-giving.* Sharing your experiences and what has worked for you is welcomed, but no one should advise another group member what she should do. If advice-giving occurs, it should be gently pointed out by other members.

- *No criticism.* The group will only be of benefit to all members if there is a strong element of trust and acceptance. This means there should be no criticism or judgments about what another woman says, does, or doesn't do, either when she is present or when she is absent from the group. Although members are free to ask for feedback, it should never be unsolicited. In my experience it is best if each woman clarifies at the time the specific type of feedback she wants.

- *Focus on yourself.* Members need to learn to focus on themselves and their own thoughts, feelings, and behaviors rather than on their partner. It is especially important that you not talk about your partner's problems in an attempt to understand him or fix him.

- *No eating or drinking while the meeting is in progress.* These things serve as distractions from your feelings. You may choose to serve refreshments after the group, but I suggest you don't provide alcohol, since it distorts feelings and reactions and can be used as a crutch to avoid issues.

- *Some groups require that everyone read* Loving Him without Losing You *so you all start at the same level of awareness.* Decide as a group whether you require this.

5. Decide on the group format. Some groups like to use the structure of *Loving Him without Losing You* as their format, while others like to start out in a free-flowing way, simply having members share their stories and their issues. Still others prefer to have each meeting focused around a specific topic, such as:

   • how I lose myself in relationships;

   • my relationship patterns;

   • how my family history encouraged me to give myself away;

   • how our culture encourages women to lose themselves in relationships;

   • how I've lost my voice in my relationships with men;

   • why I'm so insecure with men;

   • how I handle my own anger and the anger of others;

   • how I take care of myself and meet my own needs.

6. Begin the sharing by having everyone tell why they decided to come to the group and what they would like to achieve by attending the meetings. Ask that each woman limit her sharing to no more than five to ten minutes if the group is large. Emphasize that no one has to share if she doesn't want to.

7. After everyone who wished to talk has spoken, go back to anyone who wasn't ready to talk before and gently ask if she would like to speak now. Make it clear that every woman is welcome whether or not she is ready to talk.

8. Decide how often your group will meet, and set the time and the place for the next meeting. Obviously, a group that meets once a week, at least in the beginning, has a stronger chance of becoming a viable group. When a group meets regularly, it engenders a certain level of intimacy and trust, allowing for inner work that often does not occur otherwise. But because we all have such busy schedules, meeting weekly may be prohibitive for some people.

9. Discuss whether more women should be invited to join your group and whether the women present should be able to invite other women.

10. Close your meeting by holding hands and standing silently in a circle. Ask that each woman "look around you and see the support that is here."

Do not underestimate how important your guidelines are to group cohesiveness and harmony. I recommend that you read your guidelines aloud at the beginning of each meeting. In that way, when someone new joins, she won't feel as lost, and old members need to be reminded of the guidelines from time to time. Remember that what is best for the group is also best for each individual. And do not underestimate how powerful personal sharing can be in all of your lives.

For Further Help

If you'd like more help on how to start a Women of Substance support group, you can reach me in one of two ways:

- Visit me at my web site at www.BeverlyEngel.com.
- Write me at:

  P.O. Box 6412
  Los Osos, CA 93412-6412

You may also request a list of support groups in your area, the names of women in your area who are interested in forming a new group, or announce a new group forming.

When You Need Professional Help

FOR THOSE WHO FALL ON THE EXTREME END OF THE CONTINUUM

If you fall on the extreme end of the continuum you will need help that goes beyond the scope of this book. Although this book has hopefully helped you stop losing yourself in your relationships with men, for you to alleviate more of your fear of abandonment and your tendency to merge with others, you will need specialized long-term psychotherapy.

If you were abused as a child you may suffer from Post-Traumatic Stress Disorder and need to get help for this by seeking a therapist who specializes in working with abuse survivors. But in addition, many of you also suffer from either borderline tendencies or Borderline Personality Disorder (BPD). This illness requires special treatment from a therapist who was specifically trained to work with this disorder.

Like the Disappearing Woman Syndrome, Borderline Personality Disorder has its own continuum. Those on the mild end of the BPD continuum may only suffer from "borderline tendencies," whereas those on the extreme end may be so severely affected by the disorder that they spend a great deal of time in the hospital due to severe eating disorders, substance abuse, self-mutilation, or suicide attempts. Many of those who are closer to the middle of the continuum, or those who are often called "high-functioning" borderlines, are often highly successful, well-liked people who act perfectly normal most of the time and probably only show their other side to those who are closest to them. Although they may feel the same way inside as the less-functioning borderline, they cover it up very well, often even from themselves.

I briefly discussed Borderline Personality Disorder earlier in this book, but here I will further explain this personality disorder as well as how to find a therapist who has training and experience in working with the disorder and what the therapy will entail.

Be Open to the Possibility

While many of you who read the criteria I presented in chapter 4, "The Disappearing Woman Continuum," already suspect that you have Borderline Personality Disorder, others may be reluctant to assign yourself this diagnosis. It isn't easy to admit that you suffer from an extreme version of the Disappearing Woman syndrome or that you suffer from an extreme version of *anything*, for that matter. For this reason you may attempt to whitewash your problems. But isn't it better to know what is wrong with you and to know the probable cause than to remain in a state of despair, wondering why you are the way you are, not thinking there is a way out?

Up until now you have probably felt desperately alone and hopeless about your situation, like there was something horribly wrong with you that was beyond fixing. For this reason I believe it is far better to know what is causing your problem and to know that there is help available.

Only a trained psychotherapist specifically trained to work with this disorder can give you an accurate diagnosis. But it is important for you to understand that you may have a specific psychological problem that requires more than this book can offer and that you may need very specific psychological help.

Since lists such as the one I provided in chapter 4 can sometimes be confusing, to help you alleviate any lingering doubt as to how extreme your problem is, answer the following questions, being as honest with yourself as you can:

1. Are most of your relationships unstable, chaotic, or intense?

2. Are you desperately afraid of being alone?

3. Do you suffer from extreme mood shifts that tend to only last a few hours at a time?

4. Do you often experience intense and uncontrollable anger that is inappropriate to the situation?

5. Would you consider yourself self-destructive?

6. Have you ever threatened or attempted suicide?

7. Have you ever mutilated yourself by burning, cutting, or scratching yourself until you bled or were bruised or scarred?

8. Do you abuse food, alcohol, or drugs?

9. Do you suffer from compulsive overeating, spending, gambling, or shoplifting?

10. Are you sexually promiscuous, or do you engage in sexual acts that are shame-inducing or potentially dangerous?

11. Do you suffer from persistent confusion concerning self-image, sexuality, career choice, long-term goals, friendships, or values?

12. Do you often feel empty or bored?

These are characteristics of Borderline Personality Disorder. If you answered yes to more than five of the questions, you certainly fit the criteria to place you at the extreme end of the Disappearing Woman continuum and at the very least fit the criteria for what are called "borderline tendencies."

Although the exact cause of BPD is highly controversial, most theorists agree that early family life or developmental factors help cause the illness.

One major theorist, Heinz Kohut, considers the illness to be caused by the child's belief that she has been, or will be, abandoned, and the sense of aloneness that results.

According to Janice M. Cauwels, the author of *Imbroglio: Rising to the Challenges of Borderline Personality Disorder:*

> This fear results from parental, especially maternal, failure to provide sufficient holding and soothing, enough attention to and validation of the child's feelings and experience. . . . Her primary feeling is a terror of utter aloneness, emptiness, hunger, coldness, and annihilation. The fear or actuality of such abandonment also produces rage.
>
> The borderline therefore uses other people to help evoke soothing images or to perform other functions she does not have built in. Unable to recall sustained love, she becomes a reassurance addict seeking a fix of affection to help maintain her self-esteem. The loss or threatened loss of a relationship leaves the borderline feeling hollow and abandoned, bereft of self-esteem, and anxious to end these feelings through self-mutilation or suicide.

In other words, women who suffer from Borderline Personality Disorder not only lose themselves in relationships with men but never developed selves worth defending.

Many experts also believe that BPD, like many mental disorders, is caused by a combination of genetic influences and environmental circumstances. According to prominent BPD psychiatrist Kenneth R. Silk, preliminary research suggests that BPD behavior may be influenced by neurotransmitter disturbances.

How to Find the Right Treatment

Many of you have already sought help for your problems in the past, and some may have had years of individual psychotherapy. But you may not have received the right kind of therapy. While conventional, insight-based therapy can help with a wide range of psychological problems, it generally does not help with BPD. This is not to say that conventional therapy may not have helped you feel somewhat better about yourself and may have helped you resolve an immediate problem (such as leaving an abusive relationship), but in the long run you have probably continued to be plagued with the same problems you've always had—a fear of abandonment and at the same time a fear of being smothered, a fear of being alone, excessive rage, hypersensitivity to rejection, etc.

In fact, one of the ways to tell whether you likely suffer from BPD is by noticing whether the therapy you have received did you any good in terms of alleviating your major symptoms (assuming you had a good experience in therapy with a reputable, skilled therapist).

Moreover, even those who have been in therapy may not have been diagnosed correctly. Unless you have acting-out behavior such as self-mutilation or suicide attempts, no one but an experienced therapist can tell whether you suffer from BPD. Typically, BPD shows up primarily in relationships—how you relate to other people—so unless a person is in a relationship with you, including a therapeutic relationship, he or she will not recognize your symptoms. Even then, many therapists are just not skilled enough to diagnose this problem correctly.

In addition, many therapists resist giving this diagnosis because insurance companies are notorious for denying claims when the diagnosis is given. This is because some believe those suffering from BPD are untreatable, but most deny claims because it requires long-term care.

Medication

Some medications have been used successfully to help people with BPD, but they do not cure it. What they can do, in optimum situations, is reduce depression, minimize emotional ups and downs, and curb excessive impulsivity. By alleviating these symptoms a patient can participate more fully in psychotherapy and gain much more from it.

The Modalities of Therapy

There are several modalities of therapy that are used for the treatment of BPD. These can be broken down into two general categories: exploratory (or intrapsychic) and supportive techniques.

EXPLORATORY THERAPY

Exploratory or intrapsychic psychotherapy is a modification of classical analysis. Recommended by experts in BPD such as Otto Kernberg and James Masterson, this form of therapy is more intensive than regular "supportive" therapy and has a more ambitious goal—to alter personality structure.

Unlike supportive therapy, there is little direct guidance provided by the therapist. Instead the therapist uses confrontation to point out the destructiveness of specific behaviors of the client and interprets unconscious behaviors in the hope of eliminating them.

In this form of therapy there is less focus on childhood and developmental issues than in classical psychoanalysis, particularly in the early stages of treatment, when the focus is on diminishing behaviors that are self-destructive or disruptive to the treatment process (including prematurely terminating therapy), solidifying the patient's commitment to change, and establishing a trusting, reliable relationship between patient and therapist. Later stages emphasize the processes of formulating a separate, self-accepting sense of identity, establishing constant and trusting relationships, and tolerating aloneness and separations (including those from the therapist).

In some forms of exploratory therapy, primarily those based on the concept of object relations, the therapist will not ask questions or try to elicit information in any way. Instead the therapist, with his or her silence, encourages the client to step out on her own—to take the risk of expressing her true self instead of performing or attempting to please the therapist—and, in essence, begin to individuate. This is radically different from most therapies, particularly supportive therapy, in which the therapist often asks questions to get therapy sessions under way or to express caring or concern. Some clients, especially those who have experienced supportive therapy in the past, will feel abandoned, hurt, and angry when met with the therapist's silence.

Silence in the presence of a therapist can be very healing. In such moments of accompanied solitude, the client has the time and the space necessary to sense out her own impulses and to sense out things going on inside herself. The quality of this presence of the other is the critical point: It must be felt, and at the same time not be intrusive. This means that no demands be made and no expectations expressed, not even well-meaning interventions.

Sessions are usually conducted two or more times a week, and the duration of treatment is a minimum of four years but often lasts as long as six to ten years.

SUPPORTIVE THERAPY

Even though this form of therapy is often referred to as "supportive," it is not to be confused with conventional insight-based therapy, which can help alleviate some symptoms but generally does not help to restructure the personality, as is needed for BPD. Supportive therapy is the most common type of therapy used for borderline personality. Instead of confrontation and interpretation of unconscious material, therapists offer direct advice, education, and reassurance.

Meant to be less intense and to bolster more adaptive defenses, this form of therapy may reinforce suppression of emotions and discourages discussion of painful memories that cannot be resolved. As opposed to discovering the roots of defenses and then eradicating them, as in psychoanalysis, defenses may be acknowledged as useful ways of retaining a sense of mastery and control.

Supportive therapy most often continues on a once-a-week basis for approximately four to five years before proceeding to an as-needed basis. Therapy gradually terminates when the patient forms other lasting relationships and when gratifying activities become more important in the patient's life.

Although some experts have insisted that supportive therapy is not effective in treating borderline patients since it is less likely that lasting changes will occur, others insist that significant behavioral modifications can occur.

The Cognitive Behavioral Approach

Not everyone has the financial means for the long-term, intensive treatment that is most often recommended for those suffering from BPD, especially since insurance companies usually don't pay for treatment (unless you are hospitalized for such problems as an eating disorder, a sexual addiction disorder, or for alcohol treatment). For this reason, for those with limited income I recommend the supportive therapy known as the cognitive behavioral approach.

With a cognitive behavioral approach the therapist focuses on teaching you new behaviors versus attempting to make deeper changes that take far more time. The therapist uses your ability to think (many who suffer from BPD are highly intelligent) to help you control your behavior.

Many borderlines are very enthusiastic about researcher Marsha Linehan's cognitive-behavioral method, known as Dialectical Behavior Therapy (DBT). It has been shown in empirical research to help BPD patients experience less anger, less self-mutilation, and fewer inpatient psychiatric stays than patients who received other forms of treatment.

Cost of Therapy

Unfortunately, the bottom line as to what type of therapy you choose will come down to your finances. It is a sad testament to our society that the only people who can hope for significant change are those who are financially well off or those who have excellent health insurance.

Generally speaking, BPD psychotherapy is practiced primarily by licensed psychologists who have had specialized training in the treatment of borderline personality disorder. Therefore, it will likely cost you far more than counseling by a social worker or a marriage counselor.

To prescribe medication, a therapist must be a psychiatrist or refer you to one for a psychiatric evaluation. Treatment by a psychiatrist is usually extremely expensive, but many only require you to see them once a month to track the medication.

In addition, because this treatment usually involves what is referred to as "intrapsychic" work, "reparenting," or restructuring work, it will take several years of treatment, often involving twice-a-week sessions.

The Cognitive Behavioral Approach can be conducted by social workers and marriage counselors as well as by psychologists and psychiatrists. Not only will you pay less per hour, but since this treatment focuses more on symptoms rather than on intrapsychic work, it tends to take less time.

It is important that you become educated about your choices so you can work with what is available in your community and use the resources available to you. At the end of this appendix I will provide the addresses and phone numbers of some agencies that may be able to help you.

Finding the Right Therapist

It is quite appropriate for you to "interview" several therapists before deciding which one is best for you. However, this can become quite costly and emotionally draining. Therefore, you may wish to begin your interviewing over the phone.

1. Begin by asking whether the therapist is taking on new clients. Obviously there is no need for you to talk any further if she or he does not have room

in his or her schedule to see you. Some therapists do, however, have a waiting list. If this is the case, the therapist is likely to be very good, so it might be worth your while to continue your phone interview to ascertain whether the therapist sounds like someone you might want to work with. If, after asking the following questions, you decide you would like to work with this person, ask how long the wait would be before you could start. If it is less than a month, it might be worth it for you to wait. On the other hand, if it has taken all your courage to make the decision to finally seek professional help and you are likely to back off soon, then by all means keep calling until you find someone who can be available immediately. If you don't wish to wait, this therapist is probably a very good resource for you. Ask if she or he can refer you to another therapist.

2. Next, ask whether the therapist has special training and experience working with those who have borderline tendencies. I encourage you not to say "Borderline Personality Disorder" since you do not know for certain whether you are borderline. Only a trained professional who has the experience of observing you over time will be able to make that diagnosis. What you do know, from reading this book, is that you (along with millions of other people) most likely have borderline tendencies.

   Some critics may say that by encouraging you to discuss the issue of your borderline tendencies you will prejudice the therapist against you. There are still some therapists who are afraid to work with those with borderline personalities due to the bad rap borderlines have received or negative experiences they've had with these patients in the past. But my opinion is that you wouldn't want to work with such a therapist anyway. You need someone who has the skills and the confidence to work with your symptoms, not someone who is so inept that they get caught up in them.

3. Next, ask the therapist what type of licensing and schooling she or he has, what type of therapy she or he conducts, and how many years she or he has been in practice. A good therapist should be willing to tell you all of these things without feeling resentful or defensive. There are many excellent therapists who don't have Ph.D.'s after their name, but you do want someone with training and experience in working with borderline personality disorder.

4. It is also appropriate for you to ask how much the therapist charges and whether she or he requires two or more sessions a week. Even though you realize you need this specialized therapy, if you can't afford a particular therapist's fees you will have to keep searching until you find someone more affordable. Many of my clients have made therapy a priority and have

sacrificed other, less important expenditures to pay for their therapy, but you don't want to increase your stress level by adding a financial burden.

Remember, this is not a short-term process but an ongoing one. Your budget needs to be able to accommodate your therapist's fees for several years. Even if you have insurance, it is not likely to pay for all your sessions. Most insurance will only pay for one session a week for a limited number of sessions a year, and few pay for more than a year of treatment. Check your policy, or call your insurance company and ask for their limits. *Do not, I repeat, do not say anything to your insurance company about borderline personality disorder.*

Do not expect a therapist to lower his or her fee or to offer to see you at a discounted rate (e.g., to charge less if you see the therapist twice a week).

5. If the therapist sounds like someone you could work with, make an appointment. If not, ask for a referral.

Face-to-Face Interviews

If you are fairly certain you suffer from BPD, you may wish to divulge this to the therapist during your face-to-face interview and then ask the therapist more questions concerning her or his knowledge of the subject. This is completely optional but it can be important, since there are so many therapists who are not adequately trained to work with BPD, because some still do not believe BPD patients can get better, and because many still bring negative expectations and attitudes about borderlines into treatment. Here are some suggestions for further questions:

- How do you define BPD? If the therapist doesn't seem to know that much about the disorder, or insists it is rare, you may wish to keep looking.

- What do you believe causes BPD? If the therapist believes that all BPD is caused by sexual abuse or does not mention possible biological causes, she or he may not be up to date on the latest research.

- Ask what the therapist's treatment plan is for clients with BPD. Although treatment is modified for each individual, a good therapist should be able to give you a general overview of the treatment she or he provides.

- You may also wish to ask if the therapist has special training in and experience with those who have associated problems such as substance abuse, eating disorders, or self-injury, whichever apply to you.

- Ask if the therapist believes borderlines can get better. While no one can give you a guarantee (if they do, continue to look for a therapist), you don't want to work with someone who is overly pessimistic.

- Ask about her or his views on medication. If the therapist is not a psychiatrist, ask if she or he will consider referring you to one for medication if needed.

Forming a Therapeutic Alliance

The most important factor determining whether you will be able to stick it out long enough to get better is if you and your therapist establish what professionals call a "therapeutic alliance." To form this alliance there must be a positive relationship of mutual respect between you and the therapist. In addition, there must be what is commonly referred to as a patient-therapist "fit." You should feel comfortable with the therapist's personality and style and be able to talk with her or him openly and candidly. In addition, your personal goals should coincide with the therapist's goals for therapy. (The main goal of therapy is to help you to individuate and achieve more freedom and personal dignity.)

For both you and the therapist to properly evaluate your ability and willingness to work together you will need to meet together for at least one session, possibly more. If it is determined that there isn't the proper "fit," do not blame yourself or the therapist. Instead, consider it a "no fault" exchange, since your inability to establish rapport is no one's fault.

However, if you continue to determine that each psychotherapist you meet with is unacceptable, question your commitment, and consider the strong possibility that you are merely avoiding therapy. If this is the case, choose a therapist you feel is competent, and go forward with the task of getting better.

In general, a therapist who works well with BPD possesses certain qualities that a prospective client usually can recognize. In addition to being experienced in the treatment of BPD, the therapist obviously needs to have the following qualities. She or he:

- is tolerant and accepting, as opposed to being impatient and critical;
- maintains appropriate limits and boundaries;
- is able to maintain a certain level of objectivity—that is, does not take the actions of her or his clients personally.

What to Expect from Therapy

If you suffer from BPD, therapy isn't going to make you feel better right away. In fact, it's probably going to be quite painful. This may sound odd to you—after all, isn't the purpose of therapy to make us *feel* better? The answer is no, especially for the treatment of BPD, which will probably make you feel much worse before you feel better. BPD therapy will, however, make you feel better in the long run if you make a commitment to stick with it through the pain.

If you are receiving treatment from someone who has had special training and experience in working with Borderline Personality Disorder, you will likely be expected to follow certain rules:

- In an attempt to provide you needed structure and consistency, your therapist will be very particular about starting on time and ending on time. This may seem overly rigid to you, and you may interpret this as a sign that your therapist doesn't really care about you or that she or he is just interested in money, but try to remember that there is a good reason for the therapist's behavior.

- You will be expected to commit to therapy, meaning that you make therapy a priority by attending each therapy session. This commitment is so important that some therapists require you to pay for any therapy sessions you miss, *no matter what the reason*. This may seem unreasonable to you, but this rule is in place to encourage you to continue to view therapy as a priority and to discourage you from canceling appointments when you are feeling afraid.

- You may also be expected to follow other rules, such as not calling your therapist unless it is an emergency. If you call too often, your therapist may limit the number of times you can call her or his office.

You are likely to respond to your therapist in much the same way you do in other personal relationships. Sometimes you will perceive your therapist as being capable, honest, and caring, while at other times you will see her or him as inadequate, deceitful, and uncaring. This is due to your tendency to both idealize and devalue others as well as your lack of what is called "object constancy"—the ability to understand others as complex human beings who nonetheless can relate in consistent ways.

It is not your obligation to please your therapist but to work with her or him as an equal. Therefore it is important to be as honest as possible and to feel as if you are actively collaborating with your therapist. Avoid either the extreme of assuming a totally passive role or of becoming a competitive, contentious rival who is unwilling to listen to feedback.

What's the Prognosis?

In the past, many clinicians and researchers were pessimistic about whether those suffering from BPD could recover. But today there is ample research proving that borderlines can get better. For example:

- The McGlashan Chestnut Lodge study (1986) showed that 53 percent of patients with BPD were considered "recovered" and that patients seemed to do better once they reached their forties.

- A 1990 New York State Psychiatric Institute study showed that two-thirds of patients in their thirties and forties were rated as either "good" or "recovered" on the global assessment scale, a standard tool used by clinicians to measure functioning.

While the prognosis can be good for recovery from BPD, it is also important to understand that it is common for many suffering from this disorder to consciously or unconsciously sabotage their treatment in any or all of the following ways. They might:

- discontinue therapy when faced with issues that make them feel uncomfortable;

- continually test their therapist and/or push against their limits until the clinician discontinues treatment;

- put up a false front and hide information from the therapist so that she or he continues to operate under the false assumption that the client is far healthier than the client is;

- accuse the therapist of being incompetent and refuse to go forward with treatment.

For three years Paul T. Mason and Randi Kreger, the authors of *Stop Walking on Eggshells: Taking Your Life Back When Someone You Care About Has Borderline Personality Disorder,* interviewed borderlines who greatly improved. They noticed several commonalities:

1. First and foremost, those who greatly improved accepted responsibility for their behavior and for their recovery.

2. They were willing to work through their inner pain instead of deflecting it onto other people or dealing with it through other means (drugs, self-mutilation, etc.). Even though they sometimes lapsed back into old patterns, they got back on track.

3. They had faith in themselves and believed that other people (or a Supreme Being) had faith in their inner worthiness—the "real them" behind the borderline symptoms.

4. They had access to continued therapy with a competent clinician who did not take their actions personally, believed that recovery was possible, genuinely cared about them, was willing to stick with them in the long term, and observed appropriate limits.

5. They received the appropriate medication.

If you are interested in learning more about the cognitive-behavioral model known as Dialectical Behavior Therapy (DBT) I recommend you order the book *Skills Training Manual for Treating Borderline Personality Disorder* by Marsha Linehan (The Guilford Press, 1-800-365-7006).

Although this is a workbook for clinicians using Linehan's method of cognitive-behavioral therapy, the handouts and homework sheets are extremely useful and practical, and the book teaches four valuable skills: mindfulness, interpersonal effectiveness, emotion regulation, and distress tolerance.

To locate a clinician who specializes in Dialectical Behavior Therapy, contact the following for referrals:

> Behavioral Technology Transfer Group
> (206) 675-8558

For cognitive-behavioral therapy in California:

> Mary Nowicki, LCSW
> 2628 El Camino Avenue, Suite C-1
> Sacramento, CA 95821
> (916) 482-1255

For exploratory or intrapsychic psychotherapy nationwide:

> The Masterson Institute for Psychoanalytic Psychotherapy
> 60 Sutton Place South
> New York, NY 10022
> (212) 935-1414

Among Internet and e-mail resources, there are several BPD-related Internet support groups, called "mailing lists," where you can share stories, ask for help, and offer help to others:

- bpd@mhsanctuary.com. Articles, newsletter, Ask Paul Markovitz, M.D., PhD., Ask Paul Mason, M.S., C.P.C., coauthor of *Stop Walking on Eggshells,* chatrooms, bulletin boards, ICQ lists (consumers and families), personal stories, DSM IV diagnosis, clinician's forum, resources, and more.

- BorderPD mailing list: BorderPD is a mailing list for everyone who is interested in learning more about BPD. The list owner hopes to create a warm, supportive environment for everyone on the list. To subscribe, send an e-mail message to: listserv@maelstrom.stjohns.edu and put "SUB BorderPD [your first name your last name]" in the body of the message (not the subject). The list owner is A. J. (soul@golden.net).

- DBTSkills-DG is an unmoderated discussion list that provides support and a learning environment for members to share experiences and practice effective problem-solving skills. Dialectical Behavior Therapy (DBT) skills are psychosocial skills based on the approach of Marsha Linehan, Ph.D. To subscribe, please send a message to the list owner (Kieu) at busserv@u.washington.edu and a brief message about your background, letting the list owner know why you want to subscribe to the list.

If you fall on the extreme end of the continuum, making the decision to seek professional psychotherapy will be the most important decision you can make. It can mean the difference between living a life in which you are so plagued with alternating feelings of abandonment and engulfment that you are unable to sustain a relationship, and one in which you are able to reach such a state of calmness and security within yourself that a relationship no longer throws you into a state of panic, fear, rage, or confusion.

I would appreciate hearing about how this book has affected you, how you put my suggestions into practice, and whether you have been successful in maintaining your sense of self in your relationships with men since reading the book. You can write me at:

Beverly Engel

P.O. Box 6412

Los Osos, CA 93412-6412

Now that you realize you are not alone with your problem of losing yourself in relationships, you may feel motivated to connect with other women. I have created a web site: www.BeverlyEngel.com where you can meet other Disappearing Women.

This web site will also provide more information on the problem of women losing themselves in relationships, answer questions, provide information on how to start a Woman of Substance support group, and supply a number where you can receive email or phone counseling.

References

Unattributed quotations are from interviews conducted by the author.

CHAPTER ONE: Are You a Disappearing Woman?
Salomon Grimberg, *Frida Kahlo* (New York: Barnes & Noble Books, 1997).

Martha Zamora, *Frida Kahlo: The Brush of Anguish* (San Francisco: Chronicle Books, 1990).

CHAPTER THREE: Why Women Tend to Lose Themselves in Relationships: The Cultural, Biological, and Psychological Influences
Linda Tschirhart Sanford, and Mary Ellen Donovan, *Women and Self-Esteem* (New York: Penguin, 1984).

Michael Gurian, *A Fine Young Man* (New York: Tarcher/Putnam, 1998).

Chris Evatt, *He and She: A Lively Guide to Understanding the Opposite Sex* (New York: MJF Books, 1992).

Anne Moir and David Jessel, *Brain Sex* (New York: Carol Publishing Group, 1991).

Ernest Hartmann, *Boundaries of the Mind: A New Psychology of Personality* (New York: Basic Books, 1991).

Victoria Secunda, *Women and Their Fathers* (New York: Delacorte Press, 1991).

Mary Pipher, *Reviving Ophelia: Saving the Selves of Adolescent Girls* (New York: G. P. Putnam's Sons, 1994).

DSM-IV, Diagnostic and Statistical Manual of Mental Disorders (Washington, D.C.: American Psychiatric Association, 1994).

Jerold J. Kreisman, M.D., and Hal Straus, *I Hate You, Don't Leave Me* (Los Angeles: Price Stern Sloan, 1989).

CHAPTER FOUR: The Disappearing Woman Continuum
Grimberg, *Frida Kahlo.*

CHAPTER SIX: Commitment 2: Be Yourself and Tell the Truth about Yourself
Alice Koller, *An Unknown Woman: A Journey of Self-Discovery* (New York: Bantam Books, 1981).

Secunda, *Women and Their Fathers.*

CHAPTER SEVEN: **Commitment 3: Maintain a Separate Life**

Claire Bloom, *Leaving a Doll's House* (Boston: Little, Brown, 1996).

Mia Farrow, *What Falls Away* (New York: Doubleday, 1997).

Zamora, *Frida Kahlo: The Brush of Anguish*

CHAPTER EIGHT: **Commitment 4: Stay in the Present and in Reality**

Gloria Steinem, *Revolution from Within* (Boston: Little, Brown, 1992).

Carolyn G. Heilbrun, *The Education of a Woman: The Life of Gloria Steinem* (New York: The Dial Press, 1995).

Judith Viorst, *Necessary Losses* (New York: Fawcett, 1986).

CHAPTER TWELVE: **Find Your Authentic Self**

Carol Gilligan, *In a Different Voice: Psychological Theory and Women's Development* (Cambridge, Mass.: Harvard University Press, 1993).

Drew Barrymore, *Little Girl Lost* (New York: Pocket Books, 1990).

Joanne Wieland-Burston, *Contemporary Solitude* (York Beach, Maine: Nicolas-Hays, 1996).

May Sarton, *Journal of a Solitude* (New York: W. W. Norton, 1977).

Koller, *An Unknown Woman.*

CHAPTER THIRTEEN: **Find Your Voice**

Gilligan, *In a Different Voice.*

Natalie Goldberg, *Writing Down the Bones: Freeing the Writer Within* (Boston: Shambhala, 1986).

Linda Schierse Leonard, *The Wounded Woman: Healing the Father-Daughter Relationship* (Boston: Shambhala, 1985).

CHAPTER FOURTEEN: **Find Your Shadow**

Steinem, *Revolution from Within.*

William A. Miller, *Your Golden Shadow* (San Francisco: Harper & Row, 1989).

Connie Zweig and Jeremiah Abrams, *Meeting the Shadow* (Los Angeles: Jeremy P. Tarcher, 1991).

CHAPTER FIFTEEN: **Find Your Substance**

Viorst, *Necessary Losses.*

Deena Metzger, *Writing for Your Life: A Guide and Companion to the Inner Worlds* (San Francisco: HarperSanFrancisco, 1992).

APPENDIX III

Janice M. Cauwels, *Imbroglio: Rising to the Challenges of Borderline Personality Disorder* (New York: W. W. Norton, 1992).

Paul T. Mason and Randi Kreger, *Stop Walking on Eggshells: Taking Your Life Back When Someone You Care About Has Borderline Personality Disorder* (Oakland, Calif.: New Harbinger, 1998).

Kreisman and Straus, *I Hate You, Don't Leave Me.*

Wieland-Burston, *Contemporary Solitude.*

Bibliography and
Recommended Reading

WOMEN'S PSYCHOLOGY

In a Different Voice: Psychological Theory and Women's Development by Carol Gilligan. Cambridge, Mass.: Harvard University Press, 1993.

Revolution from Within by Gloria Steinem. Boston: Little, Brown, 1992.

Women and Love by Shere Hite. New York: St. Martin's Press, 1987.

Women and Their Fathers by Victoria Secunda. New York: Delacorte Press, 1992.

The Wounded Woman: Healing the Father-Daughter Relationship by Linda Schierse Leonard. Boston: Shambhala, 1985.

The Men in Our Lives: Fathers, Lovers, Husbands, Mentors by Elizabeth Fishel. New York: William Morrow, 1985.

FEMALE DEVELOPMENT

Reviving Ophelia: Saving the Selves of Adolescent Girls by Mary Pipher. New York: G. P. Putnam's Sons, 1994.

MALE DEVELOPMENT

A Fine Young Man by Michael Gurian. New York: Tarcher/Putnam, 1998.

BOUNDARIES

Boundaries in the Mind: A New Psychology of Personality by Ernest Hartman. New York: Basic Books, 1991.

Boundaries and Relationships by Charles Whitfield. Deerfield Beach, Fla.: Health Communications, 1993.

MALE/FEMALE RELATIONSHIPS

Secrets About Men Every Woman Should Know by Barbara DeAngelis. New York: Delacorte Press, 1990.

Men Are from Mars, Women Are from Venus by John Gray. New York: HarperCollins, 1992.
He and She: A Lively Guide to Understanding the Opposite Sex by Chris Evatt. New York: MJF Books, 1992.
You Just Don't Understand by Deborah Tannen, Ph.D. New York: Ballantine Books, 1990.

PHYSIOLOGY OF SEX

Brain Sex by Anne Moir and David Jessel. New York: Carol Publishing, 1991.

SOLITUDE

An Unknown Woman: A Journey of Self-Discovery by Alice Koller. New York: Bantam Books, 1981.
Journal of a Solitude by May Sarton. New York: W. W. Norton, 1977.
Contemporary Solitude by Joanne Wieland-Burston. York Beach, Maine: Nicolas-Hays, 1996.

JOURNALING

Life's Companion: Journal Writing as a Spiritual Quest by Christina Baldwin. New York: Bantam Books, 1990.
The Creative Journal: The Art of Finding Yourself by Lucia Capacchione. North Hollywood, Calif.: Newcastle, 1979.
Harvesting Your Journals by Rosalie Deer Heart and Alison Strickland. San Cristobal, N.M.: Heart Link Publications, 1999.
The Artist's Way by Julie Cameron. New York: Tarcher, 1992.
The Creative Journal by Lucia Capacchione. North Hollywood, CA: Newcastle, 1989.

CREATIVITY

Writing Down the Bones: Freeing the Writer Within by Natalie Goldberg. Boston: Shambhala, 1986.
Writing for Your Life: A Guide and Companion to the Inner Worlds by Deena Metzger. San Francisco: HarperSanFrancisco, 1992.

SPIRITUALITY

In the Meantime: Finding Yourself and the Love That You Want by Iyanla Vanzant. New York: Simon & Schuster, 1998.
The Thirst for Wholeness: Attachment, Addiction, and the Spiritual Path by Christina Grof. San Francisco: HarperSanFrancisco, 1993.
The Care of the Soul by Thomas Moore. New York: HarperCollins, 1992.
Journey of Awakening by Ram Dass. New York: Bantam Books, 1978; rev. ed., 1990.

ANGER

The Dance of Anger by Harriet Lerner. New York: Harper & Row, 1985.

UNFINISHED BUSINESS

Getting the Love You Want by Harville Hendrix. New York: Henry Holt, 1988.

Making Peace with Your Parents by Harold Bloomfield. New York: Ballantine Books, 1983.

Cutting Loose: An Adult Guide to Coming to Terms with Your Parents by Howard Halpern. New York: Bantam Books, 1976.

Necessary Losses by Judith Viorst. New York: Fawcett, 1986.

Divorcing a Parent by Beverly Engel. New York: Fawcett, 1991.

Families in Recovery: Working Together to Heal the Damage of Childhood Sexual Abuse by Beverly Engel. Los Angeles: Lowell House, 1994; rev. ed., 2000.

FORGIVENESS

Forgive and Forget by Lewis B. Smedes. San Francisco: Harper & Row, 1984.

Forgiving and Not Forgiving by Jeanne Safer, Ph.D. New York: Avon Books, 1999.

THE SHADOW

Your Golden Shadow by William A. Miller. San Francisco: Harper & Row, 1989.

The Invisible Partners by John A. Sanford, New York: Paulist Press, 1980.

Meeting the Shadow by Connie Zweig and Jeremiah Abrams. Los Angeles: Jeremy P. Tarcher, 1991.

A Little Book of the Human Shadow by Robert Bly. San Francisco: Harper & Row, 1988.

SELF-ESTEEM AND SELF-NURTURING

The Woman's Comfort Book by Jennifer Louden. San Francisco: HarperSanFrancisco, 1992.

The Woman's Retreat Book by Jennifer Louden. San Francisco: HarperSanFrancisco, 1997.

Women and Self-Esteem by Linda Tschirhart Sanford and Mary Ellen Donovan. New York: Penguin, 1984.

BORDERLINE PERSONALITY DISORDER

I Hate You, Don't Leave Me by Jerold Kreisman, M.D., and Hal Straus. Los Angeles: Price Stern Sloan, 1989.

Imbroglio: Rising to the Challenges of Borderline Personality Disorder by Janice Cauwels. New York: W. W. Norton, 1992.

The Search for the Real Self: Unmasking the Personality Disorders of Our Age by James Masterson. New York: The Free Press, 1988.

Stop Walking on Eggshells by Paul Mason and Randi Kreger. Oakland, Calif.: New Harbinger, 1998.

CIRCLES

Calling the Circle: The First and Future Culture by Christina Baldwin. New York: Bantam Books, 1998.

The Ceremonial Circle by Sedonia Cahill and Joshua Halpern. San Francisco: HarperSanFrancisco, 1990.

Wisdom Circles by Charles Garfield, Cindy Spring, and Sedonia Cahill. New York: Hyperion, 1998.

Sacred Circles by Robin Deen Carnes and Sally Craig. San Francisco: HarperSanFrancisco, 1998.

Women Circling the Earth: Fostering Community, Healing, and Empowerment through Women's Circles by Beverly Engel. Deerfield Beach, Fla.: Health Communications, 2000.

CHILD ABUSE

Adult Children of Abusive Parents: A Healing Program for Those Who Have Been Physically, Sexually, or Emotionally Abused by Steven Farmer. Los Angeles: Lowell House, 1989.

Thou Shalt Not Be Aware: Society's Betrayal of the Child by Alice Miller. New York: New American Library, 1986.

The Drama of the Gifted Child: The Search for the True Self by Alice Miller. New York: Basic Books, 1981.

For Your Own Good: Hidden Cruelty in Child-Rearing and the Roots of Violence by Alice Miller. New York: Farrar, Straus & Giroux, 1984.

CHILDHOOD SEXUAL ABUSE

The Courage to Heal: A Guide for Women Survivors of Child Sexual Abuse by Ellen Bass and Laura Davis. New York: Harper & Row, 1988.

The Right to Innocence: Healing the Trauma of Childhood Sexual Abuse by Beverly Engel. New York: Ballantine Books, 1990.

The Sexual Healing Journey: A Guide for Survivors of Sexual Abuse by Wendy Maltz. New York: HarperPerennial, 1992.

The Emotional Incest Syndrome: What to Do When a Parent's Love Rules Your Life by Patricia Love. New York: Bantam Books, 1990.

SPOUSAL ABUSE

The Emotionally Abused Woman by Beverly Engel. New York: Fawcett Columbine, 1991.

Men Who Hate Women and the Women Who Love Them by Susan Forward. New York: Bantam Books, 1986.

Battered Wives, rev. ed., by Del Martin. San Francisco: Volcano Press, 1981.

The Battered Woman by Lenore Walker. New York: Harper & Row, 1979.

CODEPENDENCY/LOVE ADDICTION

Codependent No More by Melody Beattie. San Francisco: Harper/Hazeldon, 1987.

Beyond Codependency by Melody Beattie. San Francisco: Harper/Hazeldon, 1989.

Women Who Love Too Much: When You Keep Wishing and Hoping He'll Change by Robin Norwood. Los Angeles: Jeremy P. Tarcher, 1985.

Choice-Making: For Codependents, Adult Children, and Spirituality Seekers by Sharon Wegscheider-Cruse. Pompano Beach, Fla.: Health Communications, 1985.

Obsessive Love by Susan Forward. New York: Bantam Books, 1991.

AUTOBIOGRAPHY AND BIOGRAPHY

Little Girl Lost by Drew Barrymore. New York: Pocket Books, 1990.

Leaving a Doll's House by Claire Bloom. Boston: Little, Brown, 1996.

What Falls Away by Mia Farrow. New York: Doubleday, 1997.

Frida Kahlo by Salomon Grimberg. New York: Barnes & Noble, 1997.

The Education of a Woman: The Life of Gloria Steinem by Carolyn G. Heilbrun. New York: Dial Press, 1995.

Gloria Steinem: Her Passions, Politics, and Mystique by Sydney Ladensohn Stern. Secaucus, N.J.: Carol Publishing Group, 1997.

Frida Kahlo: The Brush of Anguish by Martha Zamora. San Francisco: Chronicle, 1990.

Index